WORKBOOK B

HOLT, RINEHART AND WINSTON
Harcourt Brace & Company
Austin • New York • Orlando • Chicago • Atlanta • San Francisco • Boston • Dallas • Toronto • London

NOTE TO THE STUDENT: Excerpted Literary Works Used in *Holt Middle School Handbook: Workbook B*

The following excerpts were used to illustrate capitalization:

from a Zuni corn-grinding song, 105
from *A Pilgrim's Solace*, by John Dowland, 105
from "Annabel Lee," by Edgar Allan Poe, 105

Printed in the United States of America

ISBN 0-03-098484-X

7 8 082 00

Table of Contents

Writer's Quick Reference

Grammar and Usage

Chapter 1 Parts of Speech

Chapter 2 Agreement

CHAPTER 3 USING VERBS

CHAPTER 4 USING PRONOUNS

CHAPTER 5 USING MODIFIERS

PHRASES, CLAUSES, SENTENCES

CHAPTER 6 PHRASES

CHAPTER 7 CLAUSES

CHAPTER 8 SENTENCES

CHAPTER 9 COMPLEMENTS

CHAPTER 10 KINDS OF SENTENCES

CHAPTER 11 WRITING EFFECTIVE SENTENCES

MECHANICS

CHAPTER 12 CAPITAL LETTERS

CHAPTER 13 PUNCTUATION

CHAPTER 14 PUNCTUATION

CHAPTER 15 PUNCTUATION

CHAPTER 16 SPELLING AND VOCABULARY

COMPOSITION

CHAPTER 17 THE WRITING PROCESS

CHAPTER 18 PARAGRAPH AND COMPOSITION STRUCTURE

CHAPTER 19 THE RESEARCH REPORT

RESOURCES

APPENDIX: DIAGRAMING SENTENCES

Name ______________ Date ________ Class ______________

Writer's Quick Reference

Common Usage Problems A

QUICK REFERENCE

The following guidelines will help you avoid errors in usage.

a, an Use *a* before words or expressions beginning with consonant sounds. Use *an* before words or expressions beginning with vowel sounds.

advice, advise The noun *advice* means "a recommendation about a course of action." The verb *advise* means "to recommend" or "to give advice."

ain't Avoid this word in speaking and writing; it is nonstandard English.

all together, altogether The expression *all together* means "everyone or everything in the same place." The adverb *altogether* means "entirely."

altar, alter The noun *altar* means "a table for a religious ceremony." The verb *alter* means "to change."

anywheres, everywheres, nowheres, somewheres Use these words without the final *s*.

at Do not use *at* after *where*.

Exercise A Underline the word or expression in parentheses that is correct according to standard usage.

1. In England, remains of ancient (altars, alters) are (everywheres, everywhere).
2. The audience was (altogether, all together) charmed by the mime.
3. The doctor's (advice, advise) was to drink plenty of fluids and to rest.
4. What do you (advice, advise) me to do?
5. The cold weather did not (altar, alter) Ling's plans.

Exercise B: Revising Most of the following sentences contain errors in usage. On the lines provided, write the corrected sentences. If a sentence is correct, write *C*.

EXAMPLE: 1. I'd advice you to alter this sentence.
I'd advise you to alter this sentence.

1. Oh, no! I can't find my wallet anywheres!

____

2. Do you know where the conference room is at?

____

3. I've been waiting for an 8:00 bus for a hour.

____

4. No, I ain't going to lend you a dollar.

____

5. Could anyone put Humpty Dumpty all together again?

____

Name ______________________ Date ____________ Class ______________________

Common Usage Problems B

The following guidelines will help you avoid errors in usage.

bad, badly *Bad* is an adjective. *Badly* is an adverb.

between, among Use *between* when referring to two things at a time, even though they may be part of a group containing more than two. *(The ties* between *those family members are strong.)* Use *among* when referring to a group rather than to separate individuals. *(Is there a practical joker* among *us?)*

brake, break The noun *brake* means "a stopping device." Used as a verb, *break* means "to fracture" or "to shatter." As a noun, *break* means "a fracture" or "a period of rest."

bring, take *Bring* means "to come carrying something." *Take* means "to go carrying something." Think of *bring* as related to *come* and of *take* as related to *go.*

bust, busted Avoid using these words as verbs. Use a form of either *burst* or *break.*

capital, capitol The noun *capital* refers to a city and means "the seat of a government." The noun *capitol* refers to a building and means "the statehouse."

choose, chose *Choose* is the present tense form of the verb *choose.* It rhymes with *whose* and means "to select." *Chose* is the past tense form of *choose.* It rhymes with *grows* and means "selected."

Exercise: Proofreading Most of the following sentences contain errors in usage. If a sentence contains an error, cross out the error and write the correct word on the line provided. If a sentence is correct, write C.

EXAMPLE: 1. Let's take a ~~brake~~ from swimming. break

1. Extra tickets will be distributed between the Glee Club members. ____________
2. Accra is the capitol of Ghana. ____________
3. What provisions did the crew of Kon Tiki take with them? ____________
4. Did he brake his promise? ____________
5. Adeola didn't do bad at all the first time she was on ice skates. ____________
6. How did I know the table would bust if I sat on it? ____________
7. The winner must choose among two prizes. ____________
8. On the dome of the capital stands a large bronze statue. ____________
9. Have you noticed that you feel bad on Monday mornings? ____________
10. Going down a steep mountain, a bicyclist can wear out a set of brakes. ____________

Name ______________________ Date ____________ Class ______________

Common Usage Problems C

The following guidelines will help you avoid errors in usage.

clothes, cloths The noun *clothes* means "wearing apparel." The noun *cloths* means "pieces of fabric."

coarse, course The adjective *coarse* means "rough" or "crude." The noun *course* means "a path of action," "a unit of study," or "a route." *Course* is also used in the expression *of course.*

consul, council, counsel The noun *consul* refers to a representative of a government in a foreign country. *Council* refers to a group of people who meet together. Used as a noun, *counsel* means "advice." Used as a verb, *counsel* means "to give advice."

could of Do not write *of* with the helping verb *could.* Write *could have.* Also avoid *ought to of, should of, would of, might of,* and *must of.*

de´sert, desert´, dessert´ The noun *de´sert* means "a dry, sandy region." The verb *desert´* means "to abandon" or "to leave." The noun *dessert´* means "the final course of a meal."

doesn't, don't *Doesn't* is the contraction of *does not. Don't* is the contraction of *do not.* Use *doesn't* (not *don't*) with *he, she, it, this, that,* and singular nouns.

fewer, less *Fewer* is used with plural words. *Less* is used with singular words. *Fewer* tells "how many"; *less* tells "how much."

Exercise A Underline the word in parentheses that is correct according to standard usage.

1. Rayon and silk would be suitable (cloths, clothes) for a shirt like this.
2. The city (council, counsel) will not meet unless seven representatives are present.
3. The patient received (council, counsel) on the best (coarse, course) to recovery.
4. When we visited Cairo, we saw the Nile River, of (coarse, course).

Exercise B: Revising The following sentences contain errors in usage. On the lines provided, write the corrected sentences.

EXAMPLE: 1. I should of known better. *I should have known better.*

1. Why don't she at least fold her own cloths?

____

2. You could of called if you were going to be late.

____

3. The new model has less moving parts and is more reliable.

____

4. A camel's large feet give it good footing in the shifting sands of the dessert.

____

QUICK REFERENCE

Name ______________________ Date ____________ Class ______________________

Common Usage Problems D

The following guidelines will help you avoid errors in usage.

good, well *Good* is always an adjective. Never use *good* as an adverb. Instead, use *well*. Although *well* is usually an adverb, *well* may also be used as an adjective to mean "healthy."

had ought, hadn't ought Unlike other verbs, *ought* is not used with *had*.

hardly, scarcely The words *hardly* and *scarcely* convey negative meanings. They should never be used with another negative word.

hear, here The verb *hear* means "to perceive sounds by ear." The adverb *here* means "in this place."

hisself *Hisself* is nonstandard English. Use *himself*.

how come In informal situations, *how come* is often used instead of *why*. In formal situations, *why* should always be used.

its, it's *Its* is a personal pronoun in the possessive form. *It's* is a contraction of *it is* or *it has*.

Exercise A: Proofreading Most of the following sentences contain errors in usage. If a sentence contains an error, cross out the error and, when necessary, write the correct word on the line provided. If a sentence is correct, write C.

1. Each family has its own traditions. ______________
2. Don't you bring that filthy dog in hear! ______________
3. To learn a language good, students had ought to speak it. ______________
4. "I don't feel good," the boy whined. ______________

Exercise B: Revising The following sentences contain errors in usage. On the lines provided, write the corrected sentences.

EXAMPLE: 1. Its good to see you looking well.
It's good to see you looking well.

1. Class hadn't hardly started when the fire alarm went off.

____

2. Its ten o'clock; you hadn't ought to be calling them this late.

____

3. How come you understand usage so well?

____

4. Don't help him; he has to learn to think for hisself one day.

____

Name ______________________ Date ____________ Class ______________

Common Usage Problems E

The following guidelines will help you avoid errors in usage.

kind of, sort of In informal situations, *kind of* and *sort of* are often used to mean "somewhat" or "rather." In formal English, *somewhat* or *rather* is preferred.

lead, led *Lead* is the present tense form of the verb *lead*. It rhymes with *feed* and means "to go first" or "to be a leader." *Led* is the past tense form of the verb *lead*. The noun *lead* rhymes with *red*. It means "a heavy metal" or "graphite used in pencils."

learn, teach *Learn* means "to gain knowledge." *Teach* means "to instruct" or "to show how."

like, as In informal situations, the preposition *like* is often used instead of the conjunction *as* to introduce a clause. In formal situations, *as* is preferred.

loose, lose The adjective *loose* rhymes with *moose*. It means "not securely attached" or "not fitting tightly." As an adverb, *loose* means "in a loose manner." *Lose* is the present tense form of the verb *lose*. It rhymes with *whose* and means "to suffer a loss."

of Do not use *of* with other prepositions such as *inside, off,* and *outside*.

passed, past *Passed* is the past tense form of the verb *pass*. It means "went by." Used as a noun, *past* means "that which has gone by." Used as a preposition, *past* means "beyond."

Exercise: Proofreading Most of the following sentences contain errors in usage. If a sentence contains an error, cross out the error and, when necessary, write the correct word on the line provided. If a sentence is correct, write C.

EXAMPLE: 1. My bicycle's back tire is ~~lose~~. loose

1. The baby is kind of cranky today because she hasn't had a nap. ______________
2. My skating instructor can learn me how to skate backward on one foot. ______________
3. I want to learn to use a calculator like my math teacher does. ______________
4. Has the school bus already gone passed our street, Tiffany? ______________
5. The workers removed the lead pipes and stacked them outside of the house. ______________
6. How did the ship break lose from both of its anchors? ______________
7. Kaya lead us to the ceremonial lodge. ______________
8. We do not expect to loose any of our backfield players this year. ______________
9. We passed three stalled cars this morning on our way to school. ______________
10. "Why did you led us inside of this warehouse?" the angry group demanded. ______________

Name ______________________ Date ____________ Class ______________________

Writer's Quick Reference

Common Usage Problems F

The following guidelines will help you avoid errors in usage.

peace, piece The noun *peace* means "security and quiet order." *Piece* means "a part of something."

plain, plane Used as an adjective, *plain* means "simple, common, undecorated." Used as a noun, *plane* means "a tool," "an airplane," or "a flat surface." Used as a verb, *plane* means "to use a plane [tool] on."

real In informal situations, *real* is often used as an adverb meaning "very" or "extremely." In formal situations, *very* or *extremely* is preferred.

some, somewhat Do not use *some* for *somewhat* as an adverb.

threw, through *Threw* is the past tense form of the verb *throw*. *Through* is a preposition.

to, too, two *To* is a preposition. It is also part of an infinitive, a verbal. *Too* is an adverb that means "also" or "overly." *Two* is the number equal to one plus one.

try and In informal situations, *try and* is often used instead of *try to*. In formal situations, *try to* should be used.

Exercise A Underline the word or expression in parentheses that is correct according to standard usage.

1. "For once," the teacher announced with a smile, "(try and, try to) enjoy your homework."
2. If you don't hurry, you'll miss your (plain, plane).
3. The principle of trust can lead to world (peace, piece).
4. On Christmas Eve we always sing carols about (peace, piece) on earth and have a (peace, piece) of fruitcake.
5. (Plain, Plane) fruits and vegetables can provide a delicious and nutritious meal.

Exercise B: Proofreading Most of the following sentences contain errors in usage. If a sentence contains an error, cross out the error and, when necessary, write the correct word on the line provided. If a sentence is correct, write C.

EXAMPLE: 1. Try ~~and~~ come up with a real solution. ___to___

1. Don't worry; these questions are real easy. ______________
2. However, one or too of them did bother me some. ______________
3. Just try and concentrate as you read each one. ______________
4. Before you answer, think threw each possibility. ______________
5. There's no need to be in a hurry. ______________

Name ____________________ Date __________ Class ______________

Common Usage Problems G

The following guidelines will help you avoid errors in usage.

weak, week *Weak* is an adjective that means "not strong" or "feeble." *Week* is a noun that means "seven days."

weather, whether *Weather* is a noun that means "the condition of the air or atmosphere." *Whether* is a conjunction that means "if."

where Do not use *where* for *that.*

who, which, that The relative pronoun *who* refers to people only; *which* refers to things only; *that* refers to either people or things.

who's, whose *Who's* is the contraction of *who is* or *who has. Whose* is the possessive form of *who.*

without, unless Do not use the preposition *without* in place of the conjunction *unless.*

your, you're *Your* is the possessive form of the pronoun *you. You're* is the contraction of *you are.*

Exercise Underline the word in parentheses that is correct according to standard usage.

1. Last (week, weak) I received a letter from Sandra, (who's, whose) my good friend.
2. When I opened the envelope, I saw (where, that) she had sent me a set of chopsticks and instructions on how to use them.
3. "I thought you'd like (you're, your) own pair of chopsticks, with instructions for how to use them," Sandra wrote.
4. Instructions like the ones Sandra sent me are helpful because chopsticks can be hard to use (unless, without) you are shown how.
5. In the letter, Sandra told me (where, that) she and her family had taken a trip to visit her grandparents, (who's, whose) home is in New York City.
6. She especially enjoyed visiting Chinatown, (which, who) is located on Manhattan Island.
7. While her family was eating in a Chinese restaurant, one of the servers, (which, who) was very helpful, showed her how to use chopsticks.
8. "(Your, You're) not going to believe this," she wrote, "but by the end of the meal, I was using chopsticks quite well."
9. Sandra claims (where, that) it is only good manners to use chopsticks to eat Chinese food.
10. I'll write Sandra that I don't know (weather, whether) or not I could have been so gracious because I still have a long way to go before I'm an expert with chopsticks.

Name ______________________ Date ____________ Class ______________________

The Double Negative

A *double negative* is the use of two negative words to express one negative idea. Avoid using double negatives.

Double negatives often contain the following words:

Common Negative Words

barely	never	none	nothing
hardly	no	no one	nowhere
neither	nobody	not (–n't)	scarcely

NONSTANDARD: They don't have no shoes on sale.
STANDARD: They don't have any shoes on sale.
STANDARD: They have no shoes on sale.

NONSTANDARD: He hadn't never heard a symphony before.
STANDARD: He hadn't ever heard a symphony before.
STANDARD: He had never heard a symphony before.

NONSTANDARD: I couldn't barely see the stage.
STANDARD: I could barely see the stage.

Exercise: Revising On the line provided, revise each of the following sentences to eliminate the double negative. Although the following sentences can be corrected in more than one way, you need to give only one revision.

EXAMPLE: 1. She didn't have no reason to be angry.
She had no reason to be angry.
or
She didn't have any reason to be angry.

1. Nobody in our family had ever eaten no enchiladas before that night.

____

2. No, I haven't seen Pia nowhere at school.

____

3. "We haven't got nothing to do," whined the bored seven-year-olds.

____

4. Neither of the children had spotted no rabbits that night.

____

5. It hardly never snows here.

____

Name ____________________ Date __________ Class ____________

WORKSHEET 9 Review

Exercise A Underline the word or expression in parentheses that is correct according to standard usage.

1. If you like to read scary stories, take my (advice, advise) and read some of Edgar Allan Poe's.
2. No doubt, Poe's strange and tragic life (lead, led) him to write many of them.
3. Gifted and handsome, Poe attended the University of Virginia but got (himself, hisself) in trouble and had to leave.
4. (Threw, Through) the efforts of his guardian John Allan, Poe was appointed to West Point.
5. However, he was also to (loose, lose) this opportunity because of misbehavior.
6. Afterwards, Poe's guardian was (real, very) angry and disowned Poe.
7. Poe married a girl named Virginia, (who, which) was his cousin.
8. As time (passed, past), his marriage also became a source of sadness, for Virginia died.
9. Poe felt that her death caused his heart to (brake, break), and he died (to, two, too) years later.
10. (Its, It's) easy to say that Poe (could have, could of) done much more with his gifts, but look how much he did accomplish!

Exercise B: Revising Most of the following sentences contain errors in usage. On the line provided, rewrite correctly each sentence containing an error or errors. If a sentence is correct, write *C*.

EXAMPLE: 1. Navajo people came to the Southwest from somewheres in the North.
Navajo people came to the Southwest from somewhere in the North.

1. Bike riders had ought to know some simple rules of safety.

   ____

2. The pilot must quickly decide weather to parachute to safety or try to land the crippled plane.

   ____

3. You're dog is to sleepy to learn any new tricks.

   ____

4. Spring break starts next weak.

   ____

Name ______________________ Date ____________ Class ______________________

5. My mother and father both took part in Operation Dessert Storm.

6. You should use soft clothes to clean silver.

7. Mr. Ramírez used a plane to smooth the board.

8. One of the purposes of the Cabinet is to advice the president.

9. Why did you chose dinosaurs for your science project?

10. Yes, there are still openings in the karate coarse that I'm taking.

Exercise C: Revising The following sentences contain errors in usage. On the lines provided, revise the sentences.

1. He don't know nothing about it.

2. That couldn't of happened nowhere around here.

3. We didn't have no directions, so we got lost.

4. The meeting hadn't hardly started when an angry man walked in.

5. Until then, none of us had never been to a circus.

Name ________________________ Date ____________ Class ____________________

Types of Nouns A

A **noun** is a word used to name a person, a place, a thing, or an idea.

PERSONS: Diana Chang, poet, police officer, Cherokees
PLACES: living room, ceiling, New South Wales, island
THINGS: sandwich, television, Father's Day, Statue of Liberty
IDEAS: fear, self-control, truth, sympathy

A **compound noun** is two or more words used together as a single noun. The parts of a compound noun may be written as one word, as separate words, or as a hyphenated word.

ONE WORD: Clean up your **bedroom**.
SEPARATE WORDS: Otis can read **Roman numerals** quickly.
HYPHENATED WORD: Did you see your **brother-in-law**?

Exercise A Underline all the nouns in the following sentences.

EXAMPLE: 1. A letter from Uncle Rufino arrived last week.

1. Our sun is actually a star.
2. My sister, a student, is studying chemistry this summer.
3. Mr. Morales was fascinated by the koalas on his trip to Australia.
4. Suke is the new goalie on the team.
5. Janell is having a party after the play.
6. Did your parents go to Hawaii for a convention?
7. The storm interrupted the final game of the World Series.
8. The actors had faith in their director.
9. Lucy, a young chimpanzee, learned several words in sign language.
10. Ryan always puts humor into his essays.

Exercise B Underline the twenty-five nouns in the following paragraph. Some nouns are used more than once, and some are compound.

EXAMPLE: [1] We have been reading about patriotic heroes in our textbook.

[1] Rebecca Motte was a great patriot. [2] During the Revolutionary War, British soldiers seized her mansion in South Carolina. [3] General Harry Lee told Motte that the Americans would have to burn her home to smoke out the enemy. [4] Motte supported the plan and was glad to help her country. [5] She even supplied fire arrows and a bow for the attack. [6] But the enemy raised the white flag of surrender, and the house was saved. [7] Afterward, Motte invited soldiers from both sides to dinner.

Name ______________________ Date ____________ Class ____________________

WORKSHEET 2

Types of Nouns B

A **common noun** is a general name for a person, a place, a thing, or an idea. A **proper noun** names a particular person, place, thing, or idea. Proper nouns always begin with a capital letter. Common nouns begin with a capital letter only when they are in titles or come at the beginning of a sentence or a line of poetry.

COMMON NOUNS: pilot, dog, fair, book, country

PROPER NOUNS: Amelia Earhart, Fido, Brown County Fair, *Black Beauty,* Japan

A **concrete noun** names a person, a place, or a thing that can be perceived by one or more of the senses (sight, hearing, taste, touch, or smell). An **abstract noun** names an idea, a feeling, a quality, or a characteristic.

CONCRETE NOUNS: song, bird, winner, oranges

ABSTRACT NOUNS: joy, freedom, honor, abundance

Exercise A: Revising Revise the following sentences by substituting a proper noun for each common noun. You may need to change some other words in each sentence. You may also make up proper names to use.

EXAMPLE: 1. An ambassador visited a local school and spoke about his country.
Ambassador Rios visited Jackson High School and spoke about Brazil.

1. That painting is in a famous museum. ______________________

____

2. The police officer directed us to the building on that street. ______________

____

3. My relatives, who are from a small town, now live in a large city. __________

____

4. The librarian asked my classmate to return the book to the library. __________

____

Exercise B Identify each of the following nouns as *concrete* or *abstract*. Then use each noun in an original sentence.

EXAMPLE: 1. truth
abstract—My mother said I should always tell the truth.

1. soy sauce

____

2. excitement

____

Name ______________________ Date ___________ Class ______________________

WORKSHEET 3 Types of Pronouns A

A **pronoun** is a word used in place of one noun or more than one noun. The word that a pronoun stands for is called its **antecedent**. Sometimes the antecedent is not stated.

> **Ms. Cato** is my math teacher. **She** made everything clear. [*Ms. Cato* is the antecedent of the pronoun *she*.]
>
> **Chim** gave **his** lunch to **her**. [*Chim* is the antecedent of the pronoun *his*. The pronoun *her* has no antecedent in this sentence.]

A **personal pronoun** refers to the one speaking *(first person)*, the one spoken to *(second person)*, or the one spoken about *(third person)*.

FIRST PERSON: **I** got some good seats for **us**.
SECOND PERSON: Can **you** tell me if this jacket is **yours**?
THIRD PERSON: **She** will help **them** with **it**.

A **reflexive pronoun** refers to the subject and directs the action of the verb back to the subject. An **intensive pronoun** emphasizes a noun or another pronoun. Notice that reflexive and intensive pronouns have the same form.

REFLEXIVE PRONOUN: Consuelo prepared **herself** for the swim meet.
INTENSIVE PRONOUN: My younger brother prepared dinner **himself**.

Exercise A On the lines provided, identify each pronoun and its antecedent in the following sentences. [Note: A sentence may have more than one pronoun.]

EXAMPLE: 1. The drama coach said he would postpone the rehearsal. *he—coach*

1. "I want you to study," Ms. Gaines said to the class. ______________________
2. The firefighter carefully adjusted her oxygen mask. ______________________
3. The children made lunch themselves. ______________________
4. Jenny and Rosa decided they would get popcorn, but Amy didn't want any popcorn. ______________________

Exercise B Underline the pronoun or pronouns in each sentence below, and decide what kind of pronoun each is. On the line provided, in the order in which the pronouns appear, write *P* for personal, *R* for reflexive, or *I* for intensive.

______ 1. We should not let ourselves overlook the plight of the homeless.

______ 2. "I will not tolerate lateness," the band leader told us.

______ 3. The principal himself called me with the good news.

______ 4. When the smoke detector sounded, the cat hid itself behind the couch.

GRAMMAR/USAGE

Name ______________________ Date ____________ Class ____________________

Types of Pronouns B

A **demonstrative pronoun** points out a person, a place, a thing, or an idea.

This is the machine we use. **These** are the instructions.

An **interrogative pronoun** introduces a question.

Which of the seats is mine? **Who** knows the words to the song?

A **relative pronoun** introduces a subordinate clause.

Chuck Yeager's plane, **which** was named *Glamorous Glennis*, flew seven hundred miles per hour.

The book **that** you need is in the reference section of the library.

An **indefinite pronoun** refers to a person, a place, or a thing that is not specifically named. Many indefinite pronouns can also serve as adjectives.

INDEFINITE PRONOUN: **Several** of the trees have already flowered.

ADJECTIVE: **Several** bushels of apples have been harvested.

Exercise On the line provided, identify the pronoun or pronouns in each sentence. Then decide what kind of a pronoun each is. Write *DEM* for demonstrative pronouns, *INT* for interrogative pronouns, *IND* for indefinite pronouns, or *REL* for relative pronouns.

EXAMPLE: 1. "Who is going to answer that?" Max asked, glancing at the phone. *Who—INT; that—DEM*

1. Jorge is the boy who wore the red wig in the first act. ____________
2. Hairstyle is one of the details that help scholars date pictures. ____________
3. Everyone who enters the lab must wear a coverall. ____________
4. Whom will the class choose as a representative? ____________
5. What should Susan bring to the party? ____________
6. Of all of the fruits, these have the most vitamin C. ____________
7. Eliot called the house, but no one answered. ____________
8. Please put away the boxes, and then help Marvin move this. ____________
9. Lily was the only one who voted against the measure. ____________
10. Think of different scenes, and decide what Alicia should paint. ____________

Name ______________________ Date __________ Class ______________

Adjectives A

An **adjective** is a word used to modify a noun or a pronoun. To *modify* a word means to describe the word or to make its meaning more definite. An adjective modifies a word by telling *what kind, which one, how much,* or *how many.*

WHAT KIND: Anzu bought a **red** dress.
HOW MUCH: There is **no** water on the moon.
WHICH ONE: Victor is the **oldest** brother.
HOW MANY: I discovered **several** boxes.

The most frequently used adjectives are *a, an,* and *the.* These adjectives are called **articles.** *A* and *an* are **indefinite articles.** They indicate that a noun refers to someone or something in general. *A* is used before a word beginning with a consonant sound. *An* is used before a word beginning with a vowel sound.

INDEFINITE ARTICLES: **An** eagle spotted **a** fish.

The adjective *the* is the **definite article.** It indicates that the noun refers to someone or something in particular.

DEFINITE ARTICLE: What are **the** colors of **the** American flag?

Exercise A Underline all adjectives in each sentence. Then decide whether the article that appears in each sentence is definite or indefinite. On the line provided, write *D* for definite or *I* for indefinite.

______ 1. Yes, Sylvia has an older brother.

______ 2. The sudden wind chilled us.

______ 3. Someday you may own a small electric car.

______ 4. Edna ordered a medium hamburger with extra onions.

______ 5. The mysterious tapping terrified everyone.

Exercise B In each of the following sentences, underline all the adjectives except *a, an,* and *the.* Then draw an arrow from each adjective to the word that it modifies.

1. Mary Shelley wrote a horror story.
2. The plot of the story was imaginative.
3. One stormy night, she had listened to several stories about ghosts.
4. Friends had made up scary stories about monsters.
5. Shelley knew she would have a terrible night.
6. Shelley thought about the stories all night and had a strange nightmare.
7. She dreamed of a young doctor who created a monster.
8. Mary Shelley wrote a story of the ghastly nightmare and called the story *Frankenstein.*
9. The eerie novel was a great success.
10. Several movies have been made from it.

Name ______________________ Date ______________ Class ______________________

WORKSHEET 6 Adjectives B

An adjective may come before or after the word it modifies.

Many swimmers found the pool **closed**. [*Closed* is an adjective modifying *pool*.]

A **proper adjective** is formed from a proper noun and begins with a capital letter. Notice that some proper nouns, such as *Rio Grande*, do not change spelling when they are used as adjectives.

PROPER NOUNS: Islam, Florida, Shakespeare

PROPER ADJECTIVES: **Islamic** beliefs, **Florida** sunshine, **Shakespearean** plays

Exercise A On the lines provided, identify the ten adjectives in the following paragraph. Then tell whether each is a common (C) or a proper (P) adjective. Do not include indefinite articles (*a*, *an*, and *the*) or possessive pronouns.

EXAMPLE: We have been studying how various animals protect themselves.

1. *various—C*

Many small animals defend themselves in clever ways. South American armadillos wear suits of armor made of small, bony scales. Armadillos may seem delicate, with their narrow faces. But their tough armor protects them well. Likewise, the Asian anteater has scales that overlap like the shingles on a roof.

1. ______________ 4. ______________ 7. ______________ 10. ______________

2. ______________ 5. ______________ 8. ______________

3. ______________ 6. ______________ 9. ______________

Exercise B Change the following proper nouns to proper adjectives, and use each proper adjective in a sentence. Use a dictionary to help you spell the adjectives.

EXAMPLE: 1. Spain *Peace Corps volunteers take Spanish lessons every Tuesday.*

1. Mexico ____

2. Memorial Day ____

3. Congress ____

4. Hawaii ____

5. Korea ____

Name ______________________ Date __________ Class ______________

Noun, Pronoun, or Adjective?

This, that, these, and *those* can be used both as adjectives and as pronouns. When they modify a noun or a pronoun, these words are called **demonstrative adjectives**. When they are used alone, they are called **demonstrative pronouns**.

ADJECTIVE: **These** bags are heavy.

PRONOUN: Please hold **these** for me.

A noun that modifies another noun or a pronoun is considered an adjective.

NOUN: My hobby is raising tropical **fish**.

ADJECTIVE: We acted fast when the **fish** tank sprung a leak.

Exercise A On the line provided, identify the italicized word in each sentence below as a noun, a pronoun, or an adjective. Write *N* for nouns, *P* for pronouns, or *A* for adjectives.

EXAMPLE: __N__ 1. We walked along the empty *beach* at sundown.

_____ 1. When the tide comes in, it brings a variety of *interesting* items from the sea.

_____ 2. When it ebbs, *it* leaves behind treasures for watchful beachcombers.

_____ 3. If you look carefully, you will find *several* tiny animals.

_____ 4. Some live in shallow burrows under the wet sand and emerge in the cool evening to dine on bits of plants and other *matter*.

_____ 5. A number of different species of beetles like *this* part of the beach.

_____ 6. Around them you can find bristly flies and *tiny* worms.

_____ 7. *You* may also see old pieces of wood with round holes and tunnels in them.

_____ 8. *These* holes are produced by shipworms.

_____ 9. If you watch the shore closely, you will see signs of *these*.

_____ 10. Low tide is a marvelous *time* to search along the shore.

Exercise B Underline all of the nouns, pronouns, and adjectives in the following sentences (do not include articles). Then label each underlined word in the space above the line. Write *N* for nouns, *P* for pronouns, or *A* for adjectives.

EXAMPLE: 1. Please give me (P) some (A) ideas (N) for a Halloween (A) costume (N).

1. Put some of this good Texas barbecue sauce on that sandwich.
2. Sam Houston was the president of Texas before it became a state.
3. Allison bought a white dress for the dance.
4. This town needs a good dress shop.
5. Many people attend many of these festivals.

GRAMMAR/USAGE

Name ______________________ Date ____________ Class ____________________

Action Verbs

A **verb** is a word used to express action or a state of being. Every sentence must have a verb. The verb says something about the subject.

John Muir **wrote** about Yosemite National Park.

Eileen **imagined** the scene.

An **action verb** may express physical action or mental action.

PHYSICAL ACTION: Slowly, the train **rumbled** into the station.

MENTAL ACTION: I **worry** about too many things.

Exercise A Underline the action verb in each of the following sentences.

EXAMPLE: 1. I saw that movie last week.

1. For a science project, Elena built a sundial.
2. Mr. Santos carefully explained the problem again.
3. I enjoy soccer more than any other sport.
4. This waterfall drops two hundred feet.
5. Leo's bicycle skidded on the pavement.
6. Mrs. Karras made us stuffed grape leaves.
7. Mix the ingredients slowly.
8. The heavy traffic delayed us.
9. For the Jewish holiday of Purim, Rachel gave a costume party.
10. The early Aztecs worshiped the sun.

Exercise B Your pen pal in another country wants to know what students at your school do at school dances. Write a letter describing the things that people do at school dances. In your letter, use at least ten action verbs. Include at least three verbs that express actions that can't be seen. Underline the action verbs in your letter.

EXAMPLE: *Everyone dances to the fast songs.*

____

____

____

____

____

____

____

Name ______________________ Date ____________ Class ____________________

WORKSHEET 9

Transitive Verbs and Intransitive Verbs

A **transitive verb** is an action verb that expresses an action directed toward a person or thing. With transitive verbs, the action passes from the doer—the subject—to the receiver of the action. Words that receive the action of a transitive verb are called **objects.**

Ingrid **left** her sneakers in the gym. [The action of *left* is directed toward *sneakers. Sneakers* is the object of the verb *left.*]

An **intransitive verb** expresses action (or tells something about the subject) without passing the action to a receiver. A verb may be transitive in one sentence and intransitive in another.

TRANSITIVE: The runner **stretched** his legs. [*Legs* is the object of *stretched.*]

INTRANSITIVE: The runner **stretched.** [The action of *stretched* is not passed to a receiver.]

Exercise A For each of the following sentences, identify the italicized action verb as transitive or intransitive. On the line provided, write *T* for transitive or *I* for intransitive.

EXAMPLE: ___*I*___ 1. She *runs* early in the morning.

______ 1. If you do different kinds of exercises, you *are exercising* in the correct way.

______ 2. You *exercise* to improve endurance, flexibility, and strength.

______ 3. Aerobic exercise *builds* endurance.

______ 4. When you *walk* quickly, you do aerobic exercise.

______ 5. Many people *attend* classes in aerobic dancing.

______ 6. They *enjoy* the fun of exercising to music.

______ 7. Exercises that *improve* flexibility require you to bend and stretch.

______ 8. *Perform* these exercises slowly for maximum benefit.

______ 9. Through isometric and isotonic exercises, your muscle strength *increases*.

______10. These exercises *contract* your muscles.

Exercise B For each verb given below, write two sentences. In one sentence, use the verb as a transitive verb, and underline its object. In the other, use the verb as an intransitive verb. You may use different tenses of the verb.

EXAMPLE: 1. write *Alex is writing a research report. (transitive)*
Alex writes in his journal every day. (intransitive)

1. fly ____

____

2. leave ____

____

GRAMMAR/USAGE

Name ____________________ Date __________ Class ____________________

Linking Verbs

A **linking verb** links or connects the subject with a noun, a pronoun, or an adjective in the predicate. The most commonly used linking verbs are *appear, become, feel, grow, look, remain, seem, smell, sound, stay, taste, turn,* and forms of the verb *be.*

Your painting **is** beautiful! The colors **are** exciting.

Linking verbs except the forms of *be* and *seem* may also be used as action verbs. Whether a verb is used to link words or to express action depends on its meaning in a sentence.

ACTION VERB: Paco **tasted** the soup.

LINKING VERB: Those vegetables **tasted** fresh.

NOTE: The verb *be* does not always link the subject with a noun, pronoun, or adjective in the predicate. *Be* can express a state of being and be followed by words or word groups that tell *when* or *where.*

Everyone is **here.** Everyone is **on time.**

Exercise A Underline the verbs in the sentences below, and decide whether each is an action or a linking verb. On the line provided, write *A* for action verb or *L* for linking verb.

EXAMPLE: __L__ 1. Aaron Burr was the third vice president of the United States.

______ 1. Although a brave man, Burr felt unhappy in the army.

______ 2. He resigned in 1779 because of ill health.

______ 3. Later, Burr seemed happy with his law practice.

______ 4. He fought an illegal duel with Alexander Hamilton.

______ 5. Hamilton's death at Burr's hands ended Burr's career.

Exercise B Underline the linking verb in each of the following sentences. Then draw an arrow between the words joined by the linking verb.

EXAMPLE: 1. The old house looked deserted.

1. The farm animals looked quite content.
2. The computerized voice sounds human.
3. After the flood, the farmers grew fearful of more rain.
4. Some of the bristlecone pines are very old.
5. The huge diamond mine is now a museum.

Name ______________________ Date ____________ Class ______________

Chapter 1: Parts of Speech

The Verb Phrase

A **helping verb** (*auxiliary verb*) helps the main verb to express an action or a state of being.

FORMS OF *BE*: am, be, being, was, are, been, is, were
FORMS OF *DO*: do, does, did
FORMS OF *HAVE*: have, has, had
OTHER HELPING VERBS: can, may, must, should, would, could, might, shall, will

A **verb phrase** consists of a main verb preceded by at least one helping verb.

The code **could have been hidden** inside an old book. [The main verb is *hidden*.]

Some helping verbs may also be used as main verbs.

I **have** the book right here.

Sometimes the verb phrase is interrupted by another part of speech, frequently by an adverb. In a question, however, the subject often interrupts the verb phrase.

Sparky **will** not **bite** you.
Our customers **can** always **use** cash, checks, or credit cards.
Did you **hear** about the new mall?

Exercise A Underline the verb phrases in the following paragraph. Then draw another line under each helping verb.

EXAMPLE: [1] Have you ever visited Redwood National Park?

[1] For centuries, the giant trees there have been an important part of the environment of the northwestern United States. [2] But more than 85 percent of the redwoods have been destroyed, and the forest is being threatened. [3] With proper planning years ago, more of the forest might already have been saved. [4] According to some scientists, all forests outside the park will have disappeared by the year 2000. [5] However, according to other experts, the redwood forests can still be saved!

Exercise B Underline the verb phrase in each sentence. Then draw another line under each main verb.

EXAMPLE: 1. People have celebrated birthdays for thousands of years.

1. Ancient Egyptians would sometimes buy birthday garlands.
2. The Persians would hold special feasts.
3. In nineteenth-century literature, birthdays were often described as sad affairs.
4. Other people have celebrated in spectacular ways.
5. On one occasion, Julius Caesar was declared a god!

GRAMMAR/USAGE

Name ______________________ Date ____________ Class ______________________

Adverbs That Modify Verbs

An **adverb** is a word used to modify a verb, an adjective, or another adverb. An adverb tells *where, when, how,* or *to what extent* (*how much* or *how long*).

WHERE: Put the bricks **there**.
WHEN: **Later,** I'll help you.
HOW: Stack them **carefully**.
TO WHAT EXTENT: My sister and I **frequently** work in the garden.

Adverbs may appear at various places in a sentence. Adverbs may come before, after, or between the verbs they modify.

Quickly, she had reached for the fire extinguisher.
She had reached **quickly** for the fire extinguisher.
She had **quickly** reached for the fire extinguisher.

Adverbs are sometimes used to ask questions.

How do you use this computer? **When** will the bell ring?

NOTE: The word *not* is an adverb. When *not* is part of a contraction like *hadn't,* the *–n't* is an adverb.

Do **not** forget the first-aid kit!

Exercise A For each of the following sentences, underline the adverb twice. Then underline the word or words it modifies.

EXAMPLE: 1. Today, many Cherokee people make their homes in Oklahoma.

1. The Cherokees once lived in Georgia, North Carolina, Alabama, and Tennessee.
2. In 1829, settlers hurried excitedly to northern Georgia for the first gold rush in the United States.
3. These settlers totally ignored the Cherokees' right to the land.
4. Later, Cherokees were forced by the U. S. government to leave their land and move to Oklahoma.
5. The people were hardly given a chance to collect their belongings before this journey, which became known as the "Trail of Tears."

Exercise B On the line provided, rewrite each of the following sentences, adding one or more adverbs.

1. The victorious knight rode his horse across the drawbridge.

____

2. People cheered as he entered.

____

Name ____________________ Date __________ Class ____________________

Adverbs That Modify Adjectives and Adverbs

An adverb may be used to modify an adjective.

Our neighbors are **extremely** kind. [The adverb *extremely* modifies the adjective *kind* and tells *to what extent*.]

An adverb may be used to modify another adverb.

My brother practices the trumpet **too loudly**. [The adverb *too* modifies the adverb *loudly*. *Loudly* modifies the verb *practices*.]

Exercise On the lines provided at the bottom of the page, write the adverbs in the following paragraphs. Then write the word or words each adverb modifies. [Note: A sentence may contain more than one adverb.]

EXAMPLE: [1] "To Build a Fire" is a dramatically suspenseful short story.

1. *dramatically—suspenseful*

[1] "To Build a Fire" is probably one of Jack London's best stories. [2] In this story, a nameless character goes outdoors on a terribly cold day in the Yukon. [3] Except for a dog, he is traveling completely alone to a mining camp. [4] Foolishly confident of his ability to survive the unusually harsh cold, he does not understand the dangers of the northern wilderness.

[5] The dog knows quite instinctively that they are in a bad situation. [6] It slinks fearfully along at the man's heels and seems to question his every movement. [7] Soon both the dog's muzzle and the man's beard are frosted with ice.

[8] Along the way, the man desperately builds a fire under a tree to avoid frostbite. [9] Unfortunately, a pile of snow suddenly falls from a tree limb and smothers the fire. [10] Based on what you now know about this story, what kind of ending would you write for "To Build a Fire"?

1. ____________________
2. ____________________
3. ____________________
4. ____________________
5. ____________________
6. ____________________
7. ____________________
8. ____________________
9. ____________________
10. ____________________

GRAMMAR/USAGE

Name ______________________ Date ____________ Class ____________________

Adjective or Adverb?

Many adverbs end in *–ly: quietly, briefly, calmly*. However, some words that end in *–ly* are adjectives: *friendly, lonely, timely*. If you're not sure whether a word is an adjective or an adverb, ask yourself what it modifies. If a word modifies a noun or a pronoun, then the word is an adjective. If a word modifies a verb, an adjective, or an adverb, then the word is an adverb.

ADJECTIVE: A **deadly** calm descended on the ship. [The adjective *deadly* modifies the noun *calm*.]

ADVERB: That snake is **deadly** poisonous. [The adverb *deadly* modifies the adjective *poisonous*.]

Exercise A On the line provided, identify the italicized word in each of the following sentences as an *adjective* or an *adverb*.

EXAMPLE: 1. For good health, exercise *daily*. adverb

1. Tours are given *hourly*. ______________
2. The riding stable has *hourly* rates. ______________
3. It's *too* hot for a hiking expedition. ______________
4. We were greeted by a *friendly* dog. ______________
5. He thanked us *kindly* for our trouble. ______________
6. Luckily, the principal was a *kindly* person. ______________
7. "Come *here*, Twink," Mary called to the puppy. ______________
8. Elm trees grow *quickly*. ______________
9. No one knew who the *mysterious* stranger was. ______________
10. Above us was a *dark* blue sky. ______________

Exercise B Supply ten different adverbs to fill the blanks in the following paragraph.

EXAMPLE: [1] I have always been a real music lover.

On Fridays I [1] ______________ go to the record store. I can [2] ______________ wait to see what new cassettes and CDs have arrived. As soon as school is out, I bicycle [3] ______________ to the store and join other [4] ______________ enthusiastic customers. [5] ______________ I stroll through the aisles and [6] ______________ study the selections. I listen [7] ______________ as the loudspeaker announces the day's specials. When I have decided what I want, I [8] ______________ figure out which items I can afford. Then I walk [9] ______________ to the cash register. I sometimes smile [10] ______________ as I think of how much I will enjoy the music.

Name ______________________ Date __________ Class ______________________

Chapter 1: Parts of Speech

Prepositions and Their Objects

A preposition is a word that shows the relationship of a noun or a pronoun to another word.

The cat jumped **through** the hoop. [The preposition *through* shows the relationship between *cat* and *hoop.*]

A preposition is always followed by a noun or a pronoun called the **object of the preposition**. A preposition may have more than one object. All together, the preposition, its object(s), and the modifiers of the object are called a **prepositional phrase**.

The room was decorated **with Japanese screens and dark wooden furniture**. [The preposition is *with*. The objects of the preposition are the nouns *screens* and *furniture*. *Japanese* modifies *screens; dark* and *wooden* modify *furniture.*]

Prepositions that consist of more than one word are called compound prepositions.

Read Chapter 12 **in addition to** Chapter 11.

Some words may be used as either prepositions or adverbs. To tell an adverb from a preposition, remember that a preposition is always followed by a noun or pronoun object.

ADVERB: A lone eagle flew **above**. PREPOSITION: A lone eagle flew **above** us.

NOTE: Be careful not to confuse a prepositional phrase that begins with *to (to town, to her club)* with a verb form that begins with *to (to run, to be seen).*

Exercise A Identify the prepositional phrases in the following paragraph. Underline each preposition once and its object twice.

EXAMPLE: [1] Lieutenant Robert Peary and Matthew Henson reached the North Pole in 1909.

[1] Lieutenant Peary looked for the North Pole for many years. [2] Matthew Henson traveled with him on every expedition except the first one. [3] For a long time, Henson received no credit for his role. [4] Peary had hired Henson as a servant on a trip to Nicaragua. [5] There, Peary discovered that Henson had experience with sailing. [6] As a result, Peary asked Henson to join an Arctic expedition. [7] The two explorers became friends during their travels. [8] On the final push to the North Pole, Henson was the only person who went along with Peary. [9] Yet because Peary was leader of the expedition, he received all the credit for the discovery. [10] Finally, after many years, Henson was honored by Congress, Maryland's state government, and two U.S. presidents.

Exercise B In the space above each line, identify each italicized word as *preposition* or *adverb.*

1. *Below* us, a huge manatee was slowly swimming *along*.
2. *Next*, read the chart on the board *above* you.

GRAMMAR/USAGE

Name ______________________ Date ____________ Class ____________________

Conjunctions

A **conjunction** is a word used to join words or groups of words. Coordinating conjunctions connect words or groups of words used in the same way.

You can pitch the tent first **or** go for a hike. [The conjunction *or* connects the verbs *can pitch* and *go*.]

When *for* is used as a conjunction, it connects groups of words that are sentences, and it is always preceded by a comma. On all other occasions, *for* is used as a preposition.

CONJUNCTION: Small craft must not sail, **for** the winds are too strong.

PREPOSITION: Please get the charts **for** the captain.

Correlative conjunctions are pairs of conjunctions that connect words or groups of words used in the same way: Your tropical fish **not only** will survive **but also** will thrive.

Exercise A On the line provided, write the conjunction(s) in each of the following sentences. Then underline the words or groups of words each conjunction joins.

EXAMPLE: 1. Both she and her mother enjoy sailing. *Both . . . and*

1. I want to see Los Lobos in concert, but I have no money. ____________
2. We recycle not only newspapers but also aluminum cans. ____________
3. He set the table with chopsticks and rice bowls. ____________
4. Have you seen either Whitney Houston or Janet Jackson? ____________
5. We learned to use neither too many adjectives nor too few. ____________
6. That diet is dangerous, for it does not meet the body's needs. ____________
7. Both the Mohawk and the Oneida are part of the Iroquois Confederacy. ____________
8. It rained all day, yet we enjoyed the trip. ____________
9. Shall we walk home or take the bus? ____________
10. Revise your paper, and proofread it carefully. ____________

Exercise B For each blank in the following sentences, choose an appropriate conjunction.

EXAMPLE: 1. *Either* solve the problem yourself *or* ask your teacher for help.

1. They were ____________ hungry ____________ thirsty.
2. ____________ turn that radio down ____________ take it into your room.

Name ______________________ Date ____________ Class ______________________

Interjections

An **interjection** is a word used to express emotion. It does not have a grammatical relation to other words in the sentence. Usually an interjection is followed by an exclamation point. Sometimes an interjection is set off by a comma.

Exercise A Underline the interjections in the following sentences.

1. Ouch! I stubbed my toe.
2. Oh, maybe we should wait.
3. Help! My experiment blew up!
4. Well, it isn't raining as hard now.
5. You won that much? Wow!
6. Eureka! I have found it!
7. Gee, it sounds like fun, but I have to work.
8. Hooray! We won first place!
9. Oops! I spilled juice on the floor.
10. Shucks, that's not so fast.

Exercise B The people at a video arcade need your help. To express their excitement, they want to use some interjections—but they don't know any. Write five sentences that they might use. In each sentence, use a different interjection from the list below. Underline the interjections you use. (Remember that an interjection may be followed by either an exclamation point or a comma.)

yea oh wow darn no oops yes whoa

1. ____

____

2. ____

____

3. ____

____

4. ____

____

5. ____

____

Name ______________________ Date ____________ Class ______________

Determining Parts of Speech

The part of speech of a word is determined by the way the word is used in a sentence.

PRONOUN: **That** is my bicycle.
ADJECTIVE: **That** bicycle is mine.
ADVERB: Write my phone number **down**.
PREPOSITION: A race car sped **down** the road.
NOUN: Give the jar a **shake** before you pour the juice.
VERB: The two contestants always **shake** hands.
INTERJECTION: **So!** That's where I took the wrong turn.
ADVERB: Summer was over **so** quickly.

Exercise A On the line provided, identify the parts of speech of the italicized words in each of the following sentences. Use these abbreviations:

N = noun	V = verb	CON = conjunction
P = pronoun	ADV = adverb	INT = interjection
ADJ = adjective	PREP = preposition	

EXAMPLE: 1. *Both* otters *and* owls hunt *from* dusk to dawn.
both . . . and—CON; from—PREP

1. *Oh!* I *just* spilled soup on the new *white* tablecloth! ______________
2. *Did* Toni Morrison *or* Toni Cade Bambara *write* that book? ______________
3. The Inuit hunters *prepared* their meal *under* the *shelter*. ______________
4. *They* were tired, *yet* they did *not* quit working. ______________

Exercise B Write eight sentences that meet the requirements in the following directions. Underline the given word in each sentence, and identify how it is used.

EXAMPLE: 1. Use *yet* as an adverb and as a conjunction.
Are we there yet?—ADV. The sky grew brighter, yet the rain continued falling.—CON

1. Use *walk* as a verb and a noun. ______________________________

____

2. Use *like* as a preposition and a verb. ______________________________

____

3. Use *inside* as an adverb and a preposition. ______________________________

____

4. Use *fast* as an adjective and an adverb. ______________________________

____

Name ____________________ Date __________ Class ____________________

WORKSHEET 19 Review

Exercise A On the lines provided, identify the nouns in the following sentences. Then write *C* for each common noun and *P* for each proper noun. Be sure to capitalize all proper nouns.

EXAMPLE: 1. Lillian Evanti sang operas in europe, latin america, and africa.
Lillian Evanti—P; operas—C; Europe—P; Latin America—P; Africa—P

1. Evanti was the first African American woman to sing opera anywhere in the world.
____

2. At the age of four, she gave a solo concert in washington, d.c.
____

3. As an adult, she performed in a special concert at the white house for president franklin roosevelt and his wife, Eleanor Roosevelt.
____

4. Her career inspired many other African American singers.
____

Exercise B Underline the pronouns in the following sentences. Then decide what kind of pronoun each is. On the line provided, write *P* for personal, *R* for reflexive, *I* for intensive, *DEM* for demonstrative, *INT* for interrogative, *IND* for indefinite, or *REL* for relative.

EXAMPLE: __*P*__ 1. Allow me to introduce Clarissa Hill.

______ 1. No, I myself have never actually seen a flying saucer.

______ 2. Wasn't something said in class about these?

______ 3. We couldn't help laughing when Dad spilled paint on himself.

______ 4. Who was the first president of Mexico?

______ 5. Sidney Lanier, who wrote many beautiful poems, is probably most famous for "The Marshes of Glynn."

Exercise C On the lines provided, identify each italicized word in the following paragraphs as either an *adverb* or a *preposition*. Underline the object of each preposition.

EXAMPLE: [1] He watches uneasily as the hunter brings the pistol *up*.
1. *adverb*

[1] "The Most Dangerous Game" is the story of Rainsford, a famous hunter who falls *off* a boat and swims to a strange island. [2] Rainsford knows that this island is feared by every sailor who passes *by*. [3] In fact, *among* sailors, the place is known as "Ship-Trap Island."

GRAMMAR/USAGE

[4] After looking *around* for several hours, Rainsford can't understand why the island is considered so dangerous. [5] Finally, he discovers a big house *on* a high bluff. [6] A man with a pistol *in* his hand answers the door. [7] Putting his pistol *down,* the man introduces Rainsford to the famous hunter General Zaroff. [8] Zaroff invites Rainsford *inside.* [9] Soon, however, Rainsford wishes he could get *out* and never see Zaroff again. [10] Rainsford has finally discovered the secret *about* the island—Zaroff likes to hunt human beings!

1. ______________________ 6. ______________________
2. ______________________ 7. ______________________
3. ______________________ 8. ______________________
4. ______________________ 9. ______________________
5. ______________________ 10. ______________________

Exercise D On the lines provided, identify the verbs in the following paragraphs. Label each verb as an *action verb* or a *linking verb.* [Note: A sentence may contain more than one verb.]

EXAMPLE: [1] Have you ever seen a play in Spanish?
1. *Have seen—action verb*

[1] The Puerto Rican Traveling Theatre presents plays about Hispanic life in the United States. [2] Over the past twenty years, this group has become a leader in Hispanic theater. [3] Some shows are musicals, while other plays seem more serious. [4] Sometimes, a production has two casts—one that performs in English and one that speaks in Spanish. [5] In this way, speakers of both languages can enjoy the play.

1. ______________________ 4. ______________________
2. ______________________ 5. ______________________
3. ______________________

Exercise E Each of the following sentences contains an italicized word that is used twice. This word may function as more than one part of speech. On the line provided, indicate the part of speech for each use of this word. Use these abbreviations:

N = noun	V = verb	CON = conjunction
P = pronoun	ADV = adverb	INT = interjection
ADJ = adjective	PREP = preposition	

EXAMPLE: 1. Grandmother noticed the faucet *in* *PREP* the kitchen was dripping, so she put a new washer *in* *ADV*.

1. Isn't *that* ______ sweater the same one *that* ______ we saw in the window?
2. Shall we *camp* ______ here or make *camp* ______ on the hill?
3. A leader must be *just* ______ or people *just* ______ will not follow him or her.
4. I haven't talked to you in *so* ______ long, *so* ______ I decided to call you.
5. The tapes weren't on sale, *but* ______ the store had sold all of them *but* ______ one.

Name ______________________ Date ____________ Class ____________________

Singular and Plural

Number is the form of a word that indicates whether the word is singular or plural. When a word refers to one person, place, thing, or idea, it is singular in number. When a word refers to more than one, it is plural in number.

SINGULAR:	circle	he	one	woman	loss
PLURAL:	circles	they	some	women	losses

Exercise A For each of the following words, write *S* if the word is singular and *P* if the word is plural.

EXAMPLE: __S__ 1. girl

______ 1. evening
______ 2. wolves
______ 3. women
______ 4. leaf
______ 5. they
______ 6. teeth
______ 7. tacos
______ 8. we
______ 9. thief
______ 10. armies
______ 11. geese
______ 12. plateau
______ 13. loaf
______ 14. cities
______ 15. mouth
______ 16. people
______ 17. many
______ 18. parentheses
______ 19. I
______ 20. mouse

Exercise B For each of the following sentences, write *S* if the subject is singular or *P* if the subject is plural.

EXAMPLE: __P__ 1. Chickens roost.

______ 1. I look.
______ 2. Ramiro enters.
______ 3. He sings.
______ 4. All dance.
______ 5. Everyone smiles.
______ 6. Each applauds.
______ 7. They bow.
______ 8. Nobody frowns.
______ 9. Some jump.
______ 10. Children laugh.

GRAMMAR/USAGE

Name ____________________ Date ____________ Class ____________________

Agreement of Subject and Verb A

A verb agrees with its subject in number. A subject and verb **agree** when they have the same number.

Singular subjects take singular verbs.

Mexican **art is** interesting. [The singular verb *is* agrees with the singular subject *art*.]

Plural subjects take plural verbs.

Mexican **holidays are** popular in the Southwest. [The plural verb *are* agrees with the plural subject *holidays*.]

The first auxiliary (helping) verb in a verb phrase must agree with its subject.

Mr. Frank has been studying Mexican culture. [The singular helping verb *has* agrees with the singular subject *Mr. Frank*.]

NOTE: Generally, nouns ending in *–s* are plural *(seasons, memories, cats, friends)*, and verbs ending in *–s* are singular *(calls, swims, rides, brings)*. However, verbs used with the singular pronouns *I* and *you* do not end in *–s*.

Exercise A For each of the following sentences, underline the form of the verb in parentheses that agrees with the subject.

EXAMPLE: 1. Gwendolyn Brooks (<u>is</u>, are) my favorite writer.

1. Her stories (seems, seem) real to me.
2. She (write, writes) about ordinary, everyday life.
3. Her poems (tells, tell) about childhood in Chicago.
4. Brooks (has, have) been writing since before she was eleven.
5. In 1969, this wonderful writer (was, were) named poet laureate of Illinois.

Exercise B: Proofreading Most of the following sentences contain errors in subject-verb agreement. If a verb does not agree with the subject, write the correct form of the verb on the line provided. If a sentence is correct, write C.

EXAMPLE: 1. Over nineteen million people lives in and around Mexico's capital. *live*

1. Mexico City have been built on Aztec ruins. ____________
2. In one of the city's subway stations, an Aztec pyramid still stand. ____________
3. Sculptures grace the Alameda, Mexico City's main park. ____________
4. Usually, tourists is fascinated by the Great Temple of the Aztecs. ____________
5. In addition, the city has one of the largest soccer stadiums in the world. ____________

Name ____________________ Date __________ Class ____________________

Agreement of Subject and Verb B

The number of a subject is not changed by a prepositional phrase following the subject.

NONSTANDARD: The mother of the kittens were somewhere nearby.
STANDARD: The **mother** of the kittens **was** somewhere nearby.
NONSTANDARD: Airplanes in the hangar is protected from storms.
STANDARD: **Airplanes** in the hangar **are** protected from storms.

Exercise A Underline the subject in each sentence. Then underline the form of the verb in parentheses that agrees with the subject.

EXAMPLE: 1. The history of the United States (is, are) largely the history of immigrants.

1. The history of Jewish Americans (begin, begins) in the 1600's.
2. New York at that time (was, were) a Dutch colony called New Amsterdam.
3. The governor of New Amsterdam (was, were) Peter Stuyvesant.
4. Jewish immigrants to our country (has, have) made many contributions.
5. The names of some Jewish American authors (is, are) well known.
6. A famous author of short stories (is, are) Bernard Malamud.
7. Jewish American writers of fiction (include, includes) Saul Bellow.
8. The winner of the Nobel Prize (was, were) Saul Bellow.
9. Another writer of Jewish descent (is, are) Philip Roth.
10. The contributions of immigrants (enrich, enriches) our country.

Exercise B: Proofreading Underline the subject in each sentence. Then decide whether or not the verb agrees with the subject. If the verb does not agree, write the correct form of the verb on the line provided. If the verb is correct, write *C*.

EXAMPLE: 1. The water in the earth's oceans cover much of the planet's surface. *covers*

1. A tidal wave, despite its name, is not caused by the tides. __________
2. An eruption beneath the sea causes a tidal wave. __________
3. A network of warning signals alert people in coastal areas of an approaching tidal wave. __________
4. The tremendous force of tidal waves cause great destruction. __________
5. Walls of earth and stone along the shore is often too weak to protect coastal villages. __________

GRAMMAR/USAGE

Name ______________________ Date ___________ Class ______________________

Agreement with Indefinite Pronouns

Some pronouns do not refer to a definite person, place, thing, or idea and are therefore called **indefinite** pronouns.

The following indefinite pronouns are singular: *anybody, anyone, each, either, everybody, everyone, neither, nobody, no one, one, somebody, and someone.*

Nobody on our street **grows** a better tomato than Otis.

The following indefinite pronouns are plural: *both, few, many,* and *several.*

Many of his tomatoes **taste** sweet and juicy.

The following indefinite pronouns may be either singular or plural: *all, any, most, none,* and *some.* The number of these pronouns is determined by the number of the word that the pronoun refers to. Indefinite pronouns that refer to singular words take singular verbs. Indefinite pronouns that refer to plural words take plural verbs.

SINGULAR: **Some** of his garden **is** ready to be planted. [*Some* refers to the singular word *garden.*]

PLURAL: **Some** of his tomatoes **are** prizewinners! [*Some* refers to the plural word *tomatoes.*]

Exercise A Underline the subject in each of the following sentences. Then underline the form of the verb in parentheses that agrees with the subject. Remember that the subject is never part of a prepositional phrase.

EXAMPLE: 1. One of these books (is, are) yours.

1. Neither of the movies (was, were) especially funny.
2. Everybody in those classes (gets, get) to see the Balinese dancers.
3. Someone among the store owners (donates, donate) the trophy each year.
4. Each of the Washington brothers (studies, study) with a Zulu dance instructor.
5. No one on either team (was, were) ever in a playoff before.

Exercise B For each of the following sentences, underline the form of the verb in parentheses that agrees with the subject.

EXAMPLE: 1. All of the new research on dreams (is, are) fascinating.

1. Most of our dreams (occur, occurs) toward morning.
2. Few of us really (understand, understands) the four cycles of sleep.
3. Some of our dreams (is, are) very clear during the cycle known as rapid eye movement (REM).
4. None of my dreams ever (make, makes) sense to me.
5. Many of them (is, are) about what happened the day before.

Name ______________________ Date ___________ Class ____________________

Agreement with Compound Subjects

Subjects joined by *and* usually take a plural verb.

Acids and bases are interesting.

A compound subject that names only one person or thing takes a singular verb.

Sweet and sour is a common style of food preparation.

When subjects are joined by *or* or *nor*, the verb agrees with the subject nearer the verb.

Unripe **apples or** sour **milk makes** you sick. [The verb agrees with the nearer subject, *milk*.]

Melon or berries are usually on the dessert menu. [The verb agrees with the nearer subject, *berries*.]

Exercise A On the line provided, indicate whether the compound subject in each of the following sentences is singular *(S)* or plural *(P)*. Then underline the form of the verb in parentheses that agrees with the compound subject.

EXAMPLE: __P__ 1. Chris and her sister (is, are) in the school band.

______ 1. My guide and companion in Bolivia (was, were) Pilar, a high school student.

______ 2. New words and new meanings for old words (is, are) included in a good dictionary.

______ 3. Mrs. Chang and her daughter (rents, rent) an apartment in San Francisco's Chinatown.

______ 4. Both iron and calcium (needs, need) to be included in a balanced diet.

______ 5. A horse and buggy (was, were) once a fashionable way to travel.

Exercise B Underline the correct form of the verb in parentheses in each of the following sentences.

EXAMPLE: 1. The club president or the officers (meets, meet) regularly with the sponsors.

1. Neither pens nor pencils (is, are) needed to mark the ballots.
2. Either my aunt or my uncle (is, are) going to drive us to the lake.
3. Index cards or a small notebook (is, are) handy for taking notes.
4. Neither that clock nor my watch (shows, show) the correct time.
5. Either Japanese poetry or Sioux folk tales (is, are) going to be the focus of my report.

GRAMMAR/USAGE

Name ______________________ Date ____________ Class ______________________

Other Problems in Agreement A

A **collective noun** is singular in form but names a group of persons, animals, or things. Collective nouns may be either singular or plural. A collective noun takes a singular verb when the noun refers to the group as a unit. A collective noun takes a plural verb when the noun refers to the individual parts or members of the group.

The **family is** closely knit. [The family as a unit is closely knit.]

The **family are meeting** in Rochester. [The individual members of the family are meeting.]

A verb agrees with its subject, not with its predicate nominative.

S V PN
His **hobby is model cars**. [The singular verb agrees with the singular subject, *hobby*, not the plural predicate nominative, *model cars*.]

S V PN
Model cars are his **hobby**. [The plural verb agrees with the plural subject, *model cars*, not the singular predicate nominative, *hobby*.]

When the subject follows the verb, find the subject, and make sure the verb agrees with it. The subject usually follows the verb in sentences beginning with *here* or *there* and in questions.

There **are** two ***p's*** in *Mississippi*. [The plural subject *p's* follows the plural verb *are*.]

NOTE: When the subject of a sentence follows the verb, the word order is said to be *inverted*. To find the subject of a sentence with inverted order, restate the sentence in usual word order.

Exercise On the line provided, write the subject in each of the following sentences. Then underline the correct form of the verb in parentheses.

EXAMPLE: 1. That flock of geese (<u>migrates</u>, migrate) each year. *flock*

1. There (is, are) at least two solutions to this Chinese puzzle. ______________
2. The Olympic team (was, were) all getting on different buses. ______________
3. (Is, Are) both of your parents from Korea? ______________
4. Here (comes, come) the six members of the dance committee. ______________
5. Those two puppies (is, are) a handful. ______________
6. Her one passion (is, are) sports. ______________
7. Here (is, are) the social studies notes I wrote about Gandhi. ______________
8. At the press conference, there (was, were) several candidates for mayor and two for governor. ______________
9. The family (has, have) announced its plans to celebrate Grandma's promotion. ______________
10. Here (is, are) some masks carved by the Haida people in Alaska. ______________

Name ____________ Date ________ Class ____________

Other Problems in Agreement B

The contractions *don't* and *doesn't* must agree with their subjects. Use *don't* with plural subjects and with the pronouns *I* and *you*. Use *doesn't* with other singular subjects.

Plaids don't match with stripes. **Milk doesn't** taste good with oranges.

The contractions *here's, there's,* and *where's* contain the verb *is* and should be used only with singular subjects.

Here**'s** the **bill** for the party. [The subject *bill* is singular.]

Words stating amounts are usually singular.

Five dollars is a good price for that football.

The title of a book or the name of an organization or country, even when plural in form, usually takes a singular verb.

***Beauty and the Beast* is** a scary but beautiful film.

A few nouns, though plural in form, are singular and take singular verbs.

Civics is the last class in my day.

Some nouns that end in *–s* and name a *pair* (such as *pants*) take a plural verb even though they refer to a singular item.

These **scissors are** dull.

Exercise A Underline the form of the verb in parentheses that agrees with the subject in each of the following sentences.

1. *The Friends* (is, are) a book about a girl from the West Indies and a girl from Harlem.
2. Two cups of broth (seems, seem) as if it is too little for that recipe.
3. (Here's, Here are) the keys to the shed.
4. My pliers (is, are) in the garage.
5. Mathematics (has, have) always been easy for me.

Exercise B Complete each sentence by writing in the blank the correct contraction, *doesn't* or *don't*.

EXAMPLE: 1. I _don't_ like radishes.

1. ____________ she want to play soccer?
2. The tomatoes ____________ look ripe.
3. Italy ____________ border Germany.
4. ____________ you want to go with us?
5. Many in the field ____________ agree with this scientist.

GRAMMAR/USAGE

Name ____________________ Date ____________ Class ____________________

Agreement of Pronoun and Antecedent

A pronoun usually refers to a noun or another pronoun that comes before it. That noun or pronoun is called the **antecedent**. A pronoun agrees with its antecedent in number and gender. Masculine pronouns (*he, him,* and *his*) refer to males. Feminine pronouns (*she, her,* and *hers*) refer to females. Neuter pronouns (*it* and *its*) refer to things and to animals.

Dolores lost **her** scarf. **Ed** walked **his** dog. The **bird** built **its** nest.

To determine the gender of a personal pronoun that refers to an indefinite pronoun, look in the phrase that follows the indefinite pronoun. Some antecedents may be either masculine or feminine. When referring to such antecedents, use both the masculine and the feminine forms.

Each of the **men** put **his** keys on the conveyor belt.

Everybody in the group wanted **his or her** own invitation.

A singular pronoun is used to refer to *anybody, anyone, each, either, everybody, everyone, neither, nobody, no one, one, someone,* or *somebody*. A plural pronoun is used to refer to *both, few, many,* or *several*. Either a singular or a plural pronoun may be used to refer to *all, any, most, none,* or *some*.

No one in the league wanted **his or her** team to lose.

Both of the teams set **their** own schedules.

All of the puzzle is in **its** box. **All** of them paid **their** dues.

A plural pronoun is used to refer to two or more antecedents joined by *and*. A singular pronoun is used to refer to two or more singular antecedents joined by *or* or *nor*.

Bill and Buddy will lend **their** microscope to the class.

Either Talasi or Wilma will share **her** room.

Exercise In the blank in each of the following sentences, write a pronoun or pronouns that will complete the meaning of the sentence. Then underline the antecedent or antecedents for that word.

1. A writer should proofread ____________________ work carefully.
2. The store sent Paula and Eric the posters that ____________________ had ordered.
3. Mark or Hector will arrive early so that ____________________ can help us cook.
4. One of the students left ____________________ calculator.
5. Each of the dogs ate ____________________ dinner.
6. My sister and her boyfriend announced ____________________ engagement.
7. Everyone in my class has ____________________ own writer's journal.
8. Neither recalled the name of ____________________ first-grade teacher.
9. Anyone may join if ____________________ collects stamps.
10. Either Kat or Liz won a prize for ____________________ design.

Name ______________ Date ______________ Class ______________

WORKSHEET 9 Review

Exercise A: Revising Most of the following sentences contain errors in subject-verb agreement. On the line provided, write each sentence correctly. If a sentence is correct, write C.

EXAMPLE: 1. Has you seen the paintings of Wang Yani?
Have you seen the paintings of Wang Yani?

1. There surely is few teenage artists as successful as Yani.
____
2. In fact, the People's Republic of China regard her as a national treasure.
____
3. She has shown her paintings throughout the world.
____
4. A painter since the age of two, Yani don't paint in just one style.
____
5. Her ideas and her art naturally changes over the years.
____
6. Several paintings shows one of Yani's favorite childhood subjects.
____
7. Many of her early paintings features monkeys.
____
8. In fact, one of her large works picture 112 monkeys.
____
9. However, most of her later paintings is of landscapes, other animals, and people.
____
10. Yani fill her paintings with energy and life.
____

Exercise B For each of the following sentences, underline the verb form or contraction in parentheses that agrees with the subject.

EXAMPLE: 1. New wheelchairs with lifts (<u>help</u>, helps) many people reach objects up high.

1. Twenty-five cents (is, are) not enough money to buy that newspaper.
2. Everyone in her company (prefers, prefer) to take winter vacations.

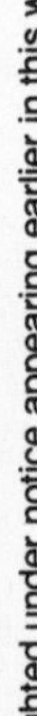

3. Allen and his parents (enjoy, enjoys) the Puerto Rican Day Parade in New York City.
4. Jan (don't, doesn't) know the rules for volleyball.
5. Neither the cassette player nor the speakers (work, works) on my stereo.
6. There (is, are) 132 islands in the state of Hawaii.
7. Many of the place names in California (comes, come) from Spanish words.
8. The principal or her assistant (is, are) the one who can help you.
9. Home economics (is, are) a required course in many schools.
10. A flock of sheep (was, were) grazing on the hill.

Exercise C Most of the sentences in the following paragraph contain errors in pronoun-antecedent agreement. On the line provided, identify each error, and give the correct pronoun or pronouns. If a sentence is correct, write C.

EXAMPLE: [1] At the meeting, each member of the Small Business Council spoke about their concerns.
1. *their—his or her*

[1] Everybody had a chance to express their opinion about the new shopping mall. [2] Mrs. Gomez and Mr. Franklin are happy about his or her new business locations at the mall. [3] Both said that his profits have increased significantly. [4] Neither Mr. Chen nor Mr. Cooper, however, feels that their customers find parking convenient enough. [5] Anyone shopping at the mall has to park their car too far from the main shopping area. [6] Several members of the council said that the mall has taken away many of their customers. [7] One of the new women on the council then presented their own idea about creating a farmers' market on weekends. [8] Many members said he or she favored the plan, and a proposal was discussed. [9] Each farmer could have their own spot near the town hall. [10] The Small Business Council then agreed to take their proposal to the mayor.

1. ______________________________
2. ______________________________
3. ______________________________
4. ______________________________
5. ______________________________
6. ______________________________
7. ______________________________
8. ______________________________
9. ______________________________
10. ______________________________

Name ______________________ Date ___________ Class ______________________

Regular Verbs

The four basic forms of a verb are called the **principal parts** of the verb. The principal parts of a verb are the *base form*, the *present participle*, the *past*, and the *past participle*. A verb's principal parts are used to show the time that the verb's action takes place. A **regular verb** forms its past and past participle by adding *–d* or *–ed* to the base form.

Base Form	Present Participle	Past	Past Participle
wish	(is) wishing	wished	(have) wished
shop	(is) shopping	shopped	(have) shopped

When forming the past or past participle of regular verbs, avoid the common error of leaving off the *–d* or *–ed* ending.

NONSTANDARD: The grocery store use to be closed on Sundays.
STANDARD: The grocery store **used** to be closed on Sundays.

Exercise For each of the following sentences, fill in the blank with the correct base form, present participle, past, or past participle form of the verb given in parentheses.

EXAMPLE: 1. Many people today are *learning* folk dances from a variety of countries. (learn)

1. In Mexico, folk dancing has been ____________ for a long time. (practice)
2. Today, professional folk dancers ____________ in colorful, native costumes. (perform)
3. Have you ever ____________ to learn any folk dances? (want)
4. Virginia reels ____________ to be popular dances in the United States. (use)
5. Mrs. Stamos, who is from Greece, ____________ to teach her daughter the Greek chain dance. (promise)
6. The Jamaican dancer ____________ backward before he went under the pole during the limbo competition. (lean)
7. The group from Estonia is ____________ a dance about a spinning wheel. (start)
8. Someone in the audience has ____________ an Irish square dance called "Sweets of May." (request)
9. During the Mexican hat dance, the girl ____________ on the rim of the sombrero. (dance)
10. The Jewish wedding dance ____________ the room with music and movement. (fill)

GRAMMAR/USAGE

Name ______________________ Date ___________ Class ______________________

Irregular Verbs

An **irregular verb** forms its past and past participle in some other way than by adding *–d* or *–ed* to the base form. An irregular verb forms its past and past participle by (1) changing vowels or consonants, (2) changing vowels and consonants, or (3) making no change.

	Base Form	Present Participle	Past	Past Participle
1.	make	(is) making	made	(have) made
2.	do	(is) doing	did	(have) done
3.	hurt	(is) hurting	hurt	(have) hurt

Exercise For each of the following sentences, give the past or past participle form of the verb given in parentheses that will fit correctly in the blank.

EXAMPLE: 1. I *wrote* a report on Jim Thorpe. (write)

1. Yesterday the wind ____________ the leaves into our yard. (blow)
2. My pen pal always ____________ his promise to write monthly. (keep)
3. I ____________ the wrong book to class. (bring)
4. The children almost ____________ with excitement. (burst)
5. The director ____________ James Earl Jones to act in her play. (choose)
6. My aunt and her friend ____________ to dinner last night. (come)
7. I have always ____________ my homework right after supper. (do)
8. The guests ____________ four quarts of fruit punch. (drink)
9. One of my Russian nesting dolls has ____________ off the shelf. (fall)
10. Has the pond ____________ yet? (freeze)
11. We have never ____________ to see the Parthenon in Nashville, Tennessee. (go)
12. Had I ____________, I would have called you sooner. (know)
13. Suddenly the fire alarm ____________. (ring)
14. Joan Samuelson certainly ____________ a good race. (run)
15. I ____________ you in line at the movies. (see)
16. We dried apples in the sun, and they ____________. (shrink)
17. After we had ____________ to George Takai, who plays Mr. Sulu, we went to the *Star Trek* convention banquet. (speak)
18. You shouldn't have ____________ the ball to second base. (throw)
19. She has ____________ me several long letters. (write)
20. We ____________ out to the float and back. (swim)

Name ______________________ Date ___________ Class ____________________

Verb Tense

The **tense** of a verb indicates the time of the action or state of being expressed by the verb.

Every verb has six tenses: *present, past, future, present perfect, past perfect,* and *future perfect.*

PRESENT: The bird **sings**.
PAST: The bird **sang**.
FUTURE: The bird **will sing**.
PRESENT PERFECT: The bird **has sung**.
PAST PERFECT: The bird **had sung**.
FUTURE PERFECT: The bird **will have sung**.

Do not change needlessly from one tense to another. When writing about events that take place in the present, use verbs in the present tense. Similarly, when writing about events that occurred in the past, use verbs in the past tense.

INCONSISTENT: We sat on the porch and gaze at the stars.
CONSISTENT: We **sit** on the porch and **gaze** at the stars.
CONSISTENT: We **sat** on the porch and **gazed** at the stars.

Exercise: Proofreading Read the following paragraph and decide whether it should be rewritten in the present or past tense. Then change the verb forms to make the verb tense consistent.

EXAMPLE: [1] I picked up the telephone receiver, but the line ~~is~~ *was* still dead.

or

I pick~~ed~~ up the telephone receiver, but the line is still dead.

[1] Lightning struck our house, and I run straight for cover. [2] "Oh, no!" I exclaim. [3] The electricity had gone out! [4] My parents light candles, and we played a game by candlelight.

[5] We know that lightning had hit our telephone answering machine because it keeps playing the same message over and over. [6] My younger brother asks me what lightning is. [7] "Lightning is a big spark of electricity from a thundercloud," I tell him. [8] He nods. [9] I started to tell him about positive and negative charges creating lightning, but he does not understand what I am talking about and walks away. [10] In the morning, we were all glad when the sun shone and our phone works again.

GRAMMAR/USAGE

Name ______________________ Date ___________ Class ______________________

Commonly Confused Verbs

Base Form	Present Participle	Past	Past Participle
sit	(is) sitting	sat	(have) sat
set	(is) setting	set	(have) set
lie	(is) lying	lay	(have) lain
lay	(is) laying	laid	(have) laid
rise	(is) rising	rose	(have) risen
raise	(is) raising	raised	(have) raised

sit, set The verb *sit* means "to rest in an upright, seated position." *Sit* seldom takes an object. The verb *set* means "to put (something) in a place." *Set* usually takes an object. Notice that *set* has the same form for the base form, past, and past participle.

lie, lay The verb *lie* means "to rest," "to recline," or "to be in a place." *Lie* never takes an object. The verb *lay* means "to put (something) in a place." *Lay* usually takes an object.

rise, raise The verb *rise* means "to go up" or "to get up." *Rise* seldom takes an object. The verb *raise* means "to lift up" or "to cause (something) to rise." *Raise* usually takes an object.

Exercise For each of the following sentences, underline the correct verb form of the two in parentheses.

EXAMPLE: 1. The bricklayer (<u>rose</u>, raised) from the patio floor and dusted himself off.

1. These rocks have (lain, laid) here for centuries.
2. (Sit, Set) there until your name is called.
3. The nurse (lay, laid) her cool hand on the sick child's forehead.
4. The cows are (lying, laying) in the pasture.
5. The senator and her advisers (sat, set) around the huge conference table.
6. After the picnic, everyone (lay, laid) on blankets to rest.
7. Smoke (rose, raised) from the chimney.
8. The farmhands (sat, set) their lunch pails under a tree.
9. Have you been (sitting, setting) there all afternoon?
10. The sun has already (risen, raised).

Name ______________________ Date ___________ Class ______________

WORKSHEET 5 **Review**

Exercise A Underline the verb in each of the following sentences. Then, on the line provided, write its tense.

EXAMPLE: 1. That is certainly a beautiful bowl. *present*

1. A bowl by Jade Snow Wong sits in the Metropolitan Museum of Art. ______________
2. In her book *No Chinese Stranger,* the artist tells of her struggle to create and sell her pottery. ______________
3. Before her success, she suffered much criticism. ______________
4. She herself destroyed many of her works. ______________
5. Next week, we will read a story about this time in her life: "A Time of Beginnings." ______________

Exercise B For each of the following sentences, give the past or past participle form of the verb that will fit correctly in the blank.

EXAMPLE: 1. Has Alameda *told* you about the book *The Indian Tipi: Its History, Construction, and Use?* (tell)

1. Reginald and Gladys Laubin ______________ that book and several others about Native American culture. (write)
2. The word *tepee,* or *tipi,* has ______________ into English from the Sioux language. (come)
3. Tepees of various sizes once ______________ all across the plains. (stand)
4. I have ______________ pictures of camps full of decorated tepees. (see)
5. For many years now, Native Americans have ______________ tepees out of cloth rather than buffalo hides. (make)
6. The Laubins ______________ their own tepee and lived in it. (build)
7. On the outside of their tepees, the Sioux and Cheyenne peoples usually ______________ designs. (draw)
8. Because the Plains peoples followed the animal herds, they needed housing that could be ______________ from place to place. (take)
9. Even before reading the book, I ______________ that tepee covers were rarely painted inside. (know)
10. Traditionally, women ______________ all the work of making tepees and putting them up. (do)

GRAMMAR/USAGE

Name ______________________ Date ___________ Class ____________________

Exercise C: Proofreading Many of the sentences in the following paragraph contain incorrect verb forms. Cross out each incorrect verb form, and write the correct form on the line provided. If the sentence is correct, write *C*.

EXAMPLE: [1] During the 1800's, many German settlers ~~choosed~~ to live in the Hill Country of central Texas.

1. *chose*

[1] These hardy, determined pioneers builded towns and cleared land for farming. [2] I have went to one town, Fredericksburg, several times. [3] This interesting town lays about eighty miles west of Austin. [4] Fredericksburg use to be in Comanche territory. [5] Early on, German settlers maked peace with the Comanche chiefs. [6] The town then growed rapidly. [7] German-style houses, churches, and public buildings raised along the town's central street. [8] On one of our visits, my family set and talked about the town with a woman who was born there. [9] She said that she had spoke German all her life. [10] When we left, she raised a hand and said, *"Auf Wiedersehen"* (until we meet again).

1. ____________ 6. ____________
2. ____________ 7. ____________
3. ____________ 8. ____________
4. ____________ 9. ____________
5. ____________ 10. ____________

Exercise D: Revising Each of the following sentences contains an error in consistency of verb tense. On the line provided, rewrite each sentence, correcting the error. [Note: Some sentences may be revised in more than one way. However, you only need to provide one revision for each sentence.]

EXAMPLE: 1. We are painting the old table and repaired the chairs.
We are painting the old table and repairing the chairs.
or
We painted the old table and repaired the chairs.

1. By the time the frontier closed in 1890, thousands of hardy pioneers have traveled across the country in Conestoga wagons.

____

2. After the President of the United States threw out the first ball, the baseball game begins.

____

3. The hungry traveler will eat some crackers and drank a cup of milk.

____

4. Eduardo was working in the garden when he hears the strange sound.

____

Name ______________________ Date ____________ Class ____________________

Case Forms

Case is the form of a noun or a pronoun that shows how it is used. There are three cases: *nominative, objective,* and *possessive.*

NOMINATIVE: The **horse** ran swiftly. [subject]
OBJECTIVE: We caught the wild **mare.** [direct object]
I gave **her** some oats. [indirect object]

The possessive case of a noun is usually formed by the addition of an apostrophe and an *s.*

POSSESSIVE: The **horse's** stable was clean.

Unlike nouns, most personal pronouns have different forms for all three cases.

		Nominative	Objective	Possessive
SINGULAR	FIRST PERSON	I	me	my, mine
	SECOND PERSON	you	you	your, yours
	THIRD PERSON	he, she, it	him, her, it	his, her, hers, its
PLURAL	FIRST PERSON	we	us	our, ours
	SECOND PERSON	you	you	your, yours
	THIRD PERSON	they	them	their, theirs

Exercise A On the line provided, write *O* if the italicized noun is in the objective case, *N* if the italicized noun is in the nominative case, or *P* if the italicized noun is in the possessive case.

EXAMPLE: ___*O*___ 1. The oceanographer prepared her *equipment.*

______ 1. Divers wear oxygen *tanks* when exploring.

______ 2. The *divers'* tanks are just one part of their equipment.

______ 3. *Divers* also wear fins and face masks.

______ 4. Sometimes divers see unusual *creatures.*

______ 5. The *ocean's* life forms are fascinating.

Exercise B On the line provided, write *O* if the italicized personal pronoun is in the objective case, *N* if it is in the nominative case, or *P* if it is in the possessive case.

EXAMPLE: ___*N*___ 1. *I* have recently become fascinated by folk-art angels.

______ 1. *My* collection so far is quite small.

______ 2. But *I've* spent many pleasant hours with it.

______ 3. Sometimes the angels need repainting, or I have to make *them* new clothes.

______ 4. I gave one to my mother; *she* keeps it on her bookshelf.

______ 5. I wonder whether other people collect *them*?

Name ________________________ Date ____________ Class ____________________

Nominative Case

A **subject of a verb** is in the nominative case.

SUBJECT: **We** locked the door.

COMPOUND SUBJECT: **Sarah** and **I** painted the scenery.

To help in choosing the correct pronoun in a compound subject, try each form of the pronoun separately.

EXAMPLE: Jamal and (them, they) are practicing skateboard tricks.
Them are practicing skateboard tricks
They are practicing skateboard tricks.

ANSWER: Jamal and **they** are practicing skateboard tricks.

A **predicate nominative** is in the nominative case. A predicate nominative follows a linking verb and explains or identifies the subject of the verb. A personal pronoun used as a predicate nominative follows a form of the verb *be* (*am, is, are, was, were, be,* or *been*).

Our best friends in the first grade were Lester and **she**. [*Lester* and *she* follow the linking verb *were* and identify the subject *friends*.]

NOTE: Expressions such as *It's me, That's her,* and *It was them* are accepted in everyday speaking. In writing, however, such expressions should be avoided.

Exercise A For each sentence in the following paragraph, underline the correct form of the pronoun or pronouns in parentheses.

EXAMPLE: [1] My friends and (I, me) like to spend time outdoors.

[1] Lou and (I, me) asked my mother to drive us to a nearby state park. [2] There (he and I, him and me) set out on a marked trail through a wooded area. [3] Before long, (he and I, him and me) were exploring a snowy area off the beaten track. [4] At dusk Lou and (I, me) reluctantly followed our tracks back to the path. [5] (We, Us) had had the best time of our lives.

Exercise B: Proofreading Most of the sentences below contain errors in pronoun usage. Cross out each error, and write the correct form of the pronoun above it. If a sentence is correct, write C on the line provided.

EXAMPLE: _______ 1. Could it be ~~them~~ *they*?

_______ 1. It must be they.

_______ 2. Two witnesses claimed that the burglar was him.

_______ 3. Is the last performer her?

_______ 4. The next speaker will be him.

_______ 5. Among the invited guests are Luther and us.

Name ______________________ Date ____________ Class ______________________

Objective Case A

A **direct object** is in the objective case. A direct object follows an action verb and tells *who* or *what* receives the action of the verb.

The sea gull attacked **me**. [*Me* tells *whom* the sea gull attacked.]

To help in choosing the correct pronoun in a compound direct object, try each form of the pronoun separately in the sentence.

EXAMPLE: Toshiro photographed Leslie and (they, them) on the steps.
Toshiro photographed *they* on the steps.
Toshiro photographed *them* on the steps.
ANSWER: Toshiro photographed Leslie and **them** on the steps.

An **indirect object** is in the objective case. An indirect object comes between an action verb and a direct object and tells *to whom* or *to what* or *for whom* or *for what*.

Grandmother told **us** tales of her younger days. [*Us* is the indirect object, telling *to whom* Grandmother told the tales.]

To help in choosing the correct pronoun in a compound indirect object, try each form of the pronoun separately in the sentence.

EXAMPLE: Mick gave Amy and (he, him) a signal.
Mick gave *he* a signal. *or* Mick gave *him* a signal.
ANSWER: Mick gave Amy and **him** a signal.

Exercise Choose appropriate pronouns for the blanks in the following sentences. Use a variety of pronouns, but do not use *you* or *it*. Then identify each pronoun you chose as a direct object (*DO*) or an indirect object (*IO*).

EXAMPLE: 1. Have you seen Kim and her—DO?

1. The manager hired Susana and ______________________.
2. Lana sent ______________________ and ______________________ invitations.
3. We gave Grandpa López and ______________________ round-trip tickets to Oaxaca.
4. The firefighters rescued ______________________ and ______________________.
5. Aunt Coretta showed my cousins and ______________________ a mask from Nigeria.
6. The show entertained the children and ______________________.
7. The waiter served ______________________ and ______________________ sushi.
8. Our team chose ______________________ and ______________________ as captains.
9. The election committee nominated Gerry and ______________________.
10. The clerk gave Misako and ______________________ the receipt for the radio.

GRAMMAR/USAGE

Name ______________________ Date ____________ Class ______________________

Objective Case B

An **object of a preposition** is in the objective case. The object of a preposition is a noun or a pronoun that follows a preposition. Together with any of the object's modifiers, the preposition and its object make a **prepositional phrase.**

by them   between you and me   before her   in front of him   with us

A pronoun used as the object of a preposition should always be in the objective case.

The dog ran right by **them**. [*Them* is the object of the preposition *by*.]

Standing between **him** and **her** was Mario. [*Him* and *her* are objects of the preposition *between*.]

To help in choosing the correct pronoun when the object of a preposition is compound, try each form of the pronoun separately in the sentence.

EXAMPLE: Behind Dr. Haddad and (she, her) stood the new patient.
Behind *she* stood the new patient.
Behind *her* stood the new patient.

ANSWER: Behind Dr. Haddad and **her** stood the new patient.

Exercise For each of the following sentences, underline the correct form of the pronoun in parentheses.

EXAMPLE: 1. Of all the people who traveled with Lewis and Clark, Sacagawea was particularly helpful to (<u>them</u>, they).

1. Sacagawea's husband, a guide named Toussaint Charbonneau, joined the expedition with (her, she) and their newborn baby.
2. The Shoshone were Sacagawea's people, and she longed to return to (them, they).
3. Captain Clark soon realized how important she would be to Lewis and (he, him).
4. The land they were traveling through was familiar to (she, her).
5. Luckily for (she, her) and the expedition, they met a group of friendly Shoshone.
6. From (they, them), Sacagawea obtained the ponies that Lewis and Clark needed.
7. Sacagawea's baby boy delighted the expedition's leaders, and they took good care of (he, him).
8. In fact, Captain Clark made a promise to (she, her) and Charbonneau that he would give the boy a good education.
9. At the age of eighteen, the boy befriended a prince and traveled with (him, he) in Europe.
10. Although sources disagree about when Sacagawea died, a gravestone for (she, her) in Wyoming bears the date April 9, 1884.

Name ______________________ Date ____________ Class ____________________

WORKSHEET 5 Who *and* Whom

The pronoun *who* has different forms in the nominative and objective cases. *Who* is the nominative form; *whom* is the objective form.

When deciding whether to use *who* or *whom* in a question, follow these steps:

STEP 1: Rephrase the question as a statement.

STEP 2: Decide how the pronoun is used in the statement—as a subject, predicate nominative, object of the verb, or object of a preposition.

STEP 3: Determine the case of the pronoun according to the rules of standard English.

STEP 4: Select the correct form of the pronoun.

EXAMPLE: (Who, Whom) do you admire?

STEP 1: The statement is *You do admire (who, whom).*

STEP 2: The subject is *you*, the verb is *do admire,* and the pronoun is a direct object.

STEP 3: A pronoun used as a direct object should be in the objective case.

STEP 4: The objective form is *whom.*

ANSWER: **Whom** do you admire?

Exercise A For each of the following sentences, underline the correct form of the pronoun in parentheses.

EXAMPLE: 1. (Who, <u>Whom</u>) will your brother invite to his party?

1. (Who, Whom) will be our substitute teacher while Mr. Chenis is away?
2. (Who, Whom) has Ms. Spears chosen to serve on the Kite Festival committee?
3. Of the three candidates, (who, whom) do you have the most confidence in?
4. To (who, whom) do you wish these flowers sent?
5. For (who, whom) is the leftover macaroni and cheese?

Exercise B On the lines provided, write the correct pronoun form, *who* or *whom.*

EXAMPLE: 1. _*Who*_ painted that beautiful still life?

1. ______________________ is captain of the football team this year?
2. To ______________________ did you give your old skateboard?
3. ______________________ will you call to come and pick us up after band practice?
4. ______________________ were the first Americans?
5. In the last play of the game, ______________________ passed the ball to ______________________?

GRAMMAR/USAGE

Name ______________________ Date ____________ Class ______________________

Chapter 4: Using Pronouns

Other Pronoun Problems

Sometimes a pronoun is followed directly by a noun that identifies the pronoun. Such a noun is called an **appositive**. To help in choosing which pronoun to use before an appositive, omit the appositive and try each form of the pronoun separately.

EXAMPLE: The crowd cheered (we, us) rodeo clowns. [*Clowns* is the appositive identifying the pronoun.]

The crowd cheered *us.* *or* The crowd cheered *we.*

ANSWER: The crowd cheered **us** rodeo clowns. [*Us* is correct because it is the object of *cheered.*]

Reflexive pronouns (such as *myself, himself,* and *yourselves*) can be used as objects. Use a reflexive pronoun only when the pronoun refers to the subject. A reflexive pronoun should not be used as a subject.

STANDARD: I allowed **myself** to read one more chapter.

NONSTANDARD: She gave the books to Maura and myself.
STANDARD: She gave the books to Maura and **me**.

NONSTANDARD: Roberto and myself like detective novels.
STANDARD: Roberto and **I** like detective novels.

Do not use the nonstandard forms *hisself* and *theirself* in place of *himself* and *themselves.*

Exercise A For each of the following sentences, underline the correct form of the pronoun in parentheses.

1. The famous golfer Lee Trevino is a symbol of pride to (we, us) Mexican Americans.
2. Miss Jefferson, (we, us) students want to thank you for all your help.
3. (We, Us) contestants shook hands warmly.
4. The best choice would be (we, us) skaters.
5. Mr. Red Cloud told (we, us) Eagle Scouts what to do.

Exercise B: Proofreading Most of the sentences below contain errors in pronoun usage. Cross out each incorrect pronoun, and write the correct form above it. If a sentence is correct, write C on the line provided.

EXAMPLE: ______ 1. He taught ~~hisself~~ *himself* how to program a computer.

______ 1. Before they started to read, Zack and himself asked three questions.

______ 2. My little brother often falls down, but he never seems to hurt hisself.

______ 3. The other guests and myself helped clean up after the party.

______ 4. John Yellowtail enjoyed himself at the festival.

______ 5. If the early settlers wanted cloth, themselves had to spin it.

Name ______________________ Date ____________ Class ____________________

Chapter 4: Using Pronouns

WORKSHEET 7 Review

Exercise A For each of the following sentences, underline the correct form of the pronoun in parentheses. Then, on the line provided, tell what part of the sentence each pronoun is—subject *(S)*, predicate nominative *(PN)*, direct object *(DO)*, indirect object *(IO)*, or object of a preposition *(OP)*.

EXAMPLE: 1. My brother Pete and (I, me) wanted to know more about Elizabeth Blackwell. __S__

1. Mom told Pete and (I, me) the fact that Elizabeth Blackwell was the first woman ever to graduate from medical school in the United States. ________
2. Geneva College granted (she, her) a degree in 1849. ________
3. At first, no male doctor would let her work for (he, him) because she was a woman. ________
4. Pete and (I, me) admire Elizabeth Blackwell for not giving up. ________
5. She wanted to help the poor and opened her own clinic for (they, them). ________
6. Wealthy citizens were soon supporting (she, her) and the clinic with donations. ________
7. Before long, one of the most talked-about topics in medical circles was (she, her) and the excellent work she was doing for the poor. ________
8. Mom and (we, us) read more about Dr. Blackwell, and we learned that she opened a medical school just for women. ________
9. Dr. Blackwell set high standards for students and gave (they, them) hard courses of study to complete. ________
10. In time, they became excellent physicians, and she was proud of (they, them). ________

Exercise B For each of the following sentences, underline the correct form of the pronoun or pronouns in parentheses.

EXAMPLE: 1. To me, the two most interesting explorers are (he, him) and Vasco da Gama.

1. The team captains will be Jack and (he, him).
2. Was the joke played on you and (him, himself)?
3. We were warned by our parents and (they, them).
4. The Washington twins and (I, me) belong to the same club.
5. Who are (they, them)?

GRAMMAR/USAGE

6. Pelé and (him, he) both played soccer for the New York Cosmos.
7. "What do you think of (he and I, him and me)?" I asked.
8. "You and (he, him) are improving," they replied.
9. When Miriam Makeba and the troupe of African musicians arrived, we gave (she and they, her and them) a party.
10. Do you remember my sister and (me, myself)?
11. The coach spoke to (we, us) players before the game.
12. The finalists in the talent contest are Alfredo, Sylvia, and (I, me).
13. Are you and (she, her) going to celebrate Kwanzaa this year?
14. Père Toussaint taught my brother and (I, me) to play a Cajun fiddle tune.
15. Mom, Andy gave (himself, hisself) the biggest piece of banana bread.
16. Both (he and she, him and her) have promised to write us this summer.
17. They congratulated (themselves, theirselves) on a job well done.
18. Don't leave without (he and I, him and me).
19. (We, Us) skiers had a beautiful view from the lift.
20. (Who, Whom) were you expecting?

Exercise C: Proofreading Most of the following sentences contain errors in pronoun usage. Cross through each incorrect pronoun, and write the correct form above it. If a sentence is correct, write C on the line provided.

EXAMPLE: ______ 1. Have you and ~~her~~ *she* finished reading the stories by William Sydney Porter?

______ 1. For a famous writer, him certainly led a tough life.

______ 2. According to the First National Bank of Austin, William Sydney Porter helped hisself to a thousand dollars.

______ 3. He escaped to Central America.

______ 4. He met some outlaws, and them and him spent the stolen money.

______ 5. However, when his wife got sick, he returned to Texas and to herself.

______ 6. Soon captured, he spent about three years in a penitentiary in Columbus, Ohio.

______ 7. The prisoners and their stories were fascinating to he, and Porter wrote many stories there.

______ 8. Did him know a guard there named Orrin Henry?

______ 9. Perhaps from the guard Porter borrowed a pen name for hisself—O. Henry.

______ 10. O. Henry left over six hundred stories for we eager readers of fiction.

Name ______________________ Date ____________ Class ______________________

Degrees of Comparison

A **modifier** is a word, a phrase, or a clause that describes or limits the meaning of another word. Two kinds of modifiers—**adjectives** and **adverbs**—may be used to compare things.

The three degrees of comparison of modifiers are **positive, comparative,** and **superlative**.

	Adjectives
POSITIVE	A boxer is a **big** dog. [no comparison]
COMPARATIVE	A mastiff is **bigger** than a boxer. [one compared with another]
SUPERLATIVE	A Great Dane is the **biggest** dog of all. [one compared with many others]
	Adverbs
POSITIVE	Juan works **carefully**. [no comparison]
COMPARATIVE	Julia works **more carefully** than Juan. [one compared with another]
SUPERLATIVE	Of all my friends, Albert works **most carefully**. [one compared with many others]

Exercise On the lines provided, write *P* if the italicized modifier is in the positive degree. Write *C* if it is in the comparative degree. Write *S* if it is in the superlative degree. Then write *1*, *2*, or *3 or more* to tell how many things are being described or compared.

EXAMPLE: 1. Who is the *tallest* basketball player on the team? S—3 or more

1. Which is *heavier*—a pound of feathers or a pound of nails? ______________
2. Of the lion, tiger, and cheetah, the cheetah can run *most rapidly*. ______________
3. Maura is the *most qualified* candidate who ever ran for president. ______________
4. Bernice dances *more gracefully* than I do. ______________
5. This math problem seems extremely *difficult*. ______________
6. *Bravely*, he stepped up and told the truth. ______________
7. It rained *harder* yesterday than it did today. ______________
8. The Yukon River is *longer* than the Rio Grande. ______________
9. Of all the players, Peder kicks the ball *most forcefully*. ______________
10. Of the six department stores in the mall, this one is the *largest*. ______________

GRAMMAR/USAGE

Name ______________________ Date ____________ Class ______________________

Regular Comparison

In comparisons, adjectives and adverbs take different forms. The specific form that is used depends on how many syllables the modifier has and how many things are being compared.

Most one-syllable modifiers form their comparative and superlative degrees by adding *–er* and *–est*. Some two-syllable modifiers form their comparative and superlative degrees by adding *–er* and *–est*. Other two-syllable modifiers form their comparative and superlative degrees by using *more* and *most*. Modifiers that have three or more syllables form their comparative and superlative degrees by using *more* and *most*.

	Modifiers with One Syllable		Modifiers with Two Syllables		Modifiers with Three or More Syllables	
POSITIVE	fast	nice	cheaply	simple	foolishly	beautiful
COMPARATIVE	faster	nicer	more cheaply	simpler	more foolishly	more beautiful
SUPERLATIVE	fastest	nicest	most cheaply	simplest	most foolishly	most beautiful

To show decreasing comparisons, all modifiers form their comparative and superlative degrees with *less* and *least*.

POSITIVE:	bright	proudly
COMPARATIVE:	less bright	less proudly
SUPERLATIVE:	least bright	least proudly

NOTE: When you are not sure how a two-syllable modifier forms its degrees of comparison, look up the word in a dictionary.

Exercise On the lines provided, write the comparative and superlative degrees of each modifier below. Use a dictionary if necessary.

EXAMPLE: 1. light *lighter* *lightest*

POSITIVE	COMPARATIVE	SUPERLATIVE
1. near	____________	____________
2. great	____________	____________
3. carefully	____________	____________
4. honestly	____________	____________
5. small	____________	____________
6. tiny	____________	____________
7. timidly	____________	____________
8. enthusiastically	____________	____________
9. safe	____________	____________
10. shady	____________	____________

Name ______________ Date __________ Class ______________

Uses of Comparative and Superlative Forms

Use the comparative degree when comparing two things. Use the superlative degree when comparing more than two.

COMPARATIVE: This pumpkin is **riper** than that one.
SUPERLATIVE: Of all the ones in the field, this pumpkin ripened **most quickly**.

Avoid the common mistake of using the superlative degree to compare two things.

NONSTANDARD: Who is the tallest twin?
STANDARD: Who is the **taller** twin?

Include the word *other* or *else* when comparing a member of a group with the rest of the group.

NONSTANDARD: Matt scored more touchdowns than anyone on the team. [Matt is a member of the team and cannot score more touchdowns than himself.]
STANDARD: Matt scored more touchdowns than anyone **else** on the team.

Exercise Write the form of the adjective or adverb in parentheses that will correctly fill the blank in each of the following sentences. You may use a dictionary.

EXAMPLE: 1. The Corn Palace in Mitchell, South Dakota, is one of the *most unusual* buildings in the United States. (unusual)

1. The Corn Palace is ______________ than I thought it would be. (big)
2. People in Mitchell try to make each year's Corn Palace ______________ than the one before. (pretty)
3. The building looks the ______________ in September after new corn and grasses are put on it. (fresh)
4. Some workers saw and nail the corn to panels, while others find it ______________ to hang the panels on the building. (easy)
5. Of two huge corn murals on the Corn Palace, I thought one was ______________. (lively)
6. The mural of the dancing figure was the ______________ to me. (mysterious)
7. The murals feature Native American scenes designed by Mitchell's ______________ artist, Oscar Howe. (famous)
8. The life of this Sioux artist is the ______________ story I've ever heard. (interesting)
9. My parents walked ______________ around the Corn Palace than I did and studied every design. (slowly)
10. The family from Mexico traveled a ______________ distance than we did to see the Corn Palace. (great)

GRAMMAR/USAGE

Name ______________________ Date ____________ Class ______________________

Irregular Comparison

Some modifiers do not form their comparative and superlative degrees by using the regular methods.

Positive	Comparative	Superlative
bad	worse	worst
far	farther	farthest
good	better	best
well	better	best
many	more	most
much	more	most

Exercise A Underline the correct form of the modifier in parentheses.

EXAMPLE: 1. They traveled (farther, farthest) into the jungle than we did.

1. Carlos likes science fiction stories (better, best) than mysteries.
2. I think Friday is the (better, best) day in the whole week.
3. (Many, More) people came to the meeting than we had expected.
4. Of all the members of the team, Inez bats (most well, best).
5. My cousin was able to save (much, more) money than I.
6. Of my four brothers, Chet has delivered the (more, most) newspapers.
7. After supper, I felt (worse, worst) than I had in the afternoon.
8. We hiked (more far, farther) today than we hiked yesterday.
9. Mom plays the (better, best) game of tennis in the family.
10. This is the (worse, worst) cold I've ever had.

Exercise B Choose a modifier from the chart above to complete each of the following sentences. Write the correct form of the modifer on the line provided.

EXAMPLE: 1. Ugh! That was the *worst* joke I've ever heard.

1. In my opinion, that was a ______________________ movie.
2. Which of the four theaters is ______________________ from your house?
3. Lita is the ______________________ speller of the three contestants.
4. Georgia plays ______________________ in all sports.
5. My tennis serve is ______________________ than it was last year.

Name ______________________ Date ____________ Class ______________________

Double Comparison and Double Negative

A **double comparison** is the use of both *–er* and *more (less)* or both *–est* and *most (least)* to form a comparison. A comparison should be formed in only one of these two ways, not both. Avoid using double comparisons.

NONSTANDARD: I have just read Carl Sagan's most latest book.
STANDARD: I have just read Carl Sagan's **latest** book.

A **double negative** is the use of two negative words to express one negative idea. Some common negative words are *never, not (–n't), hardly, no, no one, nobody,* and *none.*

Use only one negative word to express a negative idea.

NONSTANDARD: I haven't never read a book by Carl Sagan.
STANDARD: I **have never** read a book by Carl Sagan.
STANDARD: I **haven't ever** read a book by Carl Sagan.

Exercise A: Proofreading On the line provided, write the incorrect modifier in each of the following sentences. Then write the correct form of the modifier.

EXAMPLE: 1. I have been studying more harder lately.
more harder—harder

1. Sunday was more rainier than Saturday. ______________
2. That is the most saddest story I have ever heard. ______________
3. Are you exercising more longer than you used to? ______________
4. He has a more stronger backhand than his brother. ______________

Exercise B: Revising On the line provided, revise each of the following sentences to eliminate the double negative. You only need to show one possible revision.

EXAMPLE: 1. I couldn't find no one to go camping with.
I couldn't find anyone to go camping with.
or
I could find no one to go camping with.

1. I didn't see no one I knew at the game.

____

2. Early explorers searched that area of Florida for gold, but they didn't find none.

____

3. We couldn't hardly hear the guest speaker.

____

4. Double negatives don't have no place in standard English.

____

GRAMMAR/USAGE

Name ____________________ Date __________ Class ____________________

Misplaced Prepositional Phrases

A **prepositional phrase** consists of a preposition, a noun or a pronoun called the object of the preposition, and any modifiers of that object. A prepositional phrase may be used as an adjective or as an adverb.

ADJECTIVE PHRASE: A package **from Mexico** came today.
ADVERB PHRASE: This package came **from Mexico**.

An adjective phrase should be placed directly after the word it modifies.

MISPLACED: The dog belongs to that man with the black spots.
CLEAR: The dog **with the black spots** belongs to that man.

A prepositional phrase used as an adverb should be placed near the word it modifies.

MISPLACED: We talked about the football game in the cafeteria.
CLEAR: **In the cafeteria,** we talked about the football game.
CLEAR: We talked **in the cafeteria** about the football game.

Avoid placing a prepositional phrase in such a way that it appears to modify either of two words. Place the phrase so that it clearly modifies the word you intend it to modify.

MISPLACED: We decided on Tuesday we would visit you. [Does the phrase modify *decided* or *would visit*?]
CLEAR: **On Tuesday,** we decided we would visit you.
CLEAR: We decided we would visit you **on Tuesday**.

Exercise: Revising On the line provided, revise each of the sentences below by putting the misplaced modifying phrase where it belongs.

EXAMPLE: 1. The poster caught my eye on the wall.
The poster on the wall caught my eye.

1. That woman was out walking her dog in high heels and a tweed suit this morning.
____

2. I knew by the end of the year I'd need a bicycle.
____

3. Hoy taught us with chopsticks how to eat rice.
____

4. Our teacher said on Monday the class would put on a play.
____

5. Don't forget to take the box to the store with the empty bottles.
____

Name ______________ Date __________ Class ______________

Misplaced and Dangling Participial Phrases

A participial phrase consists of a verb form—either a present participle or a past participle—and its related words. A participial phrase modifies a noun or a pronoun.

Walking home, I saw a robin. [The phrase modifies the pronoun *I*.]

Built of twigs, the nest is sturdy. [The phrase modifies the noun *nest*.]

Like a prepositional phrase, a participial phrase should be placed as close as possible to the word it modifies.

MISPLACED: I saw a robin walking home. [Was the robin walking home?]

A participial phrase that does not clearly and sensibly modify any word in the sentence is a dangling participial phrase. To correct a dangling phrase, supply a word that the phrase can modify, or add a subject and a verb to the dangling modifier.

DANGLING: Walking to school, the experience was exciting.

CLEAR: **Walking to school,** I had an exciting experience. [The phrase clearly modifies *I*.]

CLEAR: I had an exciting experience **while I was walking to school.**

Exercise: Revising All of the following sentences contain misplaced or dangling participial phrases. On the line provided, revise each sentence to eliminate the misplaced or dangling phrase. [Hint: You will need to add, delete, or rearrange some words.] Participial phrases that begin or interrupt sentences should be set off by commas.

EXAMPLE: 1. Made from matzo meal, Rachel shapes tasty dumplings.
Rachel shapes tasty dumplings made from matzo meal.

1. Pacing around its kill, I watched the lion.
____
2. Wearing a bright orange suit and floppy yellow shoes, the circus featured a clown.
____
3. Filled with daisies, the girls walked through the field.
____
4. The turkey was large enough for three families stuffed with sage and bread crumbs.
____
5. Tired from the long walk through the snow, food and rest were welcomed.
____

GRAMMAR/USAGE

Name ______________________ Date ____________ Class ______________________

Misplaced Adjective Clauses

A **clause** is a group of words that contains a verb and its subject and is used as a part of a sentence. An **adjective clause** modifies a noun or a pronoun. Most adjective clauses begin with a relative pronoun, such as *that, which, who, whom,* or *whose.*

The actor **who starred in the film** gave me his autograph.

Pigs **that had escaped their pen** ran across the yard.

Like phrases, clauses should be placed as close as possible to the word or words they modify.

MISPLACED: The book was about insects that we read. [Did we read the insects?]

CLEAR: The book **that we read** was about insects.

Exercise A Underline the adjective clause in each of the following sentences. Then underline twice the noun or pronoun that the clause modifies.

EXAMPLE: 1. I have a friend who likes horror stories.

1. He is a big fan of Stephen King's stories, like *Cujo,* which was made into a movie.
2. Like King, whom my friend admires, he often writes stories of his own.
3. Yet, he had never heard of Edgar Allan Poe's stories, which are true classics and horrifying enough for anyone.
4. I love the story that is about the sound of a heartbeat.
5. Also, my friend had never heard of Mary Shelley, whose novel *Frankenstein* has terrified readers for more than a hundred years.

Exercise B: Revising Find the misplaced adjective clauses in the following sentences. Then revise each sentence, placing the clause near the word it modifies.

EXAMPLE: 1. I showed the fabric to my sister that was made in Kenya.
I showed the fabric that was made in Kenya to my sister.

1. The students received an A who made the first presentation.

 ____

2. The kitten belongs to my neighbor that is in the tree.

 ____

3. My friend Beverly visited me who lives in Sarasota, Florida.

 ____

4. The doctor said that the triplets were healthy who examined them.

 ____

5. The picnic in the park that we had was fun.

 ____

Name ____________________ Date ____________ Class ____________

Chapter 5: Using Modifiers

WORKSHEET 9 Review

Exercise A On the lines provided, complete the following chart. For each modifier in the positive degree, write the corresponding modifiers in the comparative and superlative degrees.

EXAMPLE: 1. tall *taller* *tallest*

POSITIVE	COMPARATIVE	SUPERLATIVE
1. far	____________	____________
2. many	____________	____________
3. terrific	____________	____________
4. ripe	____________	____________
5. silently	____________	____________
6. young	____________	____________
7. marvelous	____________	____________
8. shady	____________	____________
9. gently	____________	____________
10. strong	____________	____________

Exercise B: Revising The following sentences contain errors in the use of modifiers. On the line provided, revise each sentence to correct the error.

EXAMPLE: 1. My cold is worst today than it was yesterday.
My cold is worse today than it was yesterday.

1. Kendo, a Japanese martial art, is more gracefuller than many other sports.

____

2. Sylvia Yee plays chess better than anyone her age.

____

3. Time doesn't hardly move during the summer.

____

4. Which of the twins is strongest?

____

5. Some people don't seem to have no control over their tempers.

____

GRAMMAR/USAGE

Exercise C: Revising Each of the following sentences contains an error in the placement of a modifier. Revise each sentence by adding, deleting, or rearranging words.

EXAMPLE: 1. The record was the soundtrack of the movie that we heard.
The record that we heard was the soundtrack of the movie.

1. The waiter brought plates to Terrell and me piled high with spaghetti and sauce.

____

2. Barking and growling, the stranger was frightened by the dogs.

____

3. He said on Friday no one had applied for the job.

____

4. The house is about a mile from Dunbar High School that my parents want to buy.

____

5. Trees are covered with pecans all over the city at this time of year.

____

Exercise D: Revising Each of the following sentences contains an error in the form or placement of a modifier. Revise each sentence by changing the form of a modifier or by adding, deleting, or rearranging words.

EXAMPLE: 1. Of all the actors on the TV series *Life Goes On,* Chris Burke is the one I admire more.
Of all the actors on the TV series Life Goes On, Chris Burke is the one I admire the most.

1. Born with Down's syndrome, Chris is the younger of four children.

____

2. He played a character on the show whose name is Corky.

____

3. Chris certainly is one of the bestest actors that I've seen.

____

4. Chris doesn't hardly ever seem nervous about being a TV star.

____

5. Saying he has "Up syndrome," Chris's attitude is usually positive.

____

Name ______________________ Date ____________ Class ______________

Prepositional Phrases

A **phrase** is a group of related words that is used as a single part of speech and does not contain a verb and its subject. A **prepositional phrase** includes a preposition, a noun or a pronoun called the **object of the preposition,** and any modifiers of that object.

We will be reading **about King Arthur**. [The noun *King Arthur* is the object of the preposition *about*.]

Any modifier that comes between the preposition and its object is part of the prepositional phrase.

He removed a great sword **from a solid rock**. [The adjectives *a* and *solid* modify the object *rock*.]

An object of a preposition may be compound.

According to ancient legends and stories, he and his knights were dedicated to noble ideals. [Both *legends* and *stories* are objects of the preposition *according to*.]

Exercise A Underline each prepositional phrase in the following paragraph. [Note: A sentence may contain more than one prepositional phrase.]

EXAMPLE: [1] Many soldiers fought bravely during the Vietnam War.

[1] One of these soldiers was Jan C. Scruggs. [2] When the war was over, he and other veterans wondered why there was no national memorial honoring those who had served in Vietnam. [3] Scruggs decided he would raise funds for a memorial to the Vietnam veterans. [4] The memorial would include the names of all American soldiers who had died or were missing. [5] Organizing the project took years of great effort. [6] Many different people contributed their talents to the project. [7] Maya Ying Lin, a college student, designed the memorial that now stands in Washington, D.C. [8] You have probably seen the V-shaped, black granite wall that was built from Lin's design. [9] A glass company from Memphis, Tennessee, stenciled each name on the shiny granite. [10] Now, the men and women who fought and died in Vietnam will never be forgotten by the people of the United States.

Exercise B On the line provided, write a prepositional phrase to complete each sentence.

EXAMPLE: 1. We are listening *to the news* on the radio.

1. A car ______________________ pulled up in front of us.
2. ______________________ was a pile of newspapers.
3. The woman ______________________ is the one I met yesterday.
4. A cat was curled up ______________________.
5. ______________________ I found an old bag of marbles.

Name ________________________ Date ____________ Class ______________________

Adjective Phrases

An **adjective phrase** is a prepositional phrase that modifies a noun or a pronoun. An adjective phrase tells *what kind* or *which one.*

One theme **of the story *A Christmas Carol*** is kindness. [The prepositional phrase *of the story A Christmas Carol* modifies the noun *theme.*]

More than one adjective phrase may modify the same word.

This story **about Ebenezer Scrooge by Dickens** has become famous. [The two phrases *about Ebenezer Scrooge* and *by Dickens* both modify the noun *story.*]

An adjective phrase always follows the word it modifies. That word may be the object of another prepositional phrase.

One **of the ghosts in the story** frightens Scrooge. [The adjective phrase *of the ghosts* modifies the pronoun *one*. The adjective phrase *in the story* modifies the noun *ghosts,* the object of the first phrase.]

NOTE: Be careful not to confuse an infinitive with a prepositional phrase beginning with *to*. A prepositional phrase always has an object that is a noun or a pronoun. An infinitive is a verb form that usually begins with *to*.

PREPOSITIONAL PHRASE: Bob Cratchit is clerk **to Ebenezer Scrooge**.
INFINITIVE: Scrooge does not want **to celebrate** the holidays.

Exercise A Underline the adjective phrases in the following sentences.

EXAMPLE: 1. Charles Dickens wrote many tales about poverty.

1. *A Christmas Carol* is a story about a rich man's repentance.
2. Ebenezer Scrooge is a man with wealth and property.
3. His clerk, Bob Cratchit, leads a life of miserable poverty.
4. Spirits from the past, present, and future come to warn Scrooge to change his ways.
5. One of them shows Scrooge the poor yet happy Cratchit family.

Exercise B Underline the adjective phrase(s) in each of the following sentences. Then underline twice the word that each phrase modifies.

EXAMPLE: 1. Marie Sklodowska Curie was awarded the Nobel Prize for her work in science.

1. While she was still a student, Marie became friends with Pierre Curie.
2. Pierre had already gained fame as a scientist.
3. The two of them met in Paris, France.
4. Their enthusiasm for science brought them together.
5. The marriage between the two lovers of science was a true partnership.

Name ______________________ Date ___________ Class ______________________

Adverb Phrases

An **adverb phrase** is a prepositional phrase that modifies a verb, an adjective, or an adverb.

MODIFIES A VERB: The assembly line method was invented **by Henry Ford**. [The adverb phrase *by Henry Ford* modifies the verb *was invented*.]

MODIFIES AN ADJECTIVE: People were ready **for a change**. [The adverb phrase *for a change* modifies the adjective *ready*.]

MODIFIES ANOTHER ADVERB: Sid came late **in the afternoon**. [The adverb phrase *in the afternoon* modifies the adverb *late*.]

An adverb phrase tells *how, when, where, why,* or *to what extent* (that is, *how long, how many,* or *how far*).

An adverb phrase may come before or after the word it modifies.

During the 1950's, the car became increasingly important.

The car became increasingly important **during the 1950's**.

More than one adverb phrase may modify the same word or words.

They worked **for hours on the assembly line**. [The adverb phrases *for hours* and *on the assembly line* modify the verb *worked*.]

An adverb phrase may be followed by an adjective phrase modifying the object of the adverb phrase.

Ask the librarian **about books on cars**. [The adverb phrase *about books* modifies the verb *ask*. The adjective phrase *on cars* modifies the noun *books*.]

Exercise Underline the adverb phrase in each of the sentences below. On the line provided, write the word or words that each phrase modifies. [Note: Do not identify adjective phrases.]

EXAMPLE: 1. Pecos Bill still lives in the legends about him. *lives*

1. When he was only a baby, Pecos Bill fell into the Pecos River. ______________
2. His parents searched for him but couldn't find him. ______________
3. He was saved by coyotes, who raised him. ______________
4. He thought for many years that he was a coyote. ______________
5. After a long argument, a cowhand convinced him that he was not a coyote. ______________
6. During a drought he dug the bed of the Rio Grande. ______________
7. On one occasion Bill rode a cyclone. ______________
8. A mountain lion once leaped from a ledge above Bill's head. ______________
9. Bill was ready for trouble and soon had the mountain lion tamed. ______________
10. Stories like these about Pecos Bill are common in the West. ______________

Name ______________________ Date ___________ Class ______________________

Participles and Participial Phrases

A **verbal** is a form of a verb used as a noun, an adjective, or an adverb. A **participle** is a verb form that can be used as an adjective. There are two kinds of participles—*present participles* and *past participles.*

Present participles end in *–ing*.

The **crying** child asked for her mother. [*Crying* is the present participle form of the verb *cry*. The participle modifies the noun *child*.]

Most **past participles** end in *–d* or *–ed*. Others are irregularly formed.

Scattered evidence was found in the house. [The past participle *scattered* modifies the noun *evidence*.]

Sheila needed a **written** excuse from her doctor. [The irregular past participle *written* modifies the noun *excuse*.]

A **participial phrase** consists of a participle and all of the words related to the participle. The entire phrase is used as an adjective.

The record **set by Jose Canseco** is impressive. [The participle *set* is modified by the prepositional phrase *by Jose Canseco*. The participial phrase modifies *record*.]

Hammering the nails, Midori felt content. [The participle *hammering* has the direct object *nails*. The participial phrase modifies *Midori*.]

Do not confuse a participle used as an adjective with a participle used as part of a verb phrase.

PARTICIPLE: **Laughing,** we accepted her explanation.

VERB PHRASE: Soon, we **were laughing** at the kittens.

Exercise Underline the participial phrases in the following sentences. Then draw two lines under the word or words each phrase modifies.

EXAMPLE: 1. Living over four hundred years ago, Leonardo da Vinci kept journals of his many ideas and inventions.

1. The journals, written in reverse mirror writing, fill more than five thousand pages.
2. Leonardo drew many pictures showing birds in flight.
3. He designed machines based on his sketches of birds in flight.
4. His design for a helicopter was the first recorded in history.
5. Studying the eye, Leonardo understood the sense of sight.
6. He worked hard, filling his journals with sketches.
7. In his artwork, Leonardo used the solutions reached in his journals.
8. The hands sketched in the journals helped him paint the hands of the *Mona Lisa*.
9. Painting on a large wall, Leonardo created *The Last Supper*.
10. Leonardo, experimenting continually, had little time to paint in his later years.

Name ______________________ Date ____________ Class ______________________

Infinitives and Infinitive Phrases

An **infinitive** is a verb form that can be used as a noun, an adjective, or an adverb. An infinitive usually begins with *to*.

> **To swim** is refreshing. [noun, subject of sentence]
>
> The best place **to swim** is the local pool. [adjective modifying *place*]
>
> Colleen goes to the local pool **to swim**. [adverb modifying *goes*]

An **infinitive phrase** consists of an infinitive and its modifiers and complements. The entire infinitive phrase may act as an adjective, an adverb, or a noun.

> **To write well** requires hard work. [The infinitive phrase is used as a noun. The infinitive *to write* is modified by the adverb *well*.]
>
> The time **to begin a paper** is long before the paper is due. [The infinitive phrase is used as an adjective modifying the noun *time*. The infinitive *to begin* has the direct object *paper*.]
>
> Elston went to the library **to write his paper**. [The infinitive phrase is used as an adverb modifying the verb *went*. The infinitive *to write* has the direct object *paper*.]

NOTE: *To* plus a noun or a pronoun *(to class, to them, to the dance)* is a prepositional phrase, not an infinitive. Be careful not to confuse infinitives with prepositional phrases beginning with *to*.

Exercise A Underline the infinitives in the following sentences. If a sentence does not contain an infinitive, write *none* on the line provided.

EXAMPLE: ______ 1. I would like to go to New York City someday.

______ 1. My first activity would be to visit the Statue of Liberty.

______ 2. Thousands of people go to see the statue every day.

______ 3. The statue holds a torch to symbolize freedom.

______ 4. France gave the statue to the United States in 1884.

______ 5. It was a gift to express the friendship between the two nations.

Exercise B Underline the infinitive phrase in each of the following sentences.

EXAMPLE: 1. We went to the park to watch birds.

1. A bird is able to control each of its feathers.
2. Birds use their feathers to push their bodies through the air.
3. Human beings learned to build aircraft by studying birds.
4. A bird sings to claim its territory.
5. To recognize the songs of different birds takes practice.

SENTENCES

Name ________________________ Date ____________ Class ____________________

Review

Exercise A In the sentences below, underline each prepositional phrase. On the line provided, classify it as an adjective phrase *(ADJ)* or an adverb phrase *(ADV)*. Then write the word or words the phrase modifies.

EXAMPLE: 1. Here is some information about sharks.
ADJ—information

1. Did you know that there are hundreds of types? ____________
2. Scientists group these different types into twenty-eight large families. ____________
3. Sharks within the same family share many traits. ____________
4. The body shape, tail shape, and teeth mark the differences among families. ____________
5. Sharks are found throughout the world's oceans. ____________

Exercise B Underline the participial phrase or the infinitive phrase in each of the following sentences. On the line provided, label each phrase as a participial phrase *(PART)* or an infinitive phrase *(INF)*.

EXAMPLES: 1. My family is proud to celebrate our Jewish holidays. *INF*
2. Observing Jewish traditions, we celebrate each holiday in a special way. *PART*

1. During Rosh Hashanah we hear the Torah read in our synagogue. ____________
2. Celebrated in September or October, Rosh Hashanah is the Jewish New Year. ____________
3. On this holiday, the rabbi at our synagogue chooses to wear white robes instead of the usual black robes. ____________
4. Representing newness and purity, the white robes symbolize the new year. ____________
5. My favorite food of Rosh Hashanah is the honey cake baked by my grandmother. ____________
6. During this holiday everyone eats a lot, knowing that Yom Kippur, a day of fasting, is only ten days away. ____________
7. Yom Kippur, considered the holiest day of the Jewish year, is a serious holiday. ____________
8. To attend services is part of my family's Yom Kippur tradition. ____________
9. I am always pleased to see many neighbors there. ____________
10. Sunset, marking the day's end, brings Yom Kippur to a close. ____________

Name ______________________ Date ____________ Class ______________

Independent Clauses

A **clause** is a group of words that contains a verb and its subject and is used as part of a sentence. An **independent** (or **main**) **clause** expresses a complete thought and can stand by itself as a sentence.

S S V
Bands and floats lined up for the parade. [This entire sentence is an independent clause.]

S V S V
Children sat on the curb, and **adults crowded behind them**. [This sentence contains two independent clauses.]

Exercise A Identify the subject and the verb in each italicized independent clause in the sentences below. Draw one line under the subject and two lines under the verb or verb phrase.

EXAMPLE: 1. If you know any modern music history, *you are probably familiar with the Motown sound.*

1. *Can you name any of the entertainers* who helped make the Motown sound famous?
2. *These performers had hit records in the 1950's and 1960's* when the music business in Detroit (the Motor City, or "Motown") was booming.
3. *Berry Gordy,* who founded the Motown record label, *began his business in a small office.*
4. He was a songwriter and producer, and *he could spot talent.*
5. *Gordy went to clubs to hear local groups* whose sound he liked.
6. *The Miracles,* the first group he discovered, *had a lead singer named Smokey Robinson.*
7. *Robinson was also a songwriter,* and Gordy included him in the Motown team of writers and musicians.
8. *Gordy carefully managed all aspects of the Motown sound,* which is a special combination of rhythm and blues and soul.
9. *Diana Ross and the Supremes, Stevie Wonder, Marvin Gaye, The Four Tops, The Temptations, Gladys Knight and the Pips, and Michael Jackson are just some of the performers* that Gordy discovered.
10. Thinking about this time in music history, *can you remember more music legends*?

Exercise B To each item below, add an independent clause to make a complete sentence.

EXAMPLE: 1. After the game was over, we went to a pizza parlor.

1. When I graduate from high school, ______________________________
2. If you want to read a good book, ______________________________

SENTENCES

Name ______________________ Date ____________ Class ______________

Subordinate Clauses

A **subordinate** (or **dependent**) **clause** does not express a complete thought and cannot stand alone as a sentence.

SUBORDINATE CLAUSE: **if you need me** [incomplete thought] (s: you, v: need)

SUBORDINATE CLAUSE JOINED WITH AN INDEPENDENT CLAUSE: **If you need me,** I will help you.

The meaning of a subordinate clause is complete only when the clause is attached to an independent clause. A word such as *that, what,* or *since* usually begins a subordinate clause.

that he called   **what** I say   **since** we came here

Sometimes the word that begins a subordinate clause is the subject of the clause.

Did you see the movie **that was on television last night?** (s: that, v: was)

Exercise A For each of the following sentences, underline the subordinate clause.

EXAMPLE: 1. <u>When you get up in the morning</u>, do you feel sleepy?

1. A mirror is a piece of polished metal or glass that is coated with a shiny substance.
2. The most common type of mirror is the plane mirror, which is flat.
3. The image that is reflected in a plane mirror is reversed.
4. As you look into a mirror, your left hand seems to be the image's right hand.
5. When an image is reversed, it is called a mirror image.
6. A sailor who looks through a periscope is using a system of lenses and mirrors.
7. Right-hand rearview mirrors on cars, which show a wide area of the road behind, are usually convex, or curved outward.
8. Drivers must be careful because convex mirrors make reflected objects appear far away.
9. Because the mirror in a flashlight is concave, or curved inward, it strengthens the light from a small lightbulb.
10. When you look in a concave mirror, you see a magnified reflection.

Exercise B On the lines provided, add subordinate clauses to the following independent clauses.

EXAMPLE: 1. the woman is a computer programmer
The woman who lives next door is a computer programmer.

1. I bought the CD ____
2. my parents have agreed to let us go ______________________________

Name ______________________ Date ___________ Class ____________________

The Adjective Clause

An **adjective clause** is a subordinate clause that modifies a noun or a pronoun. Unlike an adjective phrase, an adjective clause has a verb and its subject.

ADJECTIVE PHRASE: a shirt **with stripes** [has no subject and verb]

ADJECTIVE CLAUSE: a shirt **that has stripes** [has subject and verb]

An adjective clause usually follows the word it modifies and tells *which one* or *what kind*.

The person **whom we elect** must represent everyone. [which person]

An adjective clause is usually introduced by a **relative pronoun,** such as *that, which, who, whom, or whose*. Sometimes, however, an adjective clause begins with a preposition.

In the cellar, I found a jar **in which hundreds of pennies had been stored**.

A relative pronoun relates an adjective clause to the word the clause modifies. A relative pronoun also has a function in the subordinate clause.

The horse **that I rode** was a palomino. [*That* relates the subordinate clause to *horse* and also functions as the direct object of the verb in the subordinate clause.]

An adjective clause may be introduced by a **relative adverb** such as *when* or *where*.

Is this the place **where** you caught that big fish?

Exercise A Underline the adjective clause in each of the following sentences. Draw another line under the relative pronoun that begins the clause. Then circle the word that the relative pronoun refers to.

EXAMPLE: 1. The (person) who wrote the Declaration of Independence was Thomas Jefferson.

1. In his later years, Jefferson lived at Monticello, which he had designed.
2. Jefferson planned a daily schedule that kept him busy all day.
3. He began each day by making a note that recorded the morning temperature.
4. Then he did his writing, which included letters to friends and businesspersons.
5. Afterward, he ate breakfast, which was served around 9:00 A.M.

Exercise B Complete each of the following sentences by adding an adjective clause that will make sense in the blank. Then underline the relative pronoun.

EXAMPLE: 1. We read the legend *that tells of the Trojan horse*.

1. You should proofread every composition ______________________________.
2. We heard a sound ______________________________.
3. Ramón wrote the song ______________________________.
4. Then she told the joke ______________________________.
5. There is the dog ______________________________.

SENTENCES

Name ______________________ Date ____________ Class ______________________

Chapter 7: Clauses

The Adverb Clause

An **adverb clause** is a subordinate clause that modifies a verb, an adjective, or an adverb. Unlike an adverb or an adverb phrase, an adverb clause has a subject and a verb. An adverb clause tells *where, when, how, why, to what extent,* or *under what condition.* When an adverb clause begins a sentence, the clause is followed by a comma.

ADVERB: Tomás ran the race **quickly**.

ADVERB PHRASE: **With great speed,** Tomás ran the race.

ADVERB CLAUSE: **Because Tomás ran the race with great speed,** he won. [The adverb clause answers the question *why.*]

An adverb clause is introduced by a *subordinating conjunction.* A **subordinating conjunction** is a word that shows the relationship between the adverb clause and whatever the clause modifies. Some common subordinating conjunctions are *after, although, as if, as soon as, because, before, if, since, so, so that, than, unless, until, when, whenever,* and *while.*

NOTE: The words *after, as, before, since,* and *until* are also commonly used as prepositions.

PREPOSITION: We will have a party **after** the race.

SUBORDINATING CONJUNCTION: We had a party **after** the race was won.

Exercise Underline the adverb clause in each sentence. Draw another line under the word or group of words that is the subordinating conjunction. On the line provided, write whether the clause tells *when, where, how, why, how much,* or *under what condition.*

EXAMPLE: 1. Before they had a written history, the Chinese made kites. *when*

1. Many people believe that a kite may have saved the people of China's Han Dynasty when they were about to be attacked by an enemy. ______________
2. As one of the emperor's advisers was thinking, his hat was blown off by a strong wind. ______________
3. He immediately called for a number of kites to be made so that they might be used to frighten the enemy. ______________
4. The Chinese attached noisemakers to the kites and flew them at night so that the enemy would hear the kites but not see them. ______________
5. According to the legend, the enemy thought the kites were gods and retreated as if they were being chased by a fire-breathing dragon. ______________

Name ______________________ Date ____________ Class ______________

Review

Exercise A On the line provided, write *IND* if the italicized clause is an independent clause or *SUB* if it is a subordinate clause. Draw one line under the subject and two lines under the verb or verb phrase.

EXAMPLE: SUB 1. *If a car does not have enough oil,* it will not run.

______ 1. The research report *that was assigned last month* is due tomorrow.

______ 2. *Since the bicycle was on sale,* I bought it.

______ 3. I voted for the candidate *who lost the election.*

______ 4. I'll let you know *as soon as your package arrives.*

______ 5. *Did you read the book* before you saw the movie?

______ 6. The flag should be brought indoors *when the weather is bad.*

______ 7. *After they performed,* the cast had a party.

______ 8. *William Shakespeare is the best-known playwright in the English language.*

______ 9. You may borrow my book overnight *if you would like.*

______10. *Please help me* when it is time to decorate the gym for the dance.

Exercise B Underline the adjective clause in each of the following sentences. Draw another line under the relative pronoun. Then circle the word that the relative pronoun refers to.

EXAMPLE: 1. The (party) that we attended last night was fun.

1. What costume did you wear to the party that Juanita had?
2. My costume, which won a prize, was a chicken suit!
3. My cousin, whom I took to the party, went as a huge mosquito.
4. I couldn't recognize many of the people who were in costume.
5. Did you recognize Hillary, who came as a gorilla?
6. The person whom I didn't recognize was Mingan.
7. His costume, which was really original, was a large cardboard box.
8. The box, which was covered with clear plastic, was very shiny.
9. Mingan, who was hidden inside the box, kept saying, "I'm melting!"
10. The box that he wore was supposed to be an ice cube!

Exercise C Underline the adverb clause in each sentence. Draw another line under the subordinating conjunction. On the line provided, write whether the clause tells *how, when, where, why, how much,* or *under what condition.*

EXAMPLE: 1. You can have a lovely garden if you plan properly. *under what condition*

1. As soon as the ground softens in the spring, plant your garden. ____________
2. Some seeds take more time to sprout than others do. ____________
3. If you want to grow morning glories, start the seeds under lights. ____________
4. When the seeds sprout, you can transplant them into the garden. ____________
5. Plant them near a fence or a wall so that the plants can climb. ____________
6. After the young plants grow strong, they will produce flowers. ____________
7. The flowers will look as if they are big blue trumpets. ____________
8. They're called morning glories because they open each morning. ____________
9. When they are warmed by the morning sun, they open. ____________
10. If the day is dark or stormy, they stay tightly shut, like umbrellas. ____________

Exercise D Underline the subordinate clause in each of the following sentences. Then on the line provided, label the clause as an *adjective clause* or an *adverb clause.*

EXAMPLE: 1. As the American colonists struggled for independence, women played important roles. *adverb clause*

1. When you study the Revolutionary War, you may learn about the adventures of a woman known as Molly Pitcher. ____________
2. Molly, whose real name is believed to have been Mary Ludwig, was the daughter of farmers. ____________
3. Although she was born in New Jersey, she moved to Pennsylvania. ____________
4. There she married John Hays, who was a barber. ____________
5. Hays joined the colonial army when the Revolution began. ____________
6. Mary Ludwig Hays went with her husband to Monmouth, New Jersey, which was the site of a battle on a hot June day in 1778. ____________
7. At first, she carried water to the soldiers so that they would not be overcome by the intense heat. ____________
8. The soldiers nicknamed her Molly Pitcher because she carried the water in pitchers. ____________
9. Later, when her husband collapsed from the heat, she took over his cannon. ____________
10. George Washington, who was the commander of the Continental Army, made Molly an honorary sergeant. ____________

Name ____________________ Date __________ Class ____________________

Sentences and Sentence Fragments

A **sentence** is a group of words that expresses a complete thought. A sentence begins with a capital letter and ends with a period, a question mark, or an exclamation point.

Lori will give a speech about whales.   Have you prepared your speech?
Speak clearly into the microphone.   What a great speech that was!

A **sentence fragment** looks like a sentence but does not express a complete thought.

SENTENCE FRAGMENT: Markings on their tails. [What about the markings?]
SENTENCE: The whales were identified by the markings on their tails.

Exercise: Revising Decide whether each group of words below is a sentence *(S)* or a sentence fragment *(F)*. Then rewrite each fragment to make it a sentence.

EXAMPLE: 1. During her vacation last summer.
F—During her vacation last summer, Bo visited Colorado.

1. She took an exciting boat trip on the Colorado River.
   ____
2. Running the rapids.
   ____
3. At first her boat drifted calmly through the Grand Canyon.
   ____
4. When the river dropped suddenly.
   ____
5. And became foaming rapids full of dangerous boulders.
   ____
6. Which can break a boat.
   ____
7. Bo's boat was actually quite small.
   ____
8. With one guide and four passengers.
   ____
9. Some people prefer large inflatable boats with outboard motors.
   ____
10. Capable of carrying eighteen passengers.
   ____

Name ______________________ Date ____________ Class ______________

Subject and Predicate

A sentence consists of two parts: a *subject* and a *predicate.*

A **subject** tells whom or what the sentence is about.

Davy Crockett is a popular legendary hero.

In folk tales, **the bigger-than-life hero** rode his tamed bear, Death Hug.

Telling many of these tall tales was **Davy Crockett himself**.

The **predicate** tells something about the subject.

Davy Crockett **died at the Battle of the Alamo.**

Killed in that attack were all the defenders of the Alamo.

Exercise A Add subjects to fill in the blanks in the following sentences. Begin each sentence with a capital letter, and end the sentence with a correct mark of punctuation.

EXAMPLE: 1. *This bag of cement* is very heavy⊙

1. ______________________________ is a difficult game to play
2. ______________________________ works in the post office
3. Luckily for me, ______________________ was easy to read
4. Tied to the end of the dock was ______________________
5. Did ______________________________ help you

Exercise B Make a sentence out of each of the following groups of words by adding a predicate to fill in the blank or blanks.

EXAMPLES: 1. A flock of geese *flew high overhead*.
2. *Over Kim's desk hung* a poster of Nelson Mandela.

1. My favorite food ______________________________.
2. A course in first aid ______________________________.
3. ______________________ our car ______________________?
4. Rock climbing ______________________________.
5. Spanish explorers in the Americas ______________________.
6. Several computers ______________________________.
7. ______________________________ a new pair of roller skates.
8. The skyscrapers of New York City ______________________.
9. Some dogs ______________________________.
10. ______________________ my family ______________________?

Name ____________________ Date __________ Class __________

Complete Subject and Simple Subject

Usually the subject comes before the predicate. Sometimes, however, the subject may appear elsewhere in the sentence. To find the subject of a sentence, ask *Who?* or *What?* before the predicate.

The **complete subject** consists of all the words needed to tell whom or what a sentence is about. A **simple subject** is the main word in the complete subject.

SENTENCE: The study of wildlife is fascinating and fun.
COMPLETE SUBJECT: The study of wildlife
SIMPLE SUBJECT: study

SENTENCE: Aunt Mai teaches an ecology course.
COMPLETE SUBJECT: Aunt Mai
SIMPLE SUBJECT: Aunt Mai

NOTE: The simple subject of a sentence is *never* part of a prepositional phrase.

One of the children has a balloon. [The complete subject is *one of the children*. The simple subject is *one*. The prepositional phrase *of the children* modifies the simple subject.]

Exercise Underline the complete subject in each of the following sentences. Then draw another line under the simple subject.

EXAMPLES: 1. Stories about time travel make exciting reading.
2. Samuel Delany writes great science fiction.

1. Ray Bradbury is also a writer of science fiction.
2. *The Golden Apples of the Sun* is a collection of his short stories.
3. My favorite story in that book is "A Sound of Thunder."
4. The main character in the story is called Mr. Eckels.
5. For ten thousand dollars, Mr. Eckels joins Time Safari, Inc.
6. He is looking for the dinosaur *Tyrannosaurus rex*.
7. With four other men, Bradbury's hero travels over sixty million years back in time.
8. Trouble develops on the safari.
9. Because of one mistake, the past is changed.
10. The results of that mistake affect the future.

Name ______________________ Date ____________ Class ______________________

Complete Predicate and Simple Predicate

A **complete predicate** consists of a verb and all the words that describe the verb and complete its meaning. A **simple predicate, or verb,** is the main word or group of words in the complete predicate.

SENTENCE: People entertained themselves one hundred years ago.
COMPLETE PREDICATE: entertained themselves one hundred years ago
SIMPLE PREDICATE (VERB): entertained

SENTENCE: They would have been astonished by television.
COMPLETE PREDICATE: would have been astonished by television
SIMPLE PREDICATE (VERB): would have been astonished

Sometimes, the complete predicate appears at the beginning of a sentence.

In the deep, blue waters of the oceans swim the killer whales.

Part of the predicate may appear on one side of the subject and the rest on the other side.

On the first Tuesday of the month, our committee **meets at the school.**

However, electric power **works equally well.**

Are you **going to the dance**?

Exercise Underline the complete predicate in each of the following sentences. Then draw another line under the verb.

EXAMPLE: 1. Nobody knows the creator of the U.S. flag.

1. Scholars are unsure about the history of the Stars and Stripes.
2. The Continental Congress approved a design for the flag.
3. The design included thirteen red stripes and thirteen white stripes.
4. The top inner quarter of the flag was a blue field with thirteen white stars.
5. The name of the designer remains a mystery.
6. During the Revolutionary War, the colonists needed a symbol of their independence.
7. George Washington wanted flags for the army.
8. Unfortunately, the flags did not arrive until after the Revolutionary War.
9. According to legend, Betsy Ross made the first flag.
10. Historians doubt the Betsy Ross story.

Name ______________________ Date ___________ Class ______________________

The Verb Phrase

A simple predicate may be a one-word verb, or it may be a *verb phrase*. A **verb phrase** consists of a main verb and its helping verbs.

A cold front **is moving** in from the north.

Thunderstorms **have been building** in its path.

Have you **been watching** the weather reports?

Small craft warnings **should have been issued** in coastal areas.

The words *not* and *never*, which are frequently used with verbs, are not part of a verb phrase. Both of these words are adverbs.

An experienced diver **would** not **dive** alone.

You **should** never **use** chlorine bleach on this shirt.

Exercise A Underline the verb or verb phrase in each of the following sentences.

EXAMPLES: 1. Look at these beautiful pictures of Hawaii.
2. They were taken by our science teacher.

1. Hawaii is called the Aloha State.
2. It was settled by Polynesians around two thousand years ago.
3. The musical heritage and rich culture of the original Hawaiians have contributed much to the islands' popularity.
4. Hawaii has the world's largest volcano, Mauna Loa.
5. This volcano may be viewed by tourists in Hawaii Volcanoes National Park.

Exercise B On the line provided, write the verb phrase in each of the following sentences.

EXAMPLE: 1. Have you finished your model yet? *Have finished*

1. Under an old tire in the abandoned lot, a small mouse had built its nest. ______________
2. I have never seen a more beautiful sunset. ______________
3. He could not have been sleeping all this time. ______________
4. The answers might be in the back of the book. ______________
5. Does the car have a carburetor or a fuel injector? ______________

Name ____________________ Date ____________ Class ____________________

Chapter 8: Sentences

Compound Subjects and Compound Verbs

A **compound subject** consists of two or more connected simple subjects that have the same verb. The usual connecting word is *and* or *or*.

Branches and **animal skins** were traditionally used to make tepees.

A **compound verb** consists of two or more verbs that have the same subject. A connecting word—usually *and, or,* or *but*—is used between the verbs.

Early plains peoples **assembled** or **dismantled** tepees quickly.

Both the simple subject and the verb of a sentence may be compound. In such a sentence, each subject goes with each verb. Note that in a compound verb phrase the helping verb(s) may not be repeated.

Silver **jewelry,** colorful **rugs,** and wool **blankets are designed** and **made** by the Navajo. [Jewelry is designed *and* made, rugs are designed *and* made, and blankets are designed *and* made.]

Exercise A Underline the compound subject in each of the following sentences.

EXAMPLE: 1. The <u>shapes</u> and <u>sizes</u> of sand dunes are determined by the wind.

1. The national parks and monuments of the United States include many of the world's most spectacular landforms.
2. The Grand Canyon and the waterfalls of Yosemite are examples of landforms shaped by erosion.
3. Water and other natural forces are continuing the age-old erosion of landforms.
4. On the Colorado Plateau, for example, natural bridges and arches have been produced by erosion.
5. Likewise, Skyline Arch and Landscape Arch in Utah are two natural arches formed by erosion.

Exercise B Underline each compound verb or verb phrase in the following sentences.

EXAMPLE: 1. Just like children today, children in ancient Egypt <u>played</u> games and <u>enjoyed</u> toys.

1. Have you heard of the game *Serpent* or learned its rules?
2. For the Egyptian board game *Serpent,* players found or carved a serpent-shaped stone.
3. Players placed the serpent in the center of the board and then began the game.
4. They used place markers and threw bones or sticks as dice.
5. The players took turns and competed with one another in a race to the center.

Name ______________________ Date ___________ Class ____________________

WORKSHEET 7 Review

Exercise A Decide whether each group of words is a sentence or a sentence fragment. Then on the line provided, write *S* if the group of words is a sentence or *F* if the group of words is a sentence fragment.

______ 1. Thought she had missed the bus.

______ 2. Pasta salad is being served for lunch today.

______ 3. In the bedroom closet behind the ironing board.

______ 4. His latest excuse but not his most original.

______ 5. Please take this note home to your family.

______ 6. I would appreciate help with this project.

______ 7. The space shuttle on the launching pad.

______ 8. Stretching for miles in every direction.

______ 9. Whenever he goes out into the sun.

______10. That was a dazzling display of fireworks!

Exercise B Make a complete sentence out of each of the following groups of words by adding a subject or a predicate to fill in the blank or blanks.

1. ______________________________ is the hardest course I have this semester.
2. Every morning before school, I ______________________________.
3. ______________________ her best friend ______________________?
4. Found behind the counter was ______________________________.
5. By the end of the day, ______________________________ is tired.
6. Marcia and Elena ______________________________.
7. At my house ______________________ is the one thing we all agree on.
8. Over the fence went ______________________________.
9. ______________________ you ______________________?
10. The books on that cart ______________________________.

Exercise C For each of the following sentences, underline the simple subject once and the verb or verb phrase twice. (Note: Some subjects or verbs may be compound.)

EXAMPLE: 1. Have you read a book by N. Scott Momaday?

1. Momaday was born in 1934 in Oklahoma and lived on Navajo and Apache reservations in the Southwest.

2. Momaday's father was a Kiowa.
3. As a young man, Momaday enrolled in and attended the University of New Mexico and Stanford University.
4. In *The Way to Rainy Mountain*, Momaday tells about the myths and history of the Kiowa people.
5. Included in the book are poems, an essay, and stories about the Kiowa people.
6. *The Way to Rainy Mountain* was published in 1969.
7. Have you read any other works by Native American writers?
8. William Least Heat-Moon traveled in a van across the United States and wrote about his journey.
9. Did his travels inspire him to write his book *Blue Highways*?
10. Readers of this Osage writer enjoy his beautiful descriptions of nature.

Exercise D Underline the simple subject once and the verb or verb phrase twice in each of the following sentences. Some of the subjects and verbs are compound.

EXAMPLE: 1. American pioneers left their homes and traveled to the West.

1. Settlers faced and overcame many dangers.
2. Mount McKinley and Mount Whitney are two very high mountains.
3. The Everglades in Florida protects many swamp creatures.
4. Every winter many skiers rush to the Grand Tetons.
5. Few Hollywood stars have been both born and raised in California.
6. Broad valleys and dense forests cool and refresh travelers through the Appalachian Mountains.
7. On Beartooth Highway in Montana, excellent campgrounds and scenic overlooks provide many views of distant glaciers.
8. Mount Evans is west of Denver and can be reached by the highest paved road in America.
9. The view from the top slopes of Mount Evans is breathtaking.
10. The name *Kentucky* comes from an Iroquois word and means "meadowland."

Name ______________________ Date ____________ Class ______________________

Recognizing Complements

A **complement** is a word or a group of words that completes the meaning of a verb. A complement may be a noun, a pronoun, or an adjective.

S V C
NOUN: Mai read a **book**.

S V C
PRONOUN: We missed **her**.

S V C
ADJECTIVE: The mood was **lively**.

An adverb is never a complement. A complement is never in a prepositional phrase.

COMPLEMENT: That snake is **deadly**. [The adjective *deadly* modifies the subject *snake* by telling what kind of snake it is.]

ADVERB: The snake hissed **dangerously**. [*Dangerously* modifies the verb *hissed* by telling how the snake hissed.]

OBJECT OF A PREPOSITION: The snake lay under a fallen **tree**. [*Tree* is the object of the preposition *under*.]

Exercise A In each item below, label the subject and verb by writing *S* and *V* above the sentence. If the sentence has a complement, underline the complement.

S V
EXAMPLES: 1. I read the newspaper.

S V
2. Sal left yesterday.

1. The computer saved the document.
2. He chose the green shirt.
3. The bus passed me at the bus stop.
4. Laurette won easily.
5. Is your sister a veterinarian?

Exercise B Write a sentence by adding a complement or complements to each subject-verb set below.

EXAMPLE: 1. film starred
The film starred Tom Cruise.

1. winter is

____

2. everyone gave

____

SENTENCES

Name ______________________ Date ______________ Class ______________________

Direct Objects

A **direct object** is a noun or a pronoun that receives the action of the verb or that shows the result of the action. A direct object tells *what* or *whom* after a transitive verb. A direct object may be compound.

Alexander Graham Bell invented the **telephone**. [*What* did Bell invent? The direct object is *telephone*.]

Ramón called my **brother** and **me** yesterday. [*Whom* did Ramón call? The compound direct object is *brother* and *me*.]

A direct object can never follow a linking verb because a linking verb does not express action.

LINKING VERB: Bell **was** an inventor. [The verb *was* does not express action. Therefore, it has no direct object.]

A direct object is never part of a prepositional phrase.

OBJECT OF A PREPOSITION: He worked in a **laboratory**. [*Laboratory* is not the direct object of the verb *worked*. *Laboratory* is the object of the preposition *in*.]

Exercise A On the line provided, label the verb in each of the following sentences as either a transitive verb *(T)* or a linking verb *(L)*. For each transitive verb, underline its direct object.

EXAMPLES: ___L___ 1. The crackers are too salty.

___T___ 2. I showed my grades to my aunt.

_______ 1. Please pour a glass of lemonade for our guest.

_______ 2. Eric read his poem to the class.

_______ 3. Next year, I will become a sophomore.

_______ 4. The bananas were still green.

_______ 5. The workers lifted sacks of grain.

Exercise B Underline the direct object in each of the following sentences. [Remember: A direct object may be compound.]

EXAMPLE: 1. Many sports test an athlete's speed and agility.

1. However, long-distance, or marathon, swimming requires strength and endurance from an athlete.
2. A swimmer in training may swim five or six miles every day.
3. Marathon swimmers smear grease on their legs and arms for protection against the cold water.
4. During a marathon, some swimmers lose seventeen pounds.
5. Fatigue, pain, and huge waves challenge marathon swimmers.

Name ______________________ Date ____________ Class ______________________

Chapter 9: Complements

Indirect Objects

The *indirect object* is another type of complement. Like a direct object, an indirect object helps to complete the meaning of a transitive verb. If a sentence has an indirect object, it always has a direct object also.

I bought **him** his **ticket**. [The indirect object is *him*. The direct object is *ticket*.]

An **indirect object** is a noun or a pronoun that comes between the verb and the direct object and tells *to what, to whom, for what,* or *for whom* the action of the verb is done.

I sent **Hortensia** a gift. [*To whom* did I send a gift?]

He gave the **chair** a coat of paint. [*To what* did he give a coat of paint?]

Linking verbs do not have indirect objects. Also, like a direct object, an indirect object may be compound.

LINKING VERB: Jaime and Alameda **are** twins. [The linking verb *are* does not express action, so it cannot have an indirect object.]

COMPOUND INDIRECT OBJECT: I wished **Jaime** and **Alameda** a happy birthday. [The nouns *Jaime* and *Alameda* tell *to whom* the action of the verb was done.]

An indirect object, like a direct object, is never in a prepositional phrase.

INDIRECT OBJECT: He fed the **dog** a biscuit.

OBJECT OF A PREPOSITION: He fed a biscuit to the **dog**.

Exercise For each of the following sentences, underline the indirect object. Draw two lines under the direct object.

EXAMPLE: 1. Did you buy Maxine a calculator for her birthday?

1. The usher found us seats near the stage.
2. I'll gladly lend you my typewriter.
3. The Nobel Committee gave Octavio Paz the Nobel Prize in literature.
4. Please show me your beaded moccasins.
5. Mai told the children stories about her family's escape from Vietnam.
6. Our teacher taught us some English words of American Indian origin.
7. I fed the horse some hay.
8. My secret pal sent me a birthday card.
9. They owe you an apology.
10. Will you please save Ricardo a seat?

Name ______________________ Date ____________ Class ____________________

Predicate Nominatives and Predicate Adjectives

A **subject complement** completes the meaning of a linking verb and identifies or describes the subject. There are two kinds of subject complements: the *predicate nominative* and the *predicate adjective*. A **predicate nominative** is a noun or a pronoun that follows a linking verb and identifies the subject or refers to it. Predicate nominatives never appear in prepositional phrases. A predicate nominative may be compound.

Maude is **one** of the team captains. [The pronoun *one* completes the meaning of the linking verb *is*.]

The forwards are **Rachel** and **Tonya**. [nouns—compound predicate nominative]

A **predicate adjective** is an adjective that follows a linking verb and describes the subject. A predicate adjective may be compound.

The cider smelled **homemade**. [The adjective *homemade* completes the meaning of the linking verb *smelled*.]

It tasted **cold** and **refreshing**. [compound predicate adjective]

Some verbs, such as *look, grow,* and *feel*, may be used as either linking verbs or action verbs.

LINKING VERB: The roses **smelled** wonderful. [*Smelled* links the subject *roses* to the predicate adjective *wonderful*.]

ACTION VERB: I **smelled** your wonderful roses! [*Smelled* is an action verb followed by the direct object *roses*, telling *what* I smelled.]

Exercise Identify the linking verb and the subject complement in each sentence below. Then identify the subject complement as a predicate nominative *(PN)* or a predicate adjective *(PA)*.

EXAMPLE: 1. Are whales mammals? *Are—mammals—PN*

1. Mount Kilimanjaro is the tallest mountain in Africa. ____________________
2. Everyone felt good about the decision. ____________________
3. That container of milk smells sour. ____________________
4. At the moment, she remains our choice for mayor. ____________________
5. When will a woman be president of the United States? ____________________
6. The kingdom of Siam became modern-day Thailand. ____________________
7. The Cuban black beans mixed with rice taste delicious. ____________________
8. Dandelions can be a problem. ____________________
9. The situation appears complicated. ____________________
10. Everyone remained calm during the emergency. ____________________

Name ____________________ Date ____________ Class ____________________

Chapter 9: Complements

WORKSHEET 5 Review

Exercise A All of the following sentences contain direct objects. Some sentences contain indirect objects, too. On the lines provided, identify the object or objects in each sentence. Then identify each object as a *direct object* or an *indirect object*.

EXAMPLE: 1. My parents gave me a choice of places to go on our camping vacation.
me—indirect object; choice—direct object

1. I told them my answer quickly. ____________________
2. I had recently read a magazine article about the Flathead Reservation in Montana. ____________________
3. We spent five days of our vacation there. ____________________
4. We liked the friendly people and the rugged land. ____________________
5. A Salishan group known as the Flatheads governs the huge reservation. ____________________
6. I especially liked the beautiful mountains and twenty-eight-mile-long Flathead Lake. ____________________
7. My parents assigned me several jobs around our camp by the lake. ____________________
8. Someone gave my father directions to the National Bison Range. ____________________
9. We also attended the Standing Arrow Pow-Wow, which was the highlight of our stay. ____________________
10. The performers showed visitors traditional Flathead dances and games. ____________________

Exercise B Underline each subject complement in the following sentences. On the lines provided, identify each complement as a *predicate nominative* or a *predicate adjective*.

EXAMPLE: 1. This soup seems too salty. *predicate adjective*

1. Reuben has become a fine pianist. ____________
2. Why does the water in that pond look green? ____________
3. She must be happy with the results of her exam. ____________

Name ______________________ Date ____________ Class ______________________

4. Variety is the spice of life. ____________
5. Sue Mishima is a lawyer. ____________
6. *Philately* is another name for stamp collecting. ____________
7. During Barbara Jordan's speech, the audience grew thoughtful. ____________
8. Alaska is the largest state in the United States. ____________
9. Jan stays cheerful most of the time. ____________
10. From here, the drums sound too loud. ____________

Exercise C Identify the complement or complements in each sentence below. Then label each complement *DO* for direct object, *IO* for indirect object, *PN* for predicate nominative, or *PA* for predicate adjective.

EXAMPLES: 1. Our teacher read us stories from *The Leather-Stocking Tales.*
us—IO; stories—DO
2. James Fenimore Cooper is the author of these tales.
author—PN

1. Leatherstocking was a fictional scout in Cooper's *The Leather-Stocking Tales.*
____
2. He was also a woodcrafter and a trapper.
____
3. He could not read, but he knew the tales of the woods.
____
4. This character gave generations of readers a hero to admire.
____
5. He could face any emergency.
____
6. He always remained faithful and fearless.
____
7. Leatherstocking loved the forest and the open country.
____
8. In later years he grew miserable.
____
9. The destruction of the wilderness by settlers and others greatly disturbed him.
____
10. He told no one his views and retreated from civilization.
____

Name ______________________ Date ____________ Class ______________________

Simple Sentences

Sentences may be classified according to **structure**—the kinds and the number of clauses they contain. A **simple sentence** has one independent clause and no subordinate clauses.

SIMPLE SENTENCES: **Ron** (S) **has found** (V) a pearl in an oyster.

He (S) **wants** (V) to make a necklace for his mother.

A simple sentence may have a compound subject, a compound verb, or both.

SIMPLE SENTENCES: **Thelma** (S) and **Leo** (S) **buy** (V) automobiles.

Then **they** (S) **repair** (V) and **sell** (V) the cars.

They (S) and **I** (S) **drove** (V) three cars to an auction and **sold** (V) them.

Exercise Identify the subject(s) and the verb(s) in each sentence of the following paragraph by writing *S* above each subject and *V* above each verb. [Note: Some sentences have a compound subject, a compound verb, or both.]

EXAMPLE: [1] I (*S*) enjoy (*V*) urban life but need (*V*) to escape from the city once in a while.

[1] My favorite escape from city life is the green world of Central Park in New York City. [2] Its beautiful woods and relaxing outdoor activities are just a few minutes from our apartment. [3] The enormous size of the park, however, can sometimes be a problem. [4] Often, I take a map along with me for guidance. [5] Using the map, I can easily find the lake, the bandshell, and the Lost Waterfall. [6] In the summertime my brothers and I row boats on the lake, climb huge rock slabs, and have picnics in the Sheep Meadow. [7] I also watch birds and often wander around the park in search of my favorite species. [8] Last month a pair of purple finches followed me along the pond. [9] Near Heckscher Playground, the birds got tired of the game and flew off. [10] In Central Park my family and I can enjoy a little bit of nature in the middle of a bustling city.

Name ______________________ Date ____________ Class ______________________

Compound Sentences

A **compound sentence** has two or more independent clauses but no subordinate clauses. The independent clauses are usually joined by a coordinating conjunction: *and, but, for, nor, or, so,* or *yet.*

INDEPENDENT CLAUSE: **Mark Twain** (S) **wrote** (V) fiction

INDEPENDENT CLAUSE: **T. S. Eliot** (S) **wrote** (V) poetry

COMPOUND SENTENCE: **Mark Twain** (S) **wrote** (V) fiction, and **T. S. Eliot** (S) **wrote** (V) poetry.

NOTE: Do not confuse a compound sentence with a simple sentence that contains a compound subject, a compound verb, or both.

SIMPLE SENTENCE: The **stallion** (S) and the **mares** (S) **leapt** (V) over the fence and **galloped** (V) out of sight.

COMPOUND SENTENCE: Some **mares** (S) **fell** (V) behind, so the **stallion** (S) **urged** (V) them on.

The independent clauses in a compound sentence may also be joined by a semicolon.

We (S) didn't **plant** (V) a garden this year**;** the **weather** (S) **was** (V) too hot.

Exercise For each of the following sentences, underline the subject(s) once and the verb(s) twice. On the lines provided, identify each sentence as either *simple* or *compound.*

EXAMPLE: 1. A tropical rain forest is an evergreen forest in the tropics and has heavy rains all year. *simple*

1. The Amazon River is located in South America and is one of the longest rivers in the world. ____________
2. The Amazon begins in Peru; it flows across Brazil to the Atlantic Ocean. ____________
3. Of all the rivers in the world, this river carries the most water and drains about one fifth of the earth's fresh water. ____________
4. The Amazon is actually a network of several rivers, but most people think of these combined rivers as only one river. ____________
5. These rivers drain the largest tropical rain forest in the world, and during the flood season, the main river often overflows its banks. ____________

Name ____________________ Date __________ Class ______________

WORKSHEET 3

Complex Sentences

A **complex sentence** has one independent clause and at least one subordinate clause.

INDEPENDENT CLAUSE: I often **go** to the library
SUBORDINATE CLAUSE: because **I like** to read
SUBORDINATE CLAUSE: **that is** down the street
COMPLEX SENTENCE: Because **I like** to read, **I** often **go** to the library **that is** down the street.

A subordinate clause can appear at the beginning, in the middle, or at the end of a complex sentence. The following words are often used to introduce subordinate clauses: *who, whose, which, that, after, as, because, if, since, before,* and *when.*

Exercise Underline the subordinate clause in each of the following sentences. On the line provided, give the word that introduces the subordinate clause.

EXAMPLE: 1. Helen Keller, who overcame severe disabilities, showed courage and determination. who

1. Helen Keller, who is famous throughout the world, became very ill as a small child. __________
2. After she recovered from the illness, she could no longer see or hear. __________
3. Because she could not hear, she also lost her ability to speak. __________
4. Helen's parents asked Alexander Graham Bell, who trained teachers of people with hearing impairments, for his advice about the child's education. __________
5. At Bell's suggestion, a special teacher, whose name was Anne Sullivan, stayed at the Kellers' home to teach Helen. __________
6. Sullivan spelled words into Helen's hand as the child touched the object represented by the word. __________
7. From this basic understanding of language, Helen went on to learn Braille, which is the alphabet used by people with visual impairments. __________
8. Sullivan, who had been partly cured of blindness herself, remained with Helen for many years. __________
9. Because she had triumphed over her disabilities, Helen Keller was awarded the Presidential Medal of Freedom. __________
10. Her autobiography, which is entitled *The Story of My Life*, tells about her remarkable achievements. __________

Name ______________________ Date ____________ Class ______________________

Chapter 10: Kinds of Sentences

Classifying Sentences by Purpose

A **declarative sentence** makes a statement. It is followed by a period.

Abraham Lincoln was elected president in 1860.

An **interrogative sentence** asks a question. It is followed by a question mark.

Did you know that John F. Kennedy was elected president in 1960?

An **imperative sentence** gives a command or makes a request. It is followed by a period. A strong command is followed by an exclamation point. The subject of an imperative sentence is always *you*. If the word *you* is not stated, it is the "understood" subject.

Denny, you tell us about these two men.

(You) Discuss the similarities between President Lincoln and President Kennedy.

(You) Consider the startling facts!

An **exclamatory sentence** shows excitement or expresses strong feeling. It is followed by an exclamation point.

How tragic that both Lincoln and Kennedy were assassinated!

Exercise Decide what kind of sentence each of the following sentences is. Add the correct punctuation mark after each sentence. Then, on the line provided, write *DEC* if the sentence is declarative, *IMP* if it is imperative, *INT* if it is interrogative, or *EXC* if it is exclamatory.

EXAMPLE: ___INT___ 1. How much do you know about our past presidents?

_______ 1. The vice-presidents under both Lincoln and Kennedy were named Johnson

_______ 2. What a strange coincidence that is

_______ 3. Read about the investigations into the deaths of both men

_______ 4. How many people believe that there was a conspiracy

_______ 5. There are still unanswered questions about these deaths

_______ 6. Will these questions ever be answered

_______ 7. Make up your own mind

_______ 8. The movie *JFK* investigates some theories about Kennedy's assassination

_______ 9. How we miss them

_______10. Never let such tragedies happen again

Name ______________________ Date ___________ Class ____________________

Chapter 10: Kinds of Sentences

Review

Exercise A Read each of the following sentences. If the sentence is simple, write *S*. If the sentence is compound, write *CD*.

EXAMPLE: __S__ 1. Boats and sometimes a canoe or raft glided along the river.

_______ 1. The talented violinist asked for the audience's attention.

_______ 2. Pandas are rare, but they are not extinct.

_______ 3. We could make a booklet, or we could post our papers on the bulletin board.

_______ 4. Elyssa came over and talked to me after the play.

_______ 5. We like our home, and we like our neighbors, too.

Exercise B Read each of the following sentences. If the sentence is compound, write *CD*. If the sentence is complex, write *CX*.

EXAMPLE: __CD__ 1. You didn't call me, so I called you.

_______ 1. When Abe Lincoln gave a stump speech, he stood on a real stump.

_______ 2. Trees lose their leaves in the fall, and they look cold and deserted.

_______ 3. While we lived in southern Maryland, we visited Annapolis.

_______ 4. Brian has a bad temper, and he doesn't make friends easily.

_______ 5. If you move your knight to that square, I will capture it.

Exercise C On the lines provided on page 96, classify each of the following sentences as *simple, compound,* or *complex.*

EXAMPLE: [1] The Iroquois people traditionally held a Green Corn Festival in August when their crops were ready for harvesting.

1. *complex*

[1] For the early Iroquois, the Green Corn Festival was a celebration that lasted several days. [2] During the celebration, all children who had been born since midwinter received their names. [3] Tribal leaders made speeches, and adults and children listened to them carefully. [4] In one traditional speech, the leader would give thanks for the harvest. [5] After they had heard the speeches, the people sang and danced.

[6] On the second day of the festival, the people performed a special dance, and during the dance they gave thanks for the sun, the moon, and the stars. [7] On the third day, the Iroquois gave thanks for the helpfulness of their neighbors and for good luck. [8] The festival ended on the fourth day when teams of young people would play a bowling game.

[9] During the festival the people renewed their friendships and rejoiced in their harmony with nature. [10] This Iroquois festival resembles the U.S. Thanksgiving holiday, which has its roots in similar American Indian celebrations.

1. ____________________ 6. ____________________
2. ____________________ 7. ____________________
3. ____________________ 8. ____________________
4. ____________________ 9. ____________________
5. ____________________ 10. ____________________

Exercise D Add the correct end mark of punctuation to each of the following sentences. Then, label each sentence as declarative *(DEC)*, imperative *(IMP)*, interrogative *(INT)*, or exclamatory *(EXC)*.

EXAMPLE: *INT* 1. Are prairie dogs social creatures*?*

______ 1. Many of these small mammals live together in underground "towns" on the prairie

______ 2. American prairie dogs dig family burrows

______ 3. These burrows sometimes cover several acres

______ 4. Have you ever seen a prairie dog

______ 5. These creatures can usually be seen at night or in the early morning

______ 6. What alert animals prairie dogs are

______ 7. At least one prairie dog always keeps a constant lookout for threats to the community

______ 8. Watch how it sits up to see better

______ 9. It makes a shrill whistle of alarm at the first sign of danger

______ 10. It then dives headfirst into the burrow and alerts the entire colony

Name ______________________ Date ___________ Class ____________________

Sentence Fragments

One of the easiest ways to make your writing clear is to use complete sentences. A **complete sentence** is a word group that (a) has a subject, (b) has a verb, and (c) expresses a complete thought. Avoid using sentence fragments. A **sentence fragment** is a part of a sentence that has been punctuated as if it were a complete sentence.

SENTENCE: Laneasha walked home.

FRAGMENT: Laneasha home. [The verb is missing. *What* did Laneasha do?]

FRAGMENT: Walked home. [The subject is missing. *Who* walked home?]

FRAGMENT: When Laneasha walked home. [This group of words has a subject and a verb but does not express a complete thought. *What happened* when Laneasha walked home?]

NOTE: Remember that the word *you* can be an *understood* subject.

SENTENCE: (You) Hold the oar with both hands.

Exercise A On the lines provided, write *F* for each sentence fragment and *S* for each sentence below.

EXAMPLE: __*F*__ 1. Reading about flying squirrels.

______ 1. A flying squirrel a squirrel that can glide through the air.

______ 2. Some Asian flying squirrels three feet long.

______ 3. Leaps from one tree to another.

______ 4. The squirrel glides downward, then straight, and finally upward.

______ 5. Some flying squirrels more than fifty feet.

______ 6. If they use a higher starting point.

______ 7. Flying squirrels live in the forests of Asia, Europe, and North America.

______ 8. Eat berries, bird eggs, insects, and nuts.

______ 9. Nest in the hollows of trees.

______10. The squirrel stretches out its legs to help it glide.

Exercise B: Revising On the lines provided, revise each fragment below to make it a complete sentence. You may need to change the punctuation and capitalization, too.

EXAMPLE: 1. As soon as we finished eating.
We left for our camping trip as soon as we finished eating.

1. The whole family into the car.

____

2. When we arrived at the campground.

____

Name ______________________ Date ____________ Class ____________________

Chapter 11: Writing Effective Sentences

Run-on Sentences

If you run together two complete sentences as if they were one sentence, you get a **run-on sentence**. A comma marks a brief pause in a sentence, but it does not show the end of a sentence. If you use a comma instead of a period between two complete sentences, you create a run-on sentence. There are two ways you can revise run-on sentences. You can make two sentences. Or you can use a comma and the coordinating conjunction *and, but,* or *or.*

RUN-ON: We ran all the way to the bus stop we made it on time.
RUN-ON: We ran all the way to the bus stop, we made it on time.
CORRECT: We ran all the way to the bus stop. We made it on time.
CORRECT: We ran all the way to the bus stop, and we made it on time.

Exercise: Revising On the lines provided, revise each sentence below that is a run-on. If the group of words is correct, write *C*.

1. Saturn is a huge planet it is almost ten times the size of Earth. ____________________
2. Saturn is covered by clouds, it is circled by bands of color. ____________________
3. Sometimes the clouds at the equator appear yellow, the clouds at the poles appear green. ____________________
4. Saturn has at least eighteen moons Titan is the largest moon. ____________________
5. Saturn rotates faster than Earth does, its day is only 10 ½ hours long. ____________________
6. Saturn's most striking feature is a group of rings that circle the planet. ____________________
7. Saturn has seven rings, they spread out far from the planet. ____________________
8. The rings are made up of billions of tiny particles. ____________________
9. Some of the rings are dark, but others are brighter. ____________________
10. Saturn is a beautiful planet you need a telescope to see its rings. ____________________

Name ________________________ Date ____________ Class ________________

Chapter 11: Writing Effective Sentences

Combining Sentences by Inserting Words and Phrases

You can combine short, choppy sentences by pulling a key word or phrase from one sentence and inserting it into another sentence.

ORIGINAL: Someone is waiting. She is **in the hallway**.
COMBINED: Someone is waiting **in the hallway**.

ORIGINAL: The dulcimer is an instrument. It has **strings**.
COMBINED: The dulcimer is a **stringed** instrument.

Exercise: Revising To combine each sentence pair below, take the italicized word or words from the second sentence and add them to the first sentence. Add commas if needed.

1. Henry David Thoreau was an individualist. He was a *thoughtful* person.
____

2. Thoreau lived near a pond in Massachusetts. It was a *peaceful* place.
____

3. In the spring of 1845, Thoreau built a home. He built his home *near Walden Pond.*
____

4. First, he dug a cellar in the soil. The soil was mostly *sand.* (Add *–y* to the inserted word.)
____

5. He cut the timbers. He cut them *from tall white pines.* ______________
____

6. His friends came to help him. They helped him *set up the framework.* ______________
____

7. Thoreau kept his weekly grocery bill to twenty-seven cents. He did this *by growing most of his food.* ______________
____

8. He would lie under a beech tree. He did this so that he could *rest from his writing.* (Write *to* before the added words.) ______________
____

9. Thoreau loved the pond. The pond was *smooth, clear,* and *deep.* ______________
____

10. He measured its depth. He measured it while *lying on its frozen surface.*
____

SENTENCES

Name ______________________ Date ___________ Class ______________

Combining by Using And, But, *or* Or

You can combine sentences by using the conjunction *and, but,* or *or* to form a compound subject, a compound verb, or a compound sentence.

ORIGINAL: Mary is my friend. Adeola is my friend.
COMPOUND SUBJECT: **Mary** and **Adeola** are my friends.

ORIGINAL: Adeola swims after school. Adeola jogs after school.
COMPOUND VERB: Adeola **swims** and **jogs** after school.

ORIGINAL: Mary sings alto. Adeola sings soprano.
COMPOUND SENTENCE: Mary sings alto**, but** Adeola sings soprano.

Exercise A: Revising Combine each of the following pairs of short, choppy sentences by using *and, but,* or *or* to make a compound subject or a compound verb. (Check your combined sentences for subject-verb agreement.)

EXAMPLE: 1. Dolphins hunt fish. Dolphins eat fish. *Dolphins hunt and eat fish.*

1. Dolphins can't smell things as people do. They can't taste things as people do.

____

2. Baby dolphins catch waves near the beach. Baby dolphins ride waves near the beach.

____

3. Sharks sometimes attack porpoises. Sharks sometimes kill porpoises.

____

4. A porpoise could outswim most sharks. A tuna could outswim most sharks.

____

Exercise B: Revising Each of the following pairs of sentences is closely related. Make each pair into a compound sentence by adding a comma and *and, but,* or *or*.

1. Some Pueblo peoples have lived in the same area for generations. They have strong ties to their land.

____

2. Many Pueblo people live in the Southwest. Some live in other parts of the country.

____

3. Some Pueblo land is desert. The people can grow crops if they irrigate.

____

4. The traditional adobe homes have several stories. Sometimes ladders are used to reach the upper levels.

____

Name ______________________ Date ____________ Class ______________

Combining by Using a Subordinate Clause

An **independent clause** can stand alone as a sentence. A **subordinate clause** cannot stand alone as a sentence because it doesn't express a complete thought.

INDEPENDENT CLAUSE: are you coming home

SUBORDINATE CLAUSE: when you come home

You can make a subordinate clause by replacing the subject of a sentence with *who, which,* or *that*. You can also make a subordinate clause by adding a word that tells time or place to a sentence.

ORIGINAL: The term *Achilles' heel* means "a weak point." *Achilles' heel* comes from Greek mythology.

COMBINED: The term *Achilles' heel,* which comes from Greek mythology, means "a weak point." [The word *which* replaces the subject, *Achilles' heel,* in the second original sentence to make a subordinate clause.]

ORIGINAL: The sun is shining. I will wash the car.

COMBINED: While the sun is shining, I will wash the car. [The word *while* has been placed at the beginning of the first original sentence to make a subordinate clause showing time.]

Exercise: Revising Combine each sentence pair by making the second sentence into a subordinate clause and attaching it to the first sentence. The hints in parentheses tell you how to begin the subordinate clause. You may need to delete a word or two from the second sentence.

EXAMPLE: 1. You are lucky. You have pearls. (Use *if*.)
You are lucky if you have pearls.

1. The pearl is a gem. It is made by certain kinds of oysters and clams. (Use *that*.)

____

2. Beautiful pearls are found in tropical seas. The best pearl oysters live there. (Use a comma and *where*.)

____

3. A valuable pearl has a shine. The shine comes from below its surface. (Use *that*.)

____

4. A pearl becomes round. It is formed in the soft part of the oyster. (Use *when*.)

____

5. Pearls should be wiped clean with a soft cloth. They are worn as jewelry. (Use *after*.)

____

Name ________________________ Date ____________ Class ______________________

Stringy Sentences and Wordy Sentences

Stringy sentences have too many independent clauses strung together with words like *and* or *but*. To fix a stringy sentence, you can break the sentence into two or more sentences, or you can turn some of the independent clauses into phrases or subordinate clauses. **Wordy sentences** are sentences that use too many words to say something simple. You can revise wordy sentences in three different ways: (1) replace a group of words with one word; (2) replace a clause with a phrase; or (3) take out a whole group of unnecessary words.

Exercise A: Revising Identify the stringy sentences below. Then, revise them, using the methods discussed above. If the sentence doesn't need to be improved, write C.

EXAMPLE: 1. Mercedes O. Cubría was born in Cuba, but her mother died, and she moved to the United States, and she moved with her two sisters.
Mercedes O. Cubría was born in Cuba. When her mother died, she moved to the United States with her two sisters.

1. She worked as a nurse, and then she joined the Women's Army Corps, and she soon became an officer in the army. ______________________________

2. Cubría was the first Cuban-born woman to become an officer in the U.S. Army.

3. The war ended, and she was promoted to captain, and later her official rank rose to major.

4. Then there was the Korean War, and she worked as an intelligence officer, and she studied information about the enemy. ______________________________

Exercise B: Revising Decide which of the sentences below are wordy; then, revise them, using the methods discussed above. If a sentence is effective as it is, write C.

1. What I want to say is that starfish are fascinating creatures.

2. A starfish has little feet tipped with suction cups that have suction power.

3. At the end of each arm is a sensitive eyespot.

4. In spite of the fact that the eyespot cannot see things, it can tell light from dark.

Name ________________________ Date ____________ Class ______________________

Review

Exercise A: Revising Identify the fragments and run-ons in the following paragraph. Then, revise the paragraph on the lines provided.

EXAMPLE: 1. Many deserts have no plant life, some do.
Many deserts have no plant life, but some do.

Many plants can survive. Where the climate is hot and dry. Cacti, Joshua trees, palm trees, and wildflowers grow in deserts. These plants. Do not grow close together. Are spread out, each plant gets water and minerals from a large area.

____

____

____

____

____

Exercise B: Revising To combine each pair of sentences below, take the italicized key word or phrase from the second sentence and insert it into the first sentence. Follow the directions in parentheses to change the form of the key word if applicable.

EXAMPLE: 1. Peanuts are the tiny seeds of the peanut plant. They have a good taste. (Change *taste* to *tasty*.)
Peanuts are the tiny, tasty seeds of the peanut plant.

1. Peanuts are a major crop. They are a crop *grown in many warm regions.* ______________

____

2. Peanuts are a food for snacking. Peanuts are good for your *health.* (Add *-ful* to *health.*)

____

3. The oil from peanuts is used in many dressings. The dressings are *for salads.*

____

4. Grades of peanut oil are used to make soap. The *low* grades are used for this purpose.

____

Exercise C: Revising This paragraph sounds choppy because it has too many short sentences. Use the methods you've learned in this section to combine sentences in the paragraph. The revised paragraph should sound much better.

EXAMPLE: 1. Pegasus is a winged horse. He is a beautiful horse. He is a horse from Greek mythology. Pegasus was created by Poseidon. Poseidon was the god of the sea.
Pegasus, a beautiful winged horse from Greek mythology, was created by Poseidon, the god of the sea.

Athena caught Pegasus. Athena tamed Pegasus. Athena was the goddess of wisdom. A hero could ride Pegasus. A true poet could ride Pegasus. These were the only kinds of people who could ride him. The first person to ride the winged horse was a Greek youth named Bellerophon. Bellerophon was sent by a king to kill a monster. Bellerophon destroyed the monster. Bellerophon became a hero.

____

____

____

____

____

____

Exercise D: Revising Identify the stringy and wordy sentences in the following paragraph. Then, revise the paragraph by using the methods you've learned. Notice how your revisions improve the style of the paragraph.

EXAMPLE: 1. The movie *The Dark Crystal* features a lot of strange characters, and the characters are actually puppets, and they were designed by Jim Henson, and he was the man who created the Muppets.

The movie The Dark Crystal features a lot of strange characters that are actually puppets designed by Jim Henson, the man who created the Muppets.

The puppets used in *The Dark Crystal* were different from the original Muppets, having things about them that were different. One thing is that they weren't as brightly colored as the TV Muppets. They also had legs and could move through a scene with their whole bodies showing. Some of the characters in *The Dark Crystal* were radio-controlled, and others were operated by puppeteers, and the puppeteers were hidden under the movie set.

____

____

____

____

____

____

____

____

Name ______________________ Date ___________ Class ______________________

Using Capital Letters A

Capitalize the first word in every sentence.

Two years ago, my sister graduated from high school.

The first word of a sentence that is a direct quotation is capitalized even if the quotation begins within a sentence.

Have you heard the expression, "**A**ll's well that ends well"?

Traditionally, the first word in a line of poetry is capitalized.

Lovely! See the cloud, the cloud appear!
Lovely! See the rain, the rain draw near!
—Zuni corn-grinding song

Capitalize the pronoun *I*.

My grandfather and **I** walked in his garden; then **I** showed him my computer.

Capitalize the interjection *O*, which is most often used on solemn or formal occasions, and sometimes in poetry or songs. It is usually followed by a word in direct address.

Stay, **O** sweet and do not rise!
The light that shines comes from thine eyes . . .
—from *A Pilgrim's Solace*, John Dowland

The interjection *oh* requires a capital letter only at the beginning of a sentence.

Oh, was I happy to see her; but **o**h, how I cried when she left!

Exercise: Proofreading Circle the letters that should be capitalized in the following sentences.

EXAMPLE: 1. "ⓓid you hear me?" ⓘ asked.

1. last year i went to live with my aunt and uncle.
2. they love to read and asked me, "what are your favorite books?"
3. i had never read very much, so i said, "i don't know yet."
4. we started reading aloud to one another every evening.
5. we read poetry by many poets, and oh, i loved it all.
6. Edgar Allan Poe's "Annabel Lee" starts, "it was many and many a year ago. . . ."
7. my aunt would say, "what shall we read tonight, o literate one?"
8. later my uncle said, "let's read some of Robert Louis Stevenson's novels."
9. we did, and then we read Sandra Cisneros, James Thurber, and Jamaica Kincaid.
10. if you asked me "what are your favorite books?" i still would say "i don't know"; but now it's because i have too many favorites!

Name ________________ Date __________ Class ______________

Using Capital Letters B

A **common noun** is a general name for a person, a place, a thing, or an idea. A **proper noun** names a particular person, place, or thing.

A common noun is capitalized only when it begins a sentence or is part of a title. A proper noun is always capitalized.

COMMON NOUNS: actor, state, river, religion, north
PROPER NOUNS: Denzel Washington, New Mexico, Ohio River, Islam, the West

Some proper nouns consist of more than one word. In these names, prepositions with fewer than five letters and the articles *a, an,* and *the* are not capitalized.

Labor Day   Catherine the Great   Battle of the Marne

Capitalize the names of persons and animals.

Lee Trevino   Hillary Rodham Clinton   Rin Tin Tin

Capitalize geographical names.

Philadelphia   Spain   Crater Lake   Highway 101

NOTE: In a hyphenated street number, the second part of the number is not capitalized: Thirty-fourth Street. Words such as *north, east,* and *southwest* are not capitalized when they indicate direction.

Capitalize the names of planets, stars, and other heavenly bodies.

Uranus   the Milky Way   Ursa Major   Polaris

NOTE: The word *earth* is not capitalized unless it is used along with the names of other heavenly bodies. The words *sun* and *moon* are not capitalized.

Exercise: Proofreading Correct each of the following sentences by making a slash through letters that are but should not be capitalized and by circling letters that should be capitalized.

EXAMPLE: 1. The original Settlers of hawaii came from the marquesas islands and tahiti.

1. My family, including our dog rover, was lucky enough to watch the Moon rise over hawaii on the fourth of july last year.
2. The Hawaiian islands are located in the pacific ocean, nearly 2,400 miles West of san francisco, california.
3. Hawaii became the fiftieth State in the united states in 1959.
4. Our teacher, Ms. castillo, explained that the capital City is honolulu and that it is located on the southeast Coast of oahu.
5. hawaii volcanoes national park is on hawaii, the largest island.

Name ________________________ Date ____________ Class ____________________

Using Capital Letters C

Capitalize the names of teams, organizations, businesses, institutions, and government bodies.

San Diego Padres   Future Farmers of America   Northside High School

Capitalize the names of historical events and periods, special events, and calendar items.

Boer War   Age of Reason   Florida State Fair   August

NOTE: The name of a season is not capitalized unless it is part of a proper name.

Capitalize the names of nationalities, races, and peoples.

Nigerian   Chinese   Comanche   Inupiats

Capitalize the names of religions and their followers, holy days, sacred writings, and specific deities. Do not capitalize the words *god* and *goddess* when they apply to ancient deities.

Islam   Koran   Krishna   the goddess Athena

Capitalize the names of buildings and other structures.

Hancock Building   Peace Bridge   World Trade Center

Capitalize the names of monuments and awards.

Vietnam Memorial   Obie Award   Statue of Liberty

Capitalize the names of trains, ships, airplanes, and spacecraft.

Broadway Limited   USS *Missouri*   *Columbia*

Capitalize the brand names of business products.

Brother typewriters   Michelin tires   Panasonic radio

Exercise: Proofreading In the following paragraphs, circle each letter that shou be capitalized.

the branford mall is the largest in melville county. it is on jefferson parkway, tw north of duck lake state park. across the parkway from the mall is the new branfor school, home of the branford panthers. near the mall are the american legion hal bowlorama, and the beautiful new first methodist church.

the mall has two jewelry stores, nicholson's department store, the palace cine thirty-five other businesses, including a restaurant owned by jean larue from fran last year won the best chef in the midwest award. the mall also has an outlet store northwestern boating goods of chicago. for memorial day a scale model of the uss was displayed with pictures of local people who fought in world war II.

Name ______________________ Date __________ Class ______________________

Using Capital Letters D

A **proper adjective** is formed from a proper noun and is almost always capitalized.

PROPER NOUN	PROPER ADJECTIVE
Germany	a German scientist
Oklahoma City	an Oklahoma City landmark

Do *not* capitalize the names of school subjects, except languages and course names followed by a number.

Every day I have **history, Spanish, art,** and **Math II.**

Exercise On the lines provided, list the proper nouns and proper adjectives in the following sentences, adding capital letters as needed.

EXAMPLE: 1. Rosa said that we were eating real mexican *fajitas.* Rosa, Mexican

1. The program featured russian ballet dancers, hungarian singers, and polish acrobats.

____

2. The european Community helps improve international trade.

____

3. The scandinavian countries include both norway and sweden.

____

4. In geography, we learned about the platypus and the koala, two australian mammals.

____

5. Many great english plays were written during the elizabethan age.

____

I am planning to take computer I and industrial arts next year.

____

On the floor were a large persian rug and several ethiopian baskets.

____

ngland, france, scotland, russia, and the united states affected canadian history.

____

e back yard was decorated with chinese lanterns and japanese paper sculptures.

____

ve you ever tasted indian rice pudding or greek pastries?

____

Name ______________________ Date ___________ Class ______________________

Using Capital Letters E

Capitalize the title of a person when it comes before a name.

Captain Kidd **M**r. Muldoon **S**enator Benson

Capitalize a title used alone or following a person's name only when you want to emphasize the position of someone holding a high office.

CAPITALIZED: The **S**ecretary of **D**efense will speak at noon.

NOT CAPITALIZED: Marta is **s**ecretary of the business club at school.

A title used alone in direct address is usually capitalized.

When will the plane leave, **M**ajor?

Capitalize a word showing a family relationship when the word is used before or in place of a person's name. Do not capitalize a word showing a family relationship when a possessive comes before the word.

Yesterday **M**om and **U**ncle Jorge roofed our garage.

Your **a**unt Rita will take you to the boat show.

Capitalize the first and last words and all important words in titles of books, magazines, newspapers, poems, short stories, historical documents, movies, television programs, works of art, and musical compositions.

Call of the Wild *Free Willy* "**W**e **A**re the **W**orld"

NOTE: Most abbreviations, such as *Mr., Ms., U.S., TV,* state names, and organization names, are capitalized.

Exercise: Proofreading Circle the letters that should be capitalized in the following sentences.

EXAMPLE: 1. The series *ⓐll ⓒreatures ⓖreat and ⓢmall* is being rerun on TV.

1. While waiting to interview mayor ward, I read an article in *newsweek.*
2. Have you read leslie marmon silko's poem "story from bear country"?
3. Here is a picture of *the thinker,* one of rodin's finest sculptures.
4. On television last night we saw a movie called *the three faces of eve.*
5. The voters elected a president and several united states senators.
6. My uncle nick read francisco jiménez's short story "the circuit."
7. The reporter asked, "Can you tell us, general, whether you are retiring?"
8. The speaker was dr. bell, former president of the university of maine.
9. uncle don, aunt pat, aunt jean, and my grandmother were there.
10. The president met with his advisors before he spoke to the nation.

MECHANICS

Name ______________________ Date ___________ Class ______________________

Review

Exercise: Proofreading Circle the letters that should be capitalized in each of the following sentences. Make a slash through letters that should not be capitalized.

EXAMPLE: 1. ⓝext ⓢaturday ⓡachel and ⓘwill get to watch the filming of our favorite TV Show.

1. The curtis soap corporation sponsors the television show called *three is two too many.*
2. the show's theme song is "you And I might get by."
3. One actor on the show is joe fontana, jr., who plays the Physician, dr. mullins.
4. The female lead, jan bledsoe, went to our Junior High School here in houston, Texas.
5. The action takes place out West, just after the end of the civil war.
6. The program, which is loosely based on the book *two out west,* is on monday nights.
7. One episode took place at a Fourth Of July picnic, where dr. mullins approached the Sheriff and said, "hey, sheriff, i challenge you to a pie-eating contest."
8. ms. Bledsoe plays a teacher who is married to mr. Reginald wildon Foster II, President of the flint bank.
9. Mrs. Foster teaches Latin, Home Economics, and History at flintsville's one-room school, and oh, does she have problems with her students!
10. One local character, uncle Ramón, once played a practical joke on Judge Grimsby right outside the mayor's office.
11. Some people, including mom, think the program is silly, but my Father enjoys watching it occasionally.
12. I don't think it will win an emmy from the Academy Of Television Arts And Sciences.
13. grandma murray and aunt edna in mobile, Alabama, watch the program.
14. On monday night's show, an alien named romax and his pet zarrf from the planet zarko came to Town and stayed at the Sidewinder hotel.
15. The alien, who looked like United States president zachary taylor, spoke english perfectly and could read people's minds.
16. He settled a dispute between the Pacific Railroad company and the flint bank.
17. On another show a united states Senator and Romax discussed their views of justice.
18. Romax said, "i don't know when you, o Earthlings, will realize that Laws must apply equally to everyone or there is no justice."
19. A week later, mayor Murdstrone lost his only copy of his secret recipe for irish stew and saw the recipe in the next issue of the *flintsville weekly gazette.*
20. One time a mysterious buddhist priest appeared, claiming he had sailed to the east around cape horn on the ship *The Gem Of The Ocean.*

Name ________________________ Date ___________ Class ________________

Using End Marks

The three kinds of **end marks** are the *period,* the *question mark,* and the *exclamation point.*

Use a period at the end of a statement.

Charles Dickens is my favorite author**.**

Use a question mark at the end of a question.

Who can ever forget his character Oliver Twist**?**

Use an exclamation point at the end of an exclamation.

What a likable character he is**!**

Use a period or an exclamation point at the end of a request or a command.

Please return the book**.** [a request]   Don't put it there**!** [a command]

Use a period after most abbreviations.

PERSONAL NAMES:	Alfred E**.** Newman, S**.** E**.** Hinton
TITLES USED WITH NAMES:	Mr**.**, Mrs**.**, Ms**.**, Jr**.**, Sr**.**, Dr**.**
STATES (EXCEPT TWO-LETTER ZIP CODE ABBREVIATIONS):	Wyo**.**, Tex**.** *but* MA, OR
ADDRESSES:	Blvd**.**, St**.**, Ave**.**
ORGANIZATIONS AND COMPANIES:	Co**.**, Inc**.**, Corp**.**, Assn**.**
TIMES:	A.M**.**, P.M**.**, B.C**.**, A.D**.**

Exercise: Proofreading Insert periods (⊙), question marks (?), and exclamation points (!) where they belong in the following sentences.

EXAMPLE: 1. Did you know that a choreographer creates dance steps*?*

1. Why is Katherine Dunham called "the mother of African American dance"
2. She studied anthropology in college and won a scholarship to visit the Caribbean
3. In Haiti, she was inspired by the dances she saw
4. Dunham started one of the first all-black professional dance companies in the United States
5. How I admire such a talented person
6. Mrs Frazier, please find more information about Dunham for me
7. How many honors has Dunham's creativity won her
8. She's in the Hall of Fame of the National Museum of Dance in Saratoga, N Y
9. She was also honored with the National Medal of Arts Award
10. The editors of *Essence* praised Dunham for helping to break down racial barriers

Name ______________________ Date ___________ Class ______________________

Using Commas A

A **comma** is used to separate words or groups of words *within* a complete thought.

Use commas to separate items in a series.

WORDS IN A SERIES: Dad's garden produced **carrots, beans,** and **cucumbers.**

I packed a **sleeping bag, a canteen,** and **dried food.**

PHRASES IN A SERIES: I went **to the game, to the yogurt shop,** and **to Brian's house.**

The mechanic **tuned the car's engine, checked the brake fluid,** and **changed the fuel filter.**

CLAUSES IN A SERIES: **We laughed, we cried,** and **we talked until dawn.**

One flew east, one flew west, and **one flew over the cuckoo's nest.**

If all items in a series are joined by *and* or *or,* do not use commas to separate them.

We saw bats in caves and bats under bridges and some in bat houses built just for them.

Exercise: Proofreading Insert commas (^) where they are needed in the following sentences. If a sentence is correct, write C on the line provided.

EXAMPLE: ______ 1. Seal the envelope^ stamp it^ and mail the letter.

______ 1. Cleveland Toledo and Dayton are three large cities in Ohio.

______ 2. The captain entered the cockpit checked the instruments and prepared for takeoff.

______ 3. Luisa bought mangoes and papayas and oranges.

______ 4. The neighbors searched behind the garages in the bushes and along the highway.

______ 5. Eleanor Roosevelt's courage her humanity and her service to the nation will always be remembered.

______ 6. Mrs. Ortega won more votes than Mr. Harris Miss Steinberg or Dr. Gladstone.

______ 7. The chairperson's job was calling the meeting to order asking for the minutes and announcing new officers.

______ 8. Todd's uncle sold an oak chest two tables a china lamp and four paintings.

______ 9. Autos trucks and buses were stranded by the storm.

______10. The zoo director had to feed the animals guide visitors and keep the grounds safe and clean.

Name ______________________ Date ____________ Class ______________________

Using Commas B

Use a comma to separate two or more adjectives that come before a noun.

Ten **hungry, chirping** birds landed near our blanket.

We gave them **crunchy, delicious** berries.

If the final adjective in a series is closely linked to the noun, do not use a comma before the final adjective.

It's an exciting amateur production.

Use a comma before *and, but, or, nor, for, so,* or *yet* when it joins independent clauses.

Joshua's uncle drove us to the ice-skating rink**, yet** he didn't skate.

I was disappointed**, for** I had heard he used to be a competitive skater.

When the independent clauses are very short, the comma before *and, but,* or *or* may be omitted.

Mrs. Lu could have waited but she left.

Exercise: Proofreading Add commas (^) where they are needed in the following sentences. If a sentence is correct, write C on the line provided.

EXAMPLE: ______ 1. Isaac Bashevis Singer was born in Poland, and he often writes about Jewish life in eastern Europe.

______ 1. Singer writes entertaining touching short stories

______ 2. Some authors start writing as adults but Isaac Bashevis Singer began writing at the age of fifteen.

______ 3. I'm glad Singer wrote in English as well as Yiddish for I can't read Yiddish.

______ 4. My teacher assigned Singer's short story "Zlateh the Goat" to read, so I read it this morning.

______ 5. Zlateh the goat is a farm animal but she is also like a family pet.

______ 6. Zlateh is old and she doesn't produce much milk.

______ 7. The father decides to sell the patient good-natured old goat to buy Hannukah presents.

______ 8. Zlateh is almost sold but she proves that she is still valuable to the family.

______ 9. Singer is a respected writer and he won the Nobel Prize in literature in 1978.

______ 10. You can buy a book of Singer's short stories or I can lend you my copy.

Name ______________________ Date ____________ Class ______________________

Using Commas C

Use commas to set off a nonessential participial phrase or a nonessential subordinate clause.

A **nonessential** (or **nonrestrictive**) phrase or clause adds information that isn't needed to understand the meaning of the sentence. Such a phrase or clause can be omitted without changing the main idea of the sentence.

NONESSENTIAL PHRASE: The picnic**, planned for months,** is on Thursday.

NONESSENTIAL CLAUSE: My aunt**, who is a former teacher,** will drive the bus.

Do not set off an **essential** (or **restrictive**) phrase or clause. Since such a phrase or clause tells *which one(s)*, it cannot be omitted without changing the meaning of the sentence.

ESSENTIAL PHRASE: The park **with the pool** is the one we chose.

ESSENTIAL CLAUSE: Only students **who have paid their fees** can attend.

Exercise: Proofreading Add commas (‸) to the following sentences to set off the nonessential phrases or clauses. If a sentence is correct, write *C* on the line provided.

EXAMPLE: ______ 1. I have always been fascinated by Ellis Island‸ which is in Upper New York Bay.

______ 1. Millions of immigrants who came to the United States between 1892 and 1924 stopped at Ellis Island.

______ 2. Families arriving from Europe were examined and interviewed there.

______ 3. The island and its buildings which were closed to the public for many years are now part of the Statue of Liberty National Monument.

______ 4. In 1990, Ellis Island rebuilt as a museum was officially opened to the public.

______ 5. Visitors who wish to see the museum can take a ferry ride from Manhattan Island.

______ 6. The museum's lobby crowded with steamer trunks and other old baggage is the visitors' first sight.

______ 7. One special attraction in the museum consists of audiotapes and videotapes that describe the immigrants' experiences.

______ 8. The Registry Room which is on the second floor sometimes held more than eleven thousand people.

______ 9. The immigrants who came from many countries hoped to find freedom and a happier life in America.

______10. Immigrants who came to the United States brought with them a willingness to work hard and a variety of skills that helped to build the country.

Name ______________________ Date ___________ Class ______________________

Using Commas D

Use commas to set off an appositive or an appositive phrase that is nonessential.

NONESSENTIAL APPOSITIVE: Dad's boss**, Mr. Tarkov,** will be an umpire. [Dad has only one boss, so the appositive is nonessential.]

Do not set off an appositive that tells *which one(s)* about the word it identifies. Such an appositive is essential to the meaning of the sentence.

ESSENTIAL APPOSITIVE: Here is my friend **Tonya**. [Which friend?]

Use commas to set off words used in direct address.

Marie, may I borrow a pencil?

Yes**, Queta,** I have extras.

Use commas to set off a parenthetical expression, such as *after all, for example, on the other hand, I believe, in my opinion,* or *however*.

The best all-around player**, in my opinion,** is Roberto.

On the other hand, Kiyoshi runs faster.

Exercise: Proofreading Add commas (^) where they are needed for appositives, words in direct address, and parenthetical expressions in the following sentences. If a sentence is correct, write C on the line provided.

EXAMPLE: ______ 1. Mars, one of the closest planets, can be seen without a telescope.

______ 1. The whole class of course has read the novel *Old Yeller*.

______ 2. Shana Alexander a former editor of *McCall's* was the main speaker.

______ 3. Nathan do you own a thesaurus a dictionary of synonyms and antonyms?

______ 4. The Galapagos Islands a group of volcanic islands in the Pacific Ocean were named for the Spanish word meaning "tortoise."

______ 5. Rubber an elastic substance quickly restores itself to its original size and shape.

______ 6. This bowl Mary Beth is made of clay found on Kilimanjaro the highest mountain in Africa.

______ 7. For example the North Sea an arm of the Atlantic Ocean is rich in fish, natural gas, and oil.

______ 8. Jamake Highwater a Blackfoot/Eastern Band Cherokee writes about the history of his people.

______ 9. At Gettysburg a town in Pennsylvania an important battle of the Civil War was fought.

______10. My friend Juanita is teaching me to make tortillas.

Name ______________________ Date ____________ Class ______________________

Using Commas E

Use a comma after the following introductory elements:

(1) after *yes, no,* or any mild exclamation such as *well* or *why* at the beginning of a sentence

Yes, I'm the one who called. **Why,** I see you cut your hair!

(2) after an introductory prepositional phrase if the phrase is long or if two or more phrases appear together

In the back yard by the alley, I found this old horseshoe.

(3) after a participial phrase or an infinitive phrase that introduces a sentence

Coming from you, that's a compliment.

To help with your yard work, I have brought some friends.

(4) after an introductory adverb clause

After Tyrone stopped looking for his contact lens, he accidentally stepped on it.

Use commas to separate items in dates and addresses.

My grandfather was born on May 4**,** 1920**,** at 32 Walton Street**,** Dayton**,** Ohio.

Use a comma after the salutation of a friendly letter and after the closing of any letter.

Dear Grandma**,** Sincerely yours**,**

Exercise A: Proofreading Add commas (‸) to the following sentences as needed.

EXAMPLE: 1. Walking among the lions‸ the trainer seemed unafraid.

1. Although she did not win the nomination she raised many important issues.
2. On the desk in the den you will find your book.
3. Yes I enjoyed the fajitas that Ruben made.
4. Walking home from school Rosa saw a bird's nest in some bushes.

Exercise B: Proofreading Add commas (‸) to the following letter as needed.

June 24 1994

Dear Keno

Well I'm glad you finally got to visit Durango Colorado. Going to my summer class I thought about your trip. Hey on your way back did you stop by your aunt's farm as you planned? When I heard you describe her horses I couldn't believe she has so many. I've moved, so write to me at 478 Maybird Street Athens Georgia.

Your friend

Marta

Name ______________________ Date ___________ Class ______________________

Chapter 13: Punctuation

Using Semicolons

MECHANICS

A **semicolon** separates complete thoughts as a period does and items within a sentence as a comma does.

Use a semicolon instead of a comma between independent clauses when they are not joined by *and, but, or, nor, for, so,* or *yet*.

Anna Mary Robertson had a goal**;** she wanted to be an artist.

Use a semicolon rather than a period between independent clauses only when the ideas in the clauses are closely related.

Some people encouraged her**;** others were critical.

Use a semicolon between independent clauses joined by a conjunctive adverb or a transitional expression. A conjunctive adverb or a transitional expression is commonly followed by a comma.

Commonly Used Conjunctive Adverbs

accordingly	furthermore	instead	nevertheless
besides	however	meanwhile	otherwise
consequently	indeed	moreover	therefore

Commonly Used Transitional Expressions

as a result	for example	for instance	that is
in addition	in spite of	in conclusion	in fact

I would like to go to the concert**; however,** I have to work that afternoon.

I'm working to get a new bicycle**; in fact,** I'm saving all my money for it.

A semicolon rather than a comma may be needed to separate clauses joined by a coordinating conjunction when there are commas within the clauses.

I called Chung Sook, Van, and Ray**;** and Sam called Sarita.

Exercise: Proofreading Add semicolons (‸;) and commas (‸,) where necessary in the following sentences.

EXAMPLE: 1. Human beings have walked on the moon‸; they have not yet walked on any of the planets.

1. Tie these newspapers together with string put the aluminum cans in a bag.
2. I called Tom, Paul, and Francine and Fred called Amy, Carlos, and Brad.
3. Reading is my favorite pastime consequently I love to begin a new book.
4. We haven't seen the movie in fact we've never even heard of it.
5. Simone, Rita, and Hector use charcoal Anita uses paints.

Name ______________________ Date ____________ Class ______________________

Using Colons

Use a colon before a list of items, especially after expressions like *as follows* or *the following*.

The things to buy for the picnic are as follows: fruit, drinks, cheese, and crackers.

My father likes these activities: cooking, fishing, and quilting.

NOTE: Never use a colon directly after a verb or a preposition.

Use a colon before a statement that explains or clarifies a preceding statement.

The counselor gave me some good advice: "Never put off until tomorrow what you can do today."

I know why Karen isn't here: She's visiting her grandfather.

Use a colon between the hour and the minute.

8:00 A.M. 2:15 P.M.

Use a colon after the salutation of a business letter.

Dear Mrs. Cramer: To Whom It May Concern:

Use a colon between chapter and verse in referring to passages from the Bible.

Matthew 5:3–11 Exodus 2:6

Exercise A: Proofreading Write the missing colons in the following items.

EXAMPLE: 1. These students won awards: Tasha Zimmer, Blake Sanders, and Sam Reyes.

1. The languages the exchange student speaks are as follows English, German, French, and Spanish.
2. Our bus leaves at 6 23 A.M.
3. I learned three good watchwords for drivers courtesy, caution, and judgment.
4. Please read Luke 3 7–8.
5. Dear Mayor Winston

Exercise B: Proofreading Proofread the following memo, and add colons (:) where necessary.

To All Employees

You are invited to a luncheon at 1 30 P.M. on Friday. The speakers are as follows Dr. Pérez, Mr. Feldman, and Ms. Puccini. Bring these supplies your computer guide, a notebook, and two sharp pencils.

Name ______________________ Date ____________ Class ______________________

Review

Exercise A: Proofreading Add end marks, commas, semicolons, and colons where they are needed in the following paragraph.

EXAMPLE: [1] Animal lovers, have you heard about the Sanctuary for Animals?

[1] Founded by Leonard and Bunny Brook the Sanctuary for Animals is a safe home for all kinds of animals [2] Through the years hundreds of stray unwanted and abused animals have found a home at the sanctuary [3] It is located on the Brooks' land in Westtown N Y [4] On their two hundred acres the Brooks take care of the following animals camels lions elephants kangaroos dogs and cats [5] In addition Mr and Mrs Brook also raise chickens keep horses and look after their other farm animals [6] The Brooks their family and their friends care for the animals however they also let the animals work for themselves [7] Let me tell you how the animals work [8] The Brooks formed the Dawn Animal Agency and their animals became actors and models [9] You may have seen their animals showing off in magazines performing in movies or television shows or helping to sell products in commercials [10] What an unusual clever caring way to help animals

Exercise B: Proofreading Add end marks, commas, semicolons, and colons where they are needed in the following sentences.

EXAMPLE: 1. Snakes, lizards, and crocodiles are reptiles.

1. Toads and frogs on the other hand are amphibians
2. Some turtles live on land others live in lakes streams or oceans
3. Although turtles have no teeth they can bite with their strong hard beaks
4. Yes the terms *turtle* and *tortoise* are interchangeable but *tortoise* usually refers to a land dweller
5. The African pancake tortoise which has a flat flexible shell has a unique ability
6. Faced with a threat it takes these measures it crawls into a narrow crack in a rock it takes a deep breath and it wedges itself in tightly
7. Because some species of tortoises are endangered they cannot be sold as pets
8. The following three species of tortoises live in the United States the desert tortoise the gopher tortoise and the Texan tortoise
9. The gopher tortoise lives in the Southeast the desert tortoise lives in the Southwest
10. The Indian star tortoise considered an endangered species is very rare and I as you can imagine would like to see one

11. As this kind of tortoise grows older its shell grows larger the number of stars increases and their pattern becomes more complex
12. The Indian star tortoise an interesting animal needs warmth sun and vegetables
13. Living in fresh water soft-shelled turtles have long flexible noses and fleshy lips
14. Their shells are not really soft however they are covered by smooth skin
15. Wanda may I introduce you to my pet turtle Pokey
16. Pokey who has been part of our family for years is a red-eared turtle
17. When my parents got Pokey he was only two inches in diameter
18. Pokey has been in my family for fifteen years and he could easily live to be fifty
19. If you look at the design on Pokey's shell you can get a good idea of his age
20. What a great pet Pokey is

Exercise C: Proofreading Add punctuation to the following items as needed.

EXAMPLE: 1. near Fort Worth, Texas

1. Yours truly
2. at the Diamond Co at 10 30 A M
3. Dear Uncle Ivan
4. Genesis 12 13
5. Dear Ms. Bridges

Exercise D: Proofreading Read the following invitation to find fifteen punctuation errors. Add periods, commas, semicolons, and colons as needed.

You're invited to a Splash Party on Thursday May 26 1994.

Come to 224 Pine St Apartment 215, at 2 00 P M call if you need a ride.

Bring the following items bathing suit clogs towel soap and pool pass.

If you want to hear your favorite songs bring some tapes then we can dance.

Exercise E On the lines provided, make each of the following word groups into a complete sentence by supplying an appropriate list or time. Insert colons and commas where they are needed.

EXAMPLE: 1. The test will begin at *9:30 on Friday morning*.

1. My classes this year are as follows ____
   ____.
2. You will need these supplies for your project ____
   ____.
3. So far we have studied the following punctuation marks ____
   ____.
4. Meet me at the mall at ____.
5. My favorite foods are ____.

Name ______________________ Date __________ Class ____________________

Underlining (Italics)

Use underlining (italics) for titles of books, plays, periodicals, works of art, films, television programs, recordings, long musical compositions, trains, ships, aircraft, and spacecraft.

BOOKS: *The Adventures of Tom Sawyer*
PLAYS: *Much Ado About Nothing*
WORKS OF ART: *Venus de Milo*
FILMS: *Fantasia*
PERIODICALS: *National Geographic*
RECORDINGS, LONG MUSICAL COMPOSITIONS: *Rhapsody in Blue*
SHIPS, TRAINS, AIRCRAFT, SPACECRAFT: *Challenger*

NOTE: The article *the* before the title of a magazine or a newspaper is italicized and capitalized only when it is part of the official title of the publication.

Use underlining (italics) for words, letters, and figures referred to as words, letters, and figures.

The *s* is doubled in the word *Missouri.*
Was the last number *8* or *9*?

Exercise: Proofreading In the following sentences, underline any words that should be italicized.

EXAMPLE: 1. Mike Royko writes a column for the Chicago Tribune.

1. The British spell the word humor with a u after the o.
2. In Denmark, you might see the spelling *triatlon* for the word triathlon.
3. The current issue of Newsweek has an informative article on the famine in Africa.
4. Our school paper, the Norwalk Valley News, is published weekly.
5. Luis Valdez wrote and directed La Bamba, a movie about the life of Richie Valens.
6. The Oceanic is one of the ocean liners that sail to the Caribbean.
7. The movie Dances with Wolves has some of the most beautiful cinematography that I have ever seen.
8. Our local theater group is presenting The Time of Your Life, a comedy by William Saroyan.
9. Charles Lindbergh's Spirit of St. Louis, along with the Wright brothers' Flyer and the spacecraft Gemini IV, is on display at the museum.
10. The best novel that I read during vacation was The Summer of the Swans.

Name ______________________ Date ___________ Class ______________________

Direct and Indirect Quotations

Use quotation marks to enclose a **direct quotation**—a person's exact words. Be sure to place quotation marks both before and after a person's exact words.

"Where's Mom?" Charise asked.

Do not use quotation marks for an **indirect quotation**—a rewording of a direct quotation.

Charise asked where Mom was.

A direct quotation begins with a capital letter.

George said, "Here are the new schedules."

Exercise: Proofreading Add quotation marks where necessary in the following sentences. Circle letters that should be capitalized. If a sentence is correct, write C on the line provided.

EXAMPLE: ______ 1. "Let's go to a horror movie this afternoon," said Bob.

______ 1. When I shrieked in fear, the usher warned me to be quiet.

______ 2. At the same time, Bob whispered, it's only a movie—calm down!

______ 3. He pointed out that the people around us were getting annoyed.

______ 4. I quietly replied, I'm sorry.

______ 5. You shouldn't have screamed, he complained.

______ 6. From now on I promise I'll try to be quiet, I said.

______ 7. When the lights came on, Bob said, it's time to go.

______ 8. Outside the theater he muttered something about people who shouldn't go to horror movies.

______ 9. I can't help yelling when I'm scared, I explained.

______10. Yes, but you were afraid even during the credits, Bob protested.

Name ______________________ Date ___________ Class ______________________

Setting Off Direct Quotations

When the expression identifying the speaker interrupts a quoted sentence, the second part of the quotation begins with a small letter. Each part of a divided quotation is enclosed in a set of quotation marks. In addition, the interrupting expression is followed by a comma.

"Which author," asked Lydia**,** "is your favorite?"

When the second part of a divided quotation is a full sentence, the interrupting expression ends with a period, and the second part of the quotation begins with a capital letter.

"Ashley Bryan is my favorite," Stanislav replied**.** "**H**is books are really interesting."

A direct quotation is set off from the rest of the sentence by a comma, a question mark, or an exclamation point, but not by a period.

"Then maybe you know something about his life**,**" Kara said.

"As a matter of fact, I do**!**" Stanislav exclaimed.

A comma or a period is always placed inside the closing quotation marks.

"He has been visiting schools for years**,"** Stanislav said, "to introduce students to African folk tales and culture**."**

Exercise: Proofreading Add quotation marks and other punctuation where needed in the following sentences. Circle letters that should be capitalized.

EXAMPLE: 1. "(w)hen he came to our school, Ashley Bryan wore traditional African clothing," Elton said.

1. Oh, like the clothes Mr. Johnson showed us in class Janell exclaimed
2. Elton asked have you read any Ashley Bryan books about African culture
3. Janell replied I've read *Beat the Story-Drum, Pum-Pum*
4. I really liked that one Elton said I really enjoy African folk tales
5. I think *Walk Together Children* is excellent Janell said
6. Is that one Elton asked about spirituals
7. That's right Janell answered Ashley Bryan believes that spirituals are the United States' greatest contribution to world music
8. She added he grew up in New York City and began writing stories and drawing when he was still in kindergarten
9. Did you know Elton asked that he illustrated his own books
10. Bryan made woodcuts to illustrate *Walk Together Children* he added

Name ______________________ Date ___________ Class ______________________

Punctuating Dialogue

A question mark or an exclamation point is placed inside the closing quotation marks when the quotation itself is a question or an exclamation. Otherwise, it is placed outside.

"When is the balloon fiesta in Albuquerque**?"** Terrence asked. [The quotation is a question.]

Did she say, "The meeting is Thursday**"?** [The sentence, not the quotation, is a question.]

When you write dialogue (conversation), begin a new paragraph each time you change speakers.

"Where does the city plan to build the materials recovery and recycling center?" Derek asked.

"I think," Roberto replied, "they are building it on Abbey Road."

When a quotation consists of two or more sentences, place quotation marks at the beginning and at the end of the whole quotation.

"The cave tour is quite strenuous. If you are unable to descend stairs equivalent to those in a fifty-story building, and climb stairs equivalent to those in a ten-story building, you should not go on the tour,**"** said the guide.

Exercise: Revising On the lines provided, rewrite the following dialogue, correcting any errors in paragraphing, punctuation, and capitalization.

EXAMPLE: In which act of the school play do you go on stage and say I know who the thief is?

In which act of the school play do you go on stage and say, "I know who the thief is"?

Our drama teacher is strict about play rehearsals. Did you hear her say do not miss class or rehearsals if you want to be in the play? What will happen if we miss a rehearsal? Sonia asked. You will be replaced, whatever your part is, Ms. Sibilia answered. There are more students who want to be in the play than there are parts available. If you miss rehearsal, someone will be more than glad to take your place. Does everyone understand this? Yes, and I'm one of the someones, replied Cordelia I think I'll learn everyone's lines just in case I'm called on to take over!

____

____

____

____

____

____

____

Name ______________________ Date ___________ Class ____________________

Other Uses of Quotation Marks

Use single quotation marks to enclose a quotation within a quotation.

Reginald said, "I've been trying to remember that children's song that ends 'The smile was on the crocodile.'"

Use quotation marks to enclose titles of short works such as short stories, poems, articles, songs, episodes of television programs, and chapters and other parts of books.

SHORT STORIES: "The Gift of the Magi" "The Open Window"
POEMS: "The Last Leaf" "Twilight" "Trees"
ARTICLES: "Using End Marks" "The Life of a Wombat"
SONGS: "I've Been Working on the Railroad" "Red River Valley"
EPISODES OF TELEVISION PROGRAMS: "Dr. Chan Returns" "Inside Fort Diablo"
CHAPTERS AND OTHER PARTS OF BOOKS: "The Stanfords Move to Elmira" "A Hidden Room" "Early Childhood"

Exercise: Proofreading Insert quotation marks where they are needed in each of the following sentences.

EXAMPLE: 1. "Let's sing 'The Ballad of Gregorio Cortez,'" said Young.

1. Lani yelled to me, Tracey, Mom says, Get in here right now!
2. The most interesting chapter in *The Sea Around Us* is The Birth of an Island.
3. Didn't Benjamin Franklin once say, Time is money? asked Myra.
4. My favorite Langston Hughes poem is As I Grew Older, said Mona.
5. *Nova*'s program tonight is Man on the Moon.
6. The latest issue of *Seascience* has an article entitled The Things Sharks Swallow.
7. Do you know which character asked What's in a name? in *Romeo and Juliet*? I asked.
8. Yes, answered Sylvia. My mother used to say that to me when I was a little girl. She also read the poem Who Is Sylvia.
9. If you like videos, said Van, you should read the Video Talk article in *Electro World*.
10. There is an article called The Customers Always Write in today's newspaper.

MECHANICS

Name ______________________ Date ____________ Class ______________________

WORKSHEET 6 Review

Exercise A: Proofreading On the lines provided, identify each of the following sentences as *DQ* (direct quotation) or *IQ* (indirect quotation). Then add quotation marks where needed, and circle letters that should be capitalized.

EXAMPLE: *DQ* 1. Mrs. Colby said, "(t)his certainly is a fabulous ship!"

______ 1. The captain announced that dancing begins at midnight.

______ 2. How can we dance if the sea gets rough? asked Mrs. Colby.

______ 3. My dear, her husband replied, we'll just rock with the waves.

______ 4. What's that out there? Clive asked.

______ 5. Mrs. Colby asked, did you hear the steward shout, it looks like an iceberg!?

Exercise B: Revising On the lines provided, rewrite the following dialogue in proper paragraph form. Add capital letters, quotation marks, and underlining (italics), and add or change other punctuation where needed.

Are you going to watch the programs on Classic Theater this fall? asked Thom. The Miami Herald had an article about what will be on, and the writer said, don't miss an episode. Time also recommended them, said Ginny, but I can't watch the one tonight. I have to finish my book report on To Kill a Mockingbird. I wish I could remember whether Scout's father's name has one t or two. And which adjective do you think describes the book better, suspenseful or exciting? How about intense, said Thom. By the way, have you read the poem Stopping by Woods on a Snowy Evening? It's one of my favorites. Mine, too, said Ginny. Thanks for calling, but I must get my book report finished, and it's nearly time for you to watch the first episode of Clouds over Alaska.

____

____

____

____

____

____

____

____

____

____

____

____

____

Name ______________________ Date ___________ Class ______________________

WORKSHEET 1

Using Apostrophes to Show Possession

An **apostrophe** is used to form the *possessive case* of nouns and some pronouns. The **possessive case** of a noun or a pronoun shows ownership or relationship.

OWNERSHIP: **Kalinda's** bicycle **their** job
RELATIONSHIP: **Mick's** father a **day's** wages

To form the possessive case of a singular noun, add an apostrophe and an *s*.

a **month's** work **Tess's** lunch the **elephant's** trunk

NOTE: A proper name ending in *s* may take only an apostrophe to form the possessive case if the addition of *'s* would make the name awkward to pronounce.

Manassas' battlefield the **Philippines'** largest island

To form the possessive case of a plural noun ending in *s*, add only an apostrophe.

the **Joneses'** house the **jackets'** letters the **teachers'** lounge

To form the possessive case of a plural noun that does not end in *s*, add an apostrophe and an *s*.

children's playground **oxen's** pasture **sheep's** pen

Do not use an apostrophe with possessive personal pronouns.

Is that table **theirs** or **ours**?

To form the possessive case of some indefinite pronouns, add an apostrophe and an *s*.

anybody's guess **someone's** raincoat **everybody's** party

Exercise On the line provided, rewrite each of the following expressions by using the possessive case. Add apostrophes when necessary.

EXAMPLE: 1. food for the dog *the dog's food*

1. the nominee of the party ______________________
2. the clothes of the babies ______________________
3. the grades of my sister ______________________
4. the name tags of the guests ______________________
5. the journey of Odysseus ______________________
6. the corn for the goose ______________________
7. the footprints of anyone ______________________
8. the opinions of everybody ______________________
9. the books that belong to them ______________________
10. the clothing of the women ______________________

Name ______________________ Date ___________ Class ________________

Using Apostrophes in Contractions

A **contraction** is a shortened form of a word, a figure, or a group of words. To form a contraction, use an apostrophe to show where letters or numerals have been left out.

COMMON CONTRACTIONS

I am	I'm	1999	'99
let us	let's	we are	we're
she is	she's	he will	he'll
I have	I've	she would	she'd
where is	where's	of the clock	o'clock

The word *not* can be shortened to *n't* and added to a verb, usually without any change in the spelling of the verb.

EXAMPLES: is not **isn't** was not **wasn't**
EXCEPTIONS: will not **won't** cannot **can't**

Exercise On the line provided, write the word or words from each sentence that require an apostrophe, and insert the apostrophe.

EXAMPLE: 1. Arent you going with us at one oclock? *Aren't; o'clock*

1. Wed better chain our bicycles to the rack. ________________
2. That old cars seen better days, hasnt it? ________________
3. She wasnt too happy to see us that late at night. ________________
4. Whos ringing the old cowbell in the pasture? ________________
5. We wont forget how helpful youve been. ________________
6. Im certain youll also be invited. ________________
7. Well have to tell her we wont finish on time. ________________
8. Anns an excellent swimmer, but she hasnt competed yet. ________________
9. Its almost time to leave, isnt it? ________________
10. Im sure theyll show up before its over. ________________

Name ______________________ Date ____________ Class ______________________

Using Contractions and Possessive Pronouns

Do not confuse contractions with possessive pronouns.

Contractions	Possessive Pronouns
it's [*it is*]	its
it's [*it has*]	
who's [*who is*]	whose
who's [*who has*]	
you're [*you are*]	your
they're [*they are*]	their
there's [*there is, there has*]	theirs

Exercise A On the line provided, write *CON* if the italicized word in each sentence below is a contraction or *PP* if the word is a possessive pronoun. Then insert apostrophes as needed.

EXAMPLE: __PP__ 1. How do hurricanes get *their* names?

______ 1. *Theyre* chosen by scientists from all over the world.

______ 2. Meteorologists don't just pick *their* favorite names.

______ 3. *Whose* idea is this?

______ 4. Probably *its* the idea of an international group.

______ 5. *Theres* a list of names for each coast.

______ 6. My friend Hugo thinks *hes* famous now.

______ 7. *Your* friend is right.

______ 8. But *theyre* not going to use that name again.

______ 9. *Its* devastation will be remembered for a long time.

______ 10. *Whos* going to share a name with the next hurricane?

Exercise B The following sentences have empty spaces. In each space, write a contraction or a possessive pronoun that makes sense. Choose from these five words.

their whose couldn't weren't haven't

1. ____________________ you read about the hardships of the Nez Perce?
2. They lost some of ____________________ land to settlers.
3. ____________________ land is it now?
4. Many people ____________________ understand the problems.
5. They ____________________ sure whether a treaty would help.

Name ______________________ Date ___________ Class ____________________

Using Apostrophes in Plurals

Use an apostrophe and an *s* to form the plurals of letters, numerals, and signs, and of words referred to as words.

Sam's *t*'**s** looked like *l*'**s**.

In-line skates are popular in the 1990'**s**.

Shelby uses *etc.*'**s** when she can't remember what to say.

Don't use *&*'**s** for *and*'**s** in school papers.

Exercise A In the sentences that follow, change the italicized items to their plural forms. Use the lines provided.

EXAMPLE: 1. Did you get any A on your progress report? __A's__

1. Count the *yes* and the *no*. ____________
2. How many *i* are in your name? ____________
3. My telephone number has four *2*. ____________
4. Sakura's *4* look like *9*. ____________
5. There are too many *and* in that sentence. ____________
6. Be sure to put loops in your capital *m* and *n*. ____________
7. How many *5* are in 100? ____________
8. Don't forget to write both *r* in the word. ____________
9. The game is called X and O, or tick-tack-toe. ____________
10. The *why* and *wherefore* will be covered later. ____________

Exercise B: Proofreading Insert apostrophes as needed in the following letter.

Dear Yoshi,

Im writing to tell you why 7s are lucky! Youll never believe it! I won a contest by guessing how many beans were in a jar! My winning guess was 777. Whats the prize? I won seven movie tickets. Let me know if youd like to use one.

Do you think they used all 7s in the number on purpose? Its funny if they did because the address of the theater has three 5s in it and no 7s, and the name of the theater is Super 8s! So 7s were just a lucky guess.

Your pal,

Emily

Name ______________________ Date ___________ Class ______________________

Using Hyphens

MECHANICS

Use a **hyphen** to divide a word at the end of a line. When dividing a word at the end of a line, remember the following rules:

(1) Divide the word only between syllables.

INCORRECT: Glacier Nati-
onal Park

CORRECT: Glacier **National** Park

(2) Do not divide a one-syllable word.

INCORRECT: br-
ead

CORRECT: **bread**

(3) Divide a hyphenated word at a hyphen.

INCORRECT: fath-
er-in-law

CORRECT: **father-
in-law**

(4) Do not let one letter stand alone.

INCORRECT: conten-
t

CORRECT: **con-
tent**

Use a hyphen with compound numbers from *twenty-one* to *ninety-nine* and with fractions used as adjectives.

thirty-five trees   **one-half** bushel of apples

Exercise: Proofreading On the lines provided, rewrite the following sentences, adding, deleting, or correcting the position of hyphens as needed.

1. I read twenty two books last summer.

____

2. One of my favorites was a book by Virginia Hamilton called *Paul Robeson,* a biog
raphy.

____

____

3. Paul Robeson was an African American singer and actor. He played the title role in the play *The Emperor Jones*.

____

____

4. Because of the political situation in the United States, he lived in Englan-
d for several years.

____

____

5. If I could be one tenth the singer Paul Robeson was, I would be happy.

____

Name ____________________ Date __________ Class ____________________

Using Parentheses and Dashes

Use **parentheses** to enclose material that is added to a sentence but is not considered of major importance.

Pablo Casals **(**1876–1973**)** played the cello and composed music.

Casals **(**ka salz′**)** was born in Spain.

Material enclosed in parentheses may range from a single word to a short sentence. A short sentence in parentheses may stand by itself or be contained within another sentence.

Shoshanna **(**Shanna**)** and I turned in our reports together.

My report was on bats. **(**I'm fascinated by them.**)**

Many words and phrases are used *parenthetically;* that is, they break into the main thought of a sentence. Most parenthetical elements are set off by commas or parentheses.

The tallest girl is Samantha, not Jovita.

The vacation site **(**one of many choices**)** was finally chosen.

Sometimes parenthetical elements demand a stronger emphasis. In such instances, a *dash* is used. Use a **dash** to indicate an abrupt break in thought or speech.

It's your turn**—**even though it *is* your birthday**—**to do the dishes.

My favorite outing**—**if I can afford it**—**is a day at the amusement park.

Exercise A: Proofreading Insert parentheses correctly in the following sentences.

EXAMPLE: 1. My bicycle (I've had it for three years) is a ten-speed.

1. At the age of thirteen, Jennifer Capriati began playing tennis my favorite sport professionally.
2. Elijah McCoy 1843–1929 invented a way to oil moving machinery.
3. I had to buy a new pocket calculator. My old one stopped working.
4. Charlemagne shär′ lə mān′ was one of Europe's most famous rulers.
5. Lian Young she's a friend of mine told us about her school in China.

Exercise B: Proofreading Insert dashes as needed in the following sentences.

EXAMPLE: 1. The school lunchroom—it was a dull green—has been painted a cheery yellow.

1. Fireflies I can't remember where I read this make what is called cold light.
2. Roberto has always wanted to be can't you guess? an astronaut.
3. Randy Travis I really want to see his concert has a new song out.
4. Do you mind whether Jill and Kenisha here they come now go to the mall with us?
5. The best way to learn to swim that is, after you've learned the strokes is to practice.

Name ______________ Date __________ Class ______________

Review

Exercise A On the lines provided, form the singular possessive and the plural possessive of each of the following nouns.

	Singular Possessive	Plural Possessive
EXAMPLE: 1. school	*school's*	*schools'*
1. star		
2. lady		
3. monkey		
4. mouse		
5. roof		
6. tomato		
7. family		
8. tooth		
9. dish		
10. leaf		

Exercise B On the lines provided, form the possessives of the following pronouns.

EXAMPLE: 1. no one *no one's*

1. we ______________
2. somebody ______________
3. you ______________
4. it ______________
5. who ______________

Exercise C On the line provided, form a contraction of each of the following pairs of words.

1. could not ______________
2. here is ______________
3. who has ______________
4. they are ______________
5. what is ______________
6. are not ______________
7. it is ______________
8. was not ______________
9. I am ______________
10. we are ______________

Name ______________________ Date __________ Class ______________________

Exercise D Underline the correct word in parentheses in each sentence.

EXAMPLE: 1. (There, They're) going to Washington, D.C., next week.

1. I don't think (its, it's) going to grow in this soil.
2. (Who's, Whose) poetry book is on the desk?
3. If the dog puts (its, it's) feet in the wet concrete, the marks will be there forever.
4. (They're, Their) school bus will be here soon.
5. (You're, Your) doing a good job baking bread.

Exercise E: Proofreading On the lines provided, rewrite the following sentences, adding or deleting apostrophes and hyphens as necessary.

EXAMPLE: 1. Does his address have two 5s or one?
Does his address have two 5's or one?

1. Heres the magazine article about the scientists digging up the dinosaur bone-s in Wyoming in the 1980s.

____

____

2. Someones bicycle has been out on our porch for a week, and I dont know whose it is.

____

3. Ms. Acuna hasnt decided yet whether to get the CD player for her broth-er-in-laws birthday; he'll be twenty three.

____

____

4. If you put lines through your *7*s, as they do in Europe, sometimes they look like *F*s.

____

5. Id rather use my nickname than my real name because I like to write *y*s.

____

Exercise F: Proofreading Insert parentheses or dashes in the following sentences as needed.

EXAMPLE: 1. I've lost my English paper—oh, here it is under the desk.

1. The best gift you can give Mom and Dad they'll love it is a weekend free from chores.
2. Our school's engineer Anne's uncle won an award for bravery.
3. Help me move this table I know it's heavy so we can put the bookcase by the wall.
4. Sojourner Truth 1797–1883 and Harriet Tubman 1820–1913 were famous abolitionists.
5. I have always dreamed of owning believe it or not a bright purple motorcycle.

Name ______________________ Date ____________ Class ______________________

Improving Your Spelling

The following techniques can help you spell words correctly.

Pronounce words correctly. Pronouncing words carefully can often help you spell them correctly.

sur•prise [*not* su•prise] li•brar•y [*not* li•bar•y]

Spell by syllables. When you have trouble spelling long words, divide them into syllables. A **syllable** is a word part that can be pronounced by itself.

shoe [one syllable] per•ma•nent [three syllables]
trou•ble [two syllables]

Use a dictionary. When you are not sure about the spelling of a word, look in a dictionary. A dictionary will also tell you the correct pronunciations and syllable divisions of words.

Keep a spelling notebook. The best way to master words that give you difficulty is to list the words and review them frequently. Divide each page into four columns.

COLUMN 1: Correctly spell the words you frequently misspell.
COLUMN 2: Write the words again, dividing them into syllables and marking accents. (Use a dictionary, if necessary.)
COLUMN 3: Write the words again, circling the parts that give you trouble.
COLUMN 4: Jot down any comments that may help you remember the correct spelling.

Proofread for careless spelling errors. By slowly rereading what you have written, you can correct careless errors.

Exercise A: Proofreading Read the following sentences to find spelling errors. Write each misspelled word correctly on the line provided. Use a dictionary if you need it.

1. Did you watch the documentry about bats? ______________
2. There are many difrent kinds of bats. ______________
3. One egspert said that photos make bats look vicious. ______________
4. If the bat was caged, it probly was scared. ______________
5. A scientist's labotory isn't a bat's favorite roosting place! ______________

Exercise B Look up the following words in a dictionary. Rewrite each word, using hyphens to divide it into syllables. Use the lines provided.

1. atrocious ______________
2. frightened ______________
3. habitat ______________
4. research ______________
5. scientist ______________

Name ________________ Date ____________ Class ________________

Roots

Many English words are made up of various word parts. Learning to spell the most frequently used parts can help you spell many words correctly.

The **root** is the part of the word that carries the word's core meaning. Many English word roots come from ancient Latin and Greek words. Sometimes a root has more than one form.

Word Root	Meaning	Example
–dict–	speak	predict
–duc–, –duct–	lead	induce, reduction
–ject–	throw	project
–ped–	foot	pedestal
–pend–	hang, weigh	pendulous
–port–	carry, bear	export
–spec–	look	inspect
–struct–	build	structure
–vid–, –vis–	see	provide, visual
–voc–	call	vocabulary

Exercise A For each of the following words, underline the root. Then on the line provided, use your own knowledge and the meaning of the root to write a definition of each word. Check your definition in a dictionary.

EXAMPLE: 1. con<u>struct</u>ion *building*

1. transportation ______________________
2. contradict ______________________
3. interject ______________________
4. revise ______________________
5. depend ______________________

Exercise B On the lines provided, write sentences using the five words that you defined in Exercise A.

EXAMPLE: 1. *The construction of the house took three months.*

1. ______________________
2. ______________________
3. ______________________
4. ______________________
5. ______________________

Name ______________________ Date ____________ Class ______________________

Prefixes

A **prefix** is one or more than one letter or syllable added to the beginning of a word to create a new word with a different meaning.

COMMONLY USED PREFIXES

Prefix	Meaning	Example
anti–	against	antibody
co–	with, together	co-worker
dis–	away, from, opposing	disallow
extra–	beyond, outside	extraordinary
fore–	before, front part of	forecast
in–	not	inability
inter–	between, among	interact
mis–	badly, not, wrongly	misshape
non–	not	nonskid
post–	after, following	postdate
pre–	before	preview
re–	back, again	review
sub–	under, beneath	subset
trans–	across, beyond	transform
un–	not, reverse of	unoriginal

Exercise Underline the prefix in each of the following words. Then use your own knowledge and the meanings of the prefix and the root to write a definition of each word. Check your definition in a dictionary.

EXAMPLE: 1. un popular *not popular*

1. disjoined ______________________
2. misguided ______________________
3. uneasy ______________________
4. transatlantic ______________________
5. prewriting ______________________
6. incurable ______________________
7. refilled ______________________
8. extraordinary ______________________
9. foremost ______________________
10. substandard ______________________

MECHANICS

Name ____________________ Date __________ Class ____________________

Suffixes

A **suffix** is one or more than one letter or syllable added to the end of a word to create a new word. Often, adding a suffix changes both a word's part of speech and its meaning.

COMMONLY USED SUFFIXES

Suffix	Meaning	Example
–able	able, likely	adaptable
–dom	state, condition	wisdom
–en	make, become	lighten
–esque	in the style of, like	statuesque
–ful	full of, characteristic of	hopeful
–fy	make, cause	nullify
–ize	make, cause to be	dramatize
–ly	characteristic of	swiftly
–ment	result, action	payment
–ness	quality, state	calmness
–or	one who	director
–ous	characterized by	courageous
–ship	condition, state	courtship
–ty	quality, state	loyalty
–y	condition, quality	handy

Exercise Underline the suffix in each of the following words. Then use your own knowledge and the meanings of the suffix and the root to write a definition of each word. Check your definition in a dictionary.

EXAMPLE: 1. dry<u>ness</u> *quality or state of being dry*

1. justifiable ____________________
2. resentful ____________________
3. moisten ____________________
4. measurement ____________________
5. ideally ____________________
6. realize ____________________
7. editor ____________________
8. picturesque ____________________
9. thrifty ____________________
10. hardship ____________________

Name ________________________ Date ____________ Class ______________________

Spelling Rules A

One way to improve your spelling is to memorize some important rules.

Except after *c,* write *ie* when the sound is long *e*. Some exceptions: *either, neither, leisure,* and *weird.*

Write *ei* when the sound is not long *e,* especially when the sound is long *a*. Some exceptions: *friend, mischief, view,* and *ancient.*

NOTE: These rules apply only when the *i* and the *e* are in the same syllable.

The only word ending in *–sede* is *supersede*. The only words ending in *–ceed* are *exceed, proceed,* and *succeed*. All other words with this sound end in *–cede*.

Exercise A The following paragraph contains ten words with missing letters. Add the letters *ie* or *ei* to spell each numbered word correctly.

EXAMPLE: Last summer I [1] rec *ei* ved an airline ticket as a birthday gift.

I flew to Puerto Rico with my [1] fr ______ nd Alicia to see my family. We arrived in San Juan, where my grandmother's [2] n ______ ghbor, Mr. Sánchez, met us and drove us to my grandmother's house. There, all of my relatives—aunts, uncles, cousins, [3] n ______ ces, and nephews—welcomed us. They couldn't [4] bel ______ ve that [5] n ______ ther of us had ever been to Puerto Rico before. The next day, they took us for a drive along the coast to Ponce, the island's [6] ch ______ f city after San Juan. From Ponce, we took a [7] l ______ surely drive on the mountain road, Ruta Panorámica. However, the road turned and twisted so much that I was [8] rel ______ ved to get back on the main road. After a [9] br ______ f rest, we explored the western part of the island. Soon, Puerto Rico no longer seemed [10] for ______ gn to us.

Exercise B: Proofreading Cross through the incorrect spellings of words ending in *–cede, –ceed,* and *–sede* in the following sentences. Then write the correct spellings on the line provided. If a sentence is correct, write C.

EXAMPLE: 1. I guess he didn't ~~succede~~ with that trick! *succeed*

1. Please prosede to the entrance. ______________
2. The canyon's beauty excedes my expectations. ______________
3. What year did Georgia secede from the Union? ______________
4. Train travel superceded stagecoach use in the area. ______________
5. We hope that the water will receed by the weekend. ______________

Name ______________________ Date ____________ Class ______________________

Spelling Rules B

When adding a prefix to a word, do not change the spelling of the word itself. Some commonly used prefixes are *il–, un–, im–, in–, pre–, mis–, dis–, over–,* and *re–.*

When adding a suffix to a word, use the following rules.

1. When adding the suffix *–ly* or *–ness,* do not change the spelling of the word itself. Exceptions: For words that end in *y* and have more than one syllable, change the *y* to *i* before adding *–ly* or *–ness.*
2. Drop the final silent *e* before a suffix beginning with a vowel. Exceptions: words ending in *ce* or *ge* before a suffix beginning with *a* or *o* and the words *dyeing, singeing,* and *mileage.*

   NOTE: When adding *–ing* to words ending in *ie,* drop the *e* and change the *i* to *y: lying, dying.*
3. Keep the final silent *e* before a suffix beginning with a consonant. Some exceptions: *argument, judgment, awful, truly,* and *ninth.*
4. For words ending in *y* preceded by a consonant, change the *y* to *i* before any suffix that does not begin with *i.*
5. For words ending in *y* preceded by a vowel, keep the *y* when adding a suffix. Some exceptions: *daily, laid, paid,* and *said.*
6. Double the final consonant before a suffix beginning with a vowel if the word (a) has only one syllable or has the accent on the last syllable *and* (b) ends in a single consonant preceded by a single vowel. Examples: *swimming, chopped.* Some exceptions: words ending in *w* or *x*: *mowing, waxed.*

Exercise A On the line provided, spell each of the following words with the given prefix.

EXAMPLE: 1. semi + circle *semicircle*

1. il + legible ______________ 6. mis + spell ______________
2. un + necessary ______________ 7. dis + satisfy ______________
3. im + partial ______________ 8. dis + approve ______________
4. in + offensive ______________ 9. mis + understand ______________
5. im + mortal ______________ 10. over + rule ______________

Exercise B On the line provided, spell each of the following words with the given suffix.

EXAMPLE: 1. joy + ful *joyful*

1. hopeful + ly ______________ 6. easy + ly ______________
2. happy + ness ______________ 7. drop + ed ______________
3. advance + ment ______________ 8. bay + ing ______________
4. desire + able ______________ 9. hurry + ed ______________
5. true + ly ______________ 10. advantage + ous ______________

Plurals of Nouns A

For most nouns you simply add *–s* to form the plural.

SINGULAR: nest PLURAL: nests

Use the following rules to form the plurals of other nouns.

1. For nouns ending in *s, x, z, ch,* or *sh,* add *–es.*

   SINGULAR: tax PLURAL: taxes

2. For nouns ending in *y* preceded by a vowel, add *–s.*

   SINGULAR: tray PLURAL: trays

3. For nouns ending in *y* preceded by a consonant, change the *y* to *i* and add *–es.*

   SINGULAR: baby PLURAL: babies

   EXCEPTIONS: For proper nouns ending in *y,* just add *–s.*

4. For some nouns ending in *f* or *fe,* add *–s.* For others, change the *f* or *fe* to *v* and add *–es.*

   SINGULAR: wolf PLURAL: wolves

5. For nouns ending in *o* preceded by a vowel, add *–s.*

   SINGULAR: radio PLURAL: radios

6. For nouns ending in *o* preceded by a consonant, add *–es.*

   SINGULAR: hero PLURAL: heroes

   EXCEPTIONS: musical terms such as *altos* and proper nouns such as *Eskimos*

NOTE: A number of nouns that end in *o* preceded by a consonant have two plural forms, such as *tornados* or *tornadoes.*

Exercise A On the line provided, spell the plural form of each of the following nouns.

EXAMPLE: 1. chimney *chimneys*

1. wish ____________________
2. piano ____________________
3. puppy ____________________
4. belief ____________________
5. self ____________________

Exercise B: Proofreading The following paragraph contains five spelling errors. Cross through each error, and write the correct spelling above it.

EXAMPLE: [1] People who live in ~~citys~~ *cities* might enjoy reading the works of J. Frank Dobie.

[1] Of the essaies I've read, "When I Was a Boy on the Ranch" is my favorite. [2] Dobie writes about life on ranchs in southwestern Texas. [3] Dobie recalls that the young ranch hands liked to copy the activitys of the cowpunchers they admired. [4] The Western heros were usually building fences and tending the livestock. [5] Dobie says that he had several horses to ride by the time he was eight yeares old.

Name ______________________ Date ____________ Class ______________________

Plurals of Nouns B

Use the following rules to form the plurals of nouns.

1. A few nouns, such as *children, oxen, geese, feet, teeth, women,* and *mice,* form their plurals irregularly.
2. For most compound nouns, form the plural of the last word in the compound.

   SINGULAR: drive-in PLURAL: drive-ins
3. For compound nouns in which one of the words is modified by the other word or words, form the plural of the word modified.

   SINGULAR: sister-in-law PLURAL: sisters-in-law
4. For some nouns, such as *Japanese* and *deer,* the singular and plural forms are the same.
5. For numbers, letters, symbols, and words used as words, it is best always to add an apostrophe and an *s.*

   and's *A*'s #'s *6*'s 1900's

Exercise A On the line provided, spell the plural form of each of the following nouns. (Note: Italics indicate words used as words or letters used as letters.)

EXAMPLE: 1. trout *trout*

1. *m* ______________
2. scissors ______________
3. 1930 ______________
4. child ______________
5. Chinese ______________
6. mother-in-law ______________
7. governor-elect ______________
8. *if* ______________
9. two-year-old ______________
10. side-wheeler ______________

Exercise B On the lines provided, write sentences using the proper plural forms of the following words and symbols.

EXAMPLE: 1. sheep *Lillian saw sheep in the meadow.*

1. merry-go-round ______________________________
2. *if* ______________________________
3. ? ______________________________
4. moose ______________________________
5. brother-in-law ______________________________

Name ____________________ Date __________ Class ______________

Spelling Numbers

Observe the following rules for spelling numbers.

1. Spell out a number that begins a sentence.

   One hundred animals were returned to the wildlife preserve.

2. Within a sentence, spell out numbers that can be written in one or two words. Use numerals for other numbers.

   Our group of **thirty-seven** students toured the preserve.

   The preserve has **3,700** animals.

   NOTE: If you use several numbers in the same sentence, some short and some long, write them all the same way. Usually, it is better to write them all as numerals.

   There are **700** birds among the **3,700** animals.

3. Spell out numbers used to indicate order.

   The **first** [*not* 1st] time I saw the preserve was on a field trip.

Exercise A: Proofreading Each of the following sentences contains an error in writing a number. Write the correct form on the line provided.

EXAMPLE: 1. 600 knights, both male and female, attend Dragonfest, a medieval festival. *Six hundred*

1. You might be interested to know that some seven hundred and thirty people take part in the event. ______________
2. The festival is actually the 3rd annual Dragonfest. ______________
3. There were 1,000 people at last year's Dragonfest. ______________
4. 5 knights got carried away with their swords, and that scared some people away this year. ______________
5. One of the knights flew more than eight hundred miles to the festival; a few knights came 1,500 miles by car. ______________

Exercise B On the lines provided, write a short paragraph about an imaginary creature. In your story, correctly spell the following numbers.

299 15 3,000 96 4th

____

____

____

____

____

Name ______________________ Date ___________ Class ______________________

Using Context Clues A

The **context** of a word consists of the words that surround it in a sentence and the whole situation in which the word is used. The context gives you clues to the meaning of a word. Types of context clues include *definitions and restatements*, and *examples*.

Definitions and restatements are clues that define the term or restate it in other words.

At the center of the engagement ring was a large *emerald*, which is **a deep-green precious stone**.

Examples used in context may also reveal the meaning of an unfamiliar word.

Gems, such as **diamonds, sapphires,** and **opals,** are used to make jewelry.

Exercise For each italicized word in the sentences below, use the list at the bottom of the page to identify the definition that is closest in meaning. Write the letter of the correct definition on the line provided.

_______ 1. They had been political *adversaries*, or foes, throughout their careers.

_______ 2. Some common *phobias* include dread of heights and of crowds.

_______ 3. The commander of the rebel forces wanted to *negotiate*, or come to verbal agreement, with the country's leaders.

_______ 4. *Precipitation*, such as rain and snow, is rare in the desert.

_______ 5. *Conifers*, such as pines, spruces, firs, and cedars, produce cones.

_______ 6. The living room had many *amenities*—a soft chair, bookshelves, and blue curtains at the windows.

_______ 7. After the auto accident, the *nape*, or back, of my neck was sore midway between and behind my ears.

_______ 8. Burglary, arson, murder, and other *felonies* are the most serious offenses.

_______ 9. *Crustaceans* such as shrimp, lobsters, and crayfish are popular food items.

_______10. Creatures that live in the desert must protect their bodies from *dehydration*, or loss of water.

a. moisture that falls to earth
b. back
c. drying out
d. desirable features
e. crimes
f. animals with hard outer shells
g. fears
h. certain trees
i. bargain
j. opponents

Name ______________________ Date ___________ Class ______________________

Using Context Clues B

The **context** of a word consists of the words that surround it in a sentence. The context gives you clues to the meaning of a word. *Synonyms,* as well as *contrast* and *cause-and-effect clues,* can help you understand new words when you read.

Synonyms are clues which indicate that an unfamiliar word is the same as, or similar to, a familiar word or phrase.

The *kohlrabi,* like its relatives **cabbages** and **turnips,** is quite tasty in soups.

Contrast clues indicate that an unfamiliar word is opposite in meaning to a familiar word or phrase.

Unlike her sister Flora, who is often **sloppy,** Elena is always *fastidious.*

Cause-and-effect clues indicate that an unfamiliar word is related to the cause or the result of an action, feeling, or idea.

The weeds are **destroying** our garden, so we'll have to *extirpate* them.

Exercise On the line provided, write the meaning of each italicized word based on the context clues in the sentence.

1. Unlike his fellow actors, who appeared anxious and distressed, the play's leading man remained *poised* when the set collapsed. ______________________
2. Mario's father couldn't drive us, so our trip to the mall was *postponed.* ______________
3. *Terns,* like gulls and other such sea birds, eat whatever they can find on the beach. ____
4. Darlene was angry, and Eduardo was equally *incensed.* ______________________
5. We had to dig through the storm's *debris,* the ruins left by the hurricane, to find the injured dog. ______________________________________
6. If you want us to understand every word you say, you will have to speak slowly and *enunciate.* ______________________________________
7. I've never had Korean *cuisine;* is it similar to Chinese cooking? ______________
8. The male peafowl is many-colored, but the female is *monochromatic.* ______________
9. New York City, like other major *urban* centers including Chicago and Los Angeles, offers many cultural attractions. ______________________________
10. I forgot to water the plant for several weeks, so it became *desiccated.* ______________

MECHANICS

Name ______________________ Date ____________ Class ______________________

Choosing the Right Word

Being alert to *synonyms, antonyms,* and *homographs* will help you identify words in context. A **synonym** is a word that means nearly the same thing as another word. However, words that are synonyms rarely have exactly the same meaning. Two words may have the same **denotation,** or dictionary definition, but a different **connotation,** or suggested meaning. For example, the word *oath* has the same denotation as *promise,* but *oath* has a more formal connotation. An **antonym** is a word that has nearly the opposite meaning of another word. For example, *friend* has an opposite meaning to *foe.*

Homographs are words that are spelled the same but have different meanings. Although the words look the same, they may not be pronounced the same.

conduct the orchestra   your **conduct** in class

Exercise A For each sentence below, underline the synonym or antonym that provides a clue to the meaning of the italicized word. On the line provided, write *S* for synonym or *A* for antonym. Then choose from the list the word closest in meaning to the italicized word. Write the letter of that word on the line.

EXAMPLE: __S, f__ 1. A hot shower will *rejuvenate* your tired body and refresh your spirits.

a. talkative   b. crumbled   c. famous   d. level   e. panic   f. restore

______ 1. The Soviet Union rapidly *disintegrated;* it simply broke into pieces.

______ 2. With strangers, Ipek was always quiet, but with her family, she was quite *loquacious.*

______ 3. The pilot advised us to stay calm, but some passengers went into a *frenzy.*

______ 4. Among well-known people in the community, no one is more *prominent* than the mayor, Mr. Chandaran.

______ 5. At each *echelon* of responsibility, you move up the steps to a good career.

Exercise B On the lines provided, write two sentences using the word *aroma* in one and *odor* in the other. Keep in mind the connotations of the words as you use them in sentences.

1. ____

2. ____

Exercise C Each sentence below contains a pair of homographs in italics. On the line provided, write a meaning for each homograph. Use a dictionary if needed.

1. The *light* was dim, but I saw the butterfly *light* on his arm.

____

2. *Lead* the children away from the *lead* pipes.

____

Name ______________________ Date ____________ Class ______________________

WORKSHEET 13

Review

Exercise A On the line provided, write each word syllable-by-syllable, using hyphens between syllables. Use a dictionary if you are unsure.

EXAMPLE: 1. college *col-lege*

1. bureau ______________________
2. embarrass ______________________
3. discipline ______________________
4. immediately ______________________
5. genuine ______________________

Exercise B On the line provided, write two words that contain each of the following roots.

EXAMPLE: 1. –pend– *suspend, depend*

1. –spec– ______________________
2. –duc– ______________________
3. –port– ______________________
4. –voc– ______________________
5. –vis– ______________________

Exercise C Underline the prefix or suffix used in each of the following words. On the line provided, give the meaning of the prefix or suffix and a meaning for each word. Use a dictionary if necessary.

EXAMPLE: 1. preheat *before; to warm beforehand*

1. antisocial ____
2. jealous ____
3. misfire ____
4. kingdom ____
5. gritty ____

Exercise D Fill in the missing letters in the following paragraph so that each word is spelled correctly.

Here's something to do in your l ______ sure time. Maybe you and a fr ______ nd can start a service. Offer to take an elderly n ______ ghbor shopping. After you load the shopping cart, proc ______ to the checkout line. Let's hope this idea will y ______ ld success!

Exercise E On the line provided, spell each of the following words with the given prefix or suffix.

EXAMPLE: 1. help + ful *helpful*

1. dis + locate ______________________
2. main + ly ______________________
3. argue + ing ______________________
4. un + natural ______________________
5. busy + ness ______________________
6. notice + able ______________________

Name ____________________ Date __________ Class ____________________

7. trap + ed ____________________
8. bare + ly ____________________
9. pay + ment ____________________
10. merry + ment ____________________

Exercise F On the line provided, write words for the instructions for each item.

EXAMPLE: 1. plural of *wish*: wishes

1. your age, at the beginning of a sentence: ____________________
2. plural of *mix*: ____________________
3. plural of *man*: ____________________
4. a number used to indicate order: ____________________
5. plural of *mother-in-law*: ____________________
6. plural of *igloo*: ____________________
7. the number 52 in a sentence containing no other numbers: ____________________
8. plural of *donkey*: ____________________
9. plural of *Sioux*: ____________________
10. an antonym for *festive*: ____________________
11. plural of *potato*: ____________________
12. plural of *country*: ____________________
13. a synonym for *solitary*: ____________________
14. plural of the letter *A*: ____________________
15. plural of *giraffe*: ____________________

Exercise G Use context clues to choose the word or phrase below that best fits the meaning of the italicized word in each of the following sentences. Write the letter on the line provided.

a. beautiful
b. nicknames
c. round
d. myths
e. dropped sharply
f. considering

______ 1. Sharria spends as much time *pondering* what to write as she does thinking about music.

______ 2. The earth is *spherical*, like a ball.

______ 3. Ludlow was known by such *monikers* as Lumpy and Pokey.

______ 4. Emiliano thought the tiny blue insect was *exquisite*, not hideous.

______ 5. Because the temperature *plummeted*, we built a fire.

Name ______________________ Date ___________ Class ____________________

WORKSHEET 1 Freewriting

Freewriting is one technique for gathering ideas for writing. In freewriting, you begin with a word or phrase and write whatever comes into your mind. Don't worry about grammar, usage, mechanics, or even organization. To freewrite, set a time limit of three to five minutes. Start with a subject that's important to you, and keep writing until the time is up. If you get stuck, just write anything. The important thing is to keep your pen moving. **Focused freewriting,** or **looping,** means taking a word or phrase from freewriting you've already done and starting to freewrite again.

Exercise A Read the following three words: *outer space, music, water*. Choose one of these words. Close your eyes and think about this word for one minute. Open your eyes, and begin to write. Don't worry about spelling, punctuation, or complete sentences. Simply write.

Exercise B Choose one word or phrase from your freewriting in Exercise A. Write that word or phrase below. Then do focused freewriting for three to five minutes on the lines provided.

Word or phrase: ______________________________

COMPOSITION

Name ______________________ Date ___________ Class ___________________

Brainstorming

Brainstorming is a technique for gathering ideas for writing. In brainstorming, you say whatever comes to mind in response to a word. You can brainstorm alone or with a group or partner. To brainstorm, write any subject at the top of a sheet of paper or on the chalkboard. List every idea about the subject that comes to your mind. (In a group, have one person list the ideas.) Keep going until you run out of ideas.

Exercise A Choose one of the following general subjects. Brainstorm about the subject alone or with one or two classmates. On the lines below, write all the ideas that you can think of about that subject.

Subjects:	space aliens	community problems	fears
	video games	outstanding Americans	rock groups

Subject you chose: ___________________________________

Brainstorming notes:

________________________ ________________________

________________________ ________________________

________________________ ________________________

________________________ ________________________

________________________ ________________________

________________________ ________________________

________________________ ________________________

________________________ ________________________

________________________ ________________________

Exercise B Choose one of the ideas that you listed in Exercise A. Explain on the lines provided why you might like to write about that topic.

Idea you chose: ___________________________________

Explanation: ____

____

____

____

____

____

____

Name ______________________ Date ____________ Class ______________

WORKSHEET 3 Clustering and Questioning

Clustering and *asking questions* are two ways to explore a subject. To **cluster,** write your subject on your paper, and circle the subject. Around the subject, write whatever ideas about it occur to you. Circle these ideas. Draw lines to connect them with the subject. When an idea in one of the outer circles makes you think of related ideas, you can do further clustering around that idea.

You can also ask the ***5W-How?* questions**—*Who? What? Where? When? Why?* and *How?*—about your subject.

Exercise A Choose a topic and write the topic on the line in the center circle below. Then complete the cluster chart by thinking of as many ideas related to that topic as you can. Write the related ideas inside the connected circles.

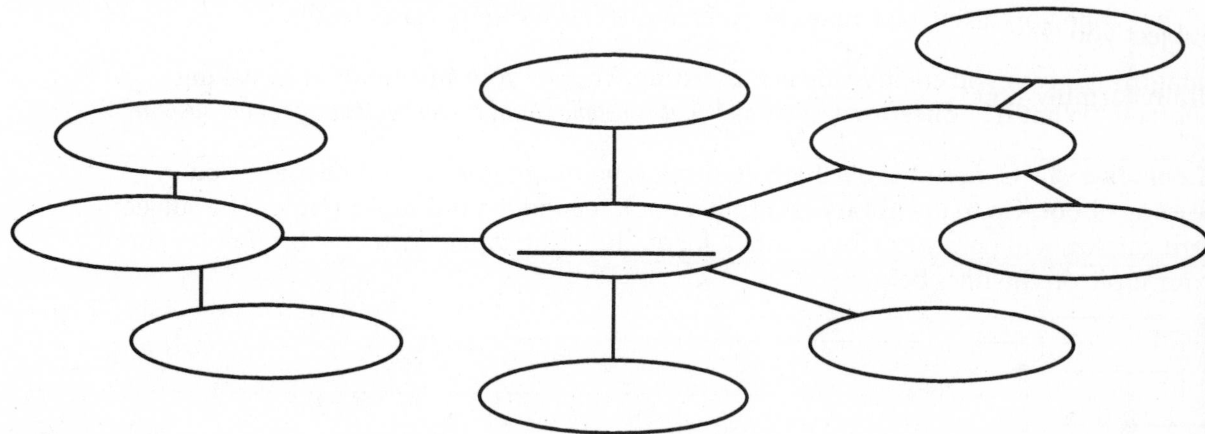

Exercise B Choose a subject from the front page of a newspaper. On the lines below, write six questions about the subject—one question for each of the *5W-How?* questions: *Who? What? When? Where? Why?* and *How?*

Subject: ______________________________

____

____

____

____

____

____

____

____

____

COMPOSITION

Name ______________________ Date __________ Class ____________________

Reading, Listening, Imagining

Reading, listening, and *imagining* are ways to gather ideas and information for your writing. **Reading** sources include books, magazines, newspapers, and brochures. Here are some tips for finding specific information.

- Check the tables of contents and indexes to find the exact pages you need to read.
- Skim the pages until you find something about your topic.
- Slow down to take notes on the main ideas and important details.

By **listening,** you can get a lot of information from speeches, radio and TV programs, interviews, audiotapes, or videotapes. Use the following hints when you listen for information.

- Before you listen, make a list of questions about your topic.
- While you listen, take notes on the main ideas and important details.

Imagining gives you creative ideas for writing. Trigger your imagination by asking yourself **"What if?" questions,** such as *What if people could travel beyond our solar system?*

Exercise A Choose a topic that you think seventh-graders would be interested in reading about. Go to the library and find a book related to your topic. (Note: The subject card catalog will help you.) Read with a focus about the topic. Write five brief notes about your topic on the lines below.

Topic: ________________________________

1. ____
   ____
2. ____
   ____
3. ____
   ____
4. ____
   ____
5. ____
   ____

Name ______________________ Date ____________ Class ______________________

Exercise B Choose an educational radio or television program about a topic that interests you. Prepare a list of questions about the topic. Have the list in front of you as you watch or listen to the program. Take notes about main ideas and important details related to the topic. After the program is over, rewrite your notes on the lines below.

Topic: ______________________________________

Exercise C You and a partner are planning a short story for your class magazine. Think of a basic idea. Imagine as many "What if?" questions about this idea as you can. Then write a brief plot outline on the lines provided.

Name ______________________ Date ___________ Class ______________________

Purpose and Audience

Before you write, always ask yourself, *Why am I writing?* You write in many different forms, but you have one or more basic **purposes:** to express your feelings, as you might in a journal or letter; to be creative, as in a short story or poem; to explain or inform, as in an essay or a news story; and to persuade, as in a letter to the editor or a political speech.

Before you write, also ask yourself, *Who will read my writing?* Consider your **audience**—the readers. Ask yourself these questions.

- Why is my audience reading my writing? Do they expect to be entertained, informed, or persuaded?
- What does my audience already know about my topic?
- What does my audience want or need to know about my topic?
- What vocabulary and type of language should I use?

Exercise A Write one purpose that you might have for doing each of the following forms of writing.

EXAMPLE: 1. campaign speech *to persuade*

1. short story ______________________
2. news story ______________________
3. advertisement ______________________
4. journal entry ______________________
5. history report ______________________

Exercise B You're writing a science report about active volcanoes in Hawaii. Your purpose is to inform, and your readers are your classmates. Which of these statements belong in your report? Which ones don't? Draw a line through the statements that do not belong.

1. Two active volcanoes in Hawaii Volcanoes National Park are Mauna Loa and Kilauea.
2. The town of Volcano, Hawaii, where many scientists live, is built right next to an active volcano.
3. I'm really afraid to even think about volcanoes ever since I saw a late-night movie about a killer volcano.
4. Mount Vesuvius in Italy is a steep-sided, symmetrical composite volcano.
5. When volcanoes erupt, they often cause much damage to homes and crops; they sometimes kill people.

Name ________________ Date ____________ Class ________________

Arranging Ideas

After gathering ideas for a piece of writing, you need to put your ideas in order. There are four common ways to order ideas.

- **Chronological order** presents events as they happen in time. You use chronological order in narration—for example, in stories, narrative poems, explanations of processes, history, biography, and drama.
- Using **spatial order,** you describe objects in order by location—near to far, left to right, top to bottom, and so on. Description may be used in any type of writing.
- When arranging ideas in **order of importance,** you give details from least to most important or the reverse. Use this type of order in persuasive, descriptive, explanatory, and evaluative writing.
- Use **logical order** to relate items to the groups they belong in. You order logically when you classify, define, or compare and contrast.

Exercise A Arrange the following items of information about writer Rudyard Kipling, author of *Rikki-tikki-tavi,* in chronological order by numbering the ideas from 1 to 5.

______ Kipling returned to India in 1882.

______ Kipling won the Nobel Prize for literature in 1907, the first time the prize had been won by an English person.

______ Kipling was born in India in 1865.

______ After Kipling's return to India, he became a journalist and soon began to write short stories, sketches, and poems.

______ When Kipling was six, he was sent to England to go to school.

Exercise B Decide how a piece of writing about each of the following subjects should be organized. Then, on the lines provided, write *L* for logical order, *S* for spatial order, or *I* for order of importance.

______ 1. an evaluation of a school dance in your town

______ 2. a description of the parts of a car engine

______ 3. a classification of Hopi pottery

______ 4. an editorial written to persuade people to vote

______ 5. a comparison and contrast of Maya Angelou's and Alice Walker's poetry

COMPOSITION

Name ______________________ Date ___________ Class ______________________

Using Visuals A

Visuals can help you bring order to your prewriting notes. Two types of **visuals** are *charts* and *Venn diagrams*. A **chart** allows you to list ideas in columns and rows. Headings for columns and rows identify the information in the body of the chart.

A **Venn diagram** uses overlapping circles to show how two subjects are similar (comparison) and different (contrast). If you are comparing two subjects, draw two overlapping circles, one for each subject. In the overlapping section, record details shared by both subjects. In the parts that don't overlap, write details that make these subjects different.

Exercise A How can you show a comparison of two countries? In the space provided below, make a chart to organize the following notes about the United States and China.

The United States has a total area of 3,600,000 square miles.

It has more than 250,000,000 people.

Its form of government is a republic.

China has a population of more than 1,100,000,000 people.

It is governed by a Communist regime.

It has a total area of more than 3,690,000 square miles.

Exercise B Use the Venn diagram below to organize information that will compare and contrast two kinds of music. Above each circle write the name of the kind of music.

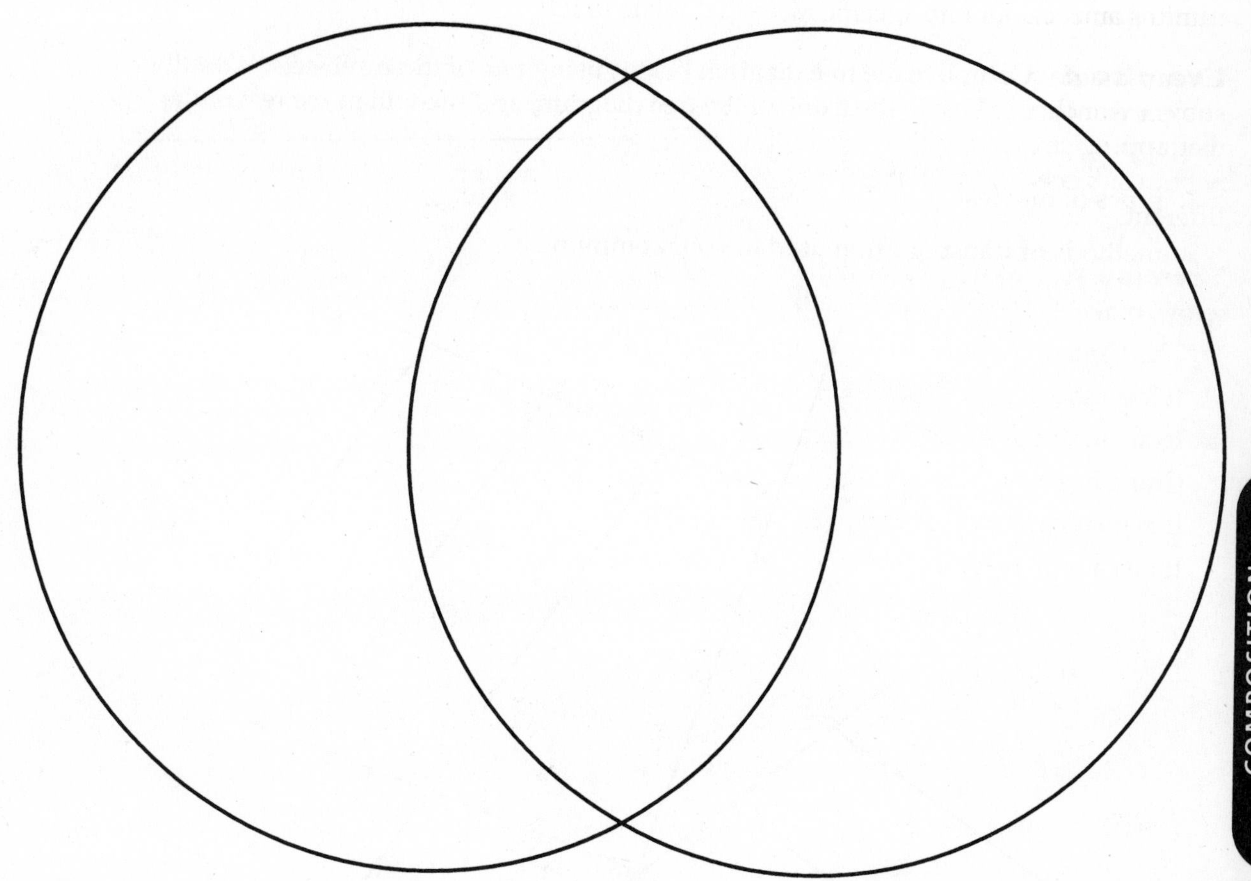

Name ______________________ Date ___________ Class ______________________

Using Visuals B

Visuals can help you bring order to your prewriting notes. Two types of visuals are *tree diagrams* and *sequence chains*. A **tree diagram** helps you to see how a general idea (the tree trunk) branches out into specific ideas that relate to it.

Exercise A Complete the tree diagram below, using one of these subjects. Write the subject you choose beside the trunk of the tree diagram, and then fill in the rest of the diagram.

1. types of movies
2. methods of transportation used in your community

Name ______________________ Date ____________ Class ____________________

A **sequence chain** can help you organize events in chronological order. You can use a sequence chain to show the steps in a process or the main events in a story. Write down a brief sketch of the first event or step, draw a box around it, and draw an arrow pointing to the next box. Follow this procedure until all events or steps are recorded.

Exercise B In the space below, fill in the boxes to create a sequence chain for one of the following assignments. You can add boxes to the chain if necessary.

1. Show the main events in a story. You can create a plot for a short story, or you can show the events in a story that you have read or in a movie or a TV show that you have seen.
2. Show the stages in the writing process.

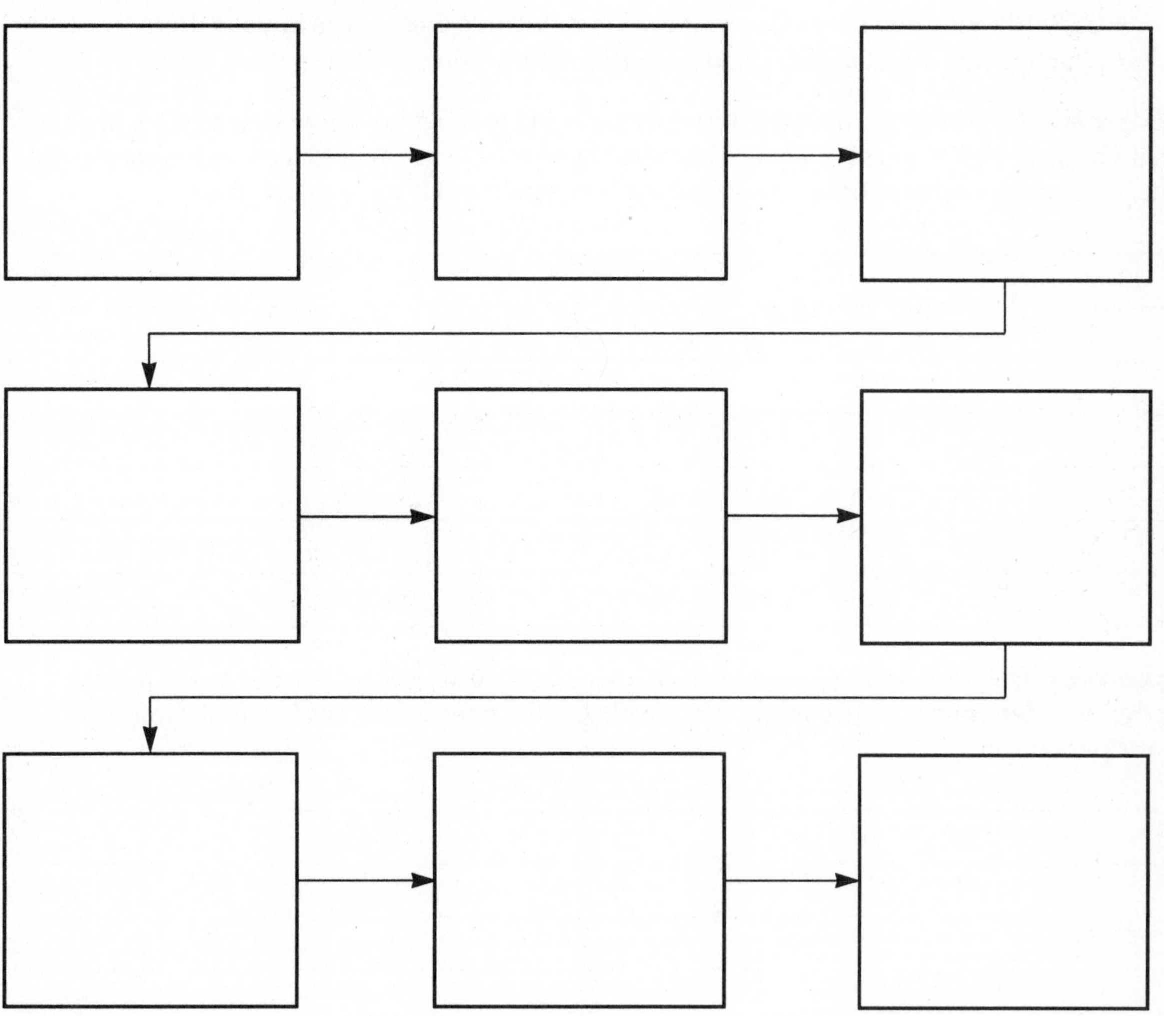

Name ______________________ Date ____________ Class ______________________

Writing a First Draft

After you have planned a piece of writing, it's time to write a **first draft**. There are no precise rules for writing a first draft. Whether people write their first drafts quickly or slowly, they are all creating something new from separate parts. This process is called **synthesizing**. To synthesize your first draft, use the following tips.

- Use your prewriting plan as a guide.
- Think about your main idea. Then write a sentence that states this main idea.
- Write freely. Focus on details that express your main idea.
- As you write, you may discover new ideas. Include these ideas in your draft.
- Don't worry about spelling and grammar errors. You can correct them later.

Exercise A Many children and adults in the world today don't know how to read. Imagine that you were never taught to read. What would you miss? How would it change your life? On the lines below, freewrite or brainstorm about how you'd feel if you couldn't read.

____

____

____

____

____

____

____

____

Exercise B Now arrange your ideas in a way that makes sense. For this topic, logical order or order of importance might work well. On the lines below, write a first draft of your paragraph.

____

____

____

____

____

____

____

____

____

____

Name ______________________ Date ____________ Class ____________________

Self-Evaluation

When you **evaluate** something, you examine its strengths and weaknesses. One way to evaluate something is to think about what it takes to make it really good. Suppose, for example, that you wanted to evaluate a guitar. You would ask yourself such questions as *What qualities does a good guitar have?*

These techniques can help you evaluate your own writing.

- **Read carefully.** Read your paper more than once. First, read for *content* (what you say), then for *organization* (how you order ideas), and then for *style* (how you use words and sentences).
- **Listen carefully.** Read your paper aloud. *Listen* to what you've said. You may notice that the ideas don't flow smoothly or that some sentences sound awkward.
- **Take time.** Set your draft aside. Come back to it later and read through it. You'll find it's easier to be objective about your writing after a little time away from it.

Exercise If you think octopuses are scary, wait until you meet the giant squid. Read the following paragraph, and then write a short evaluation of it on the lines provided. To evaluate the paragraph, ask the following questions: Is the writing interesting? Does it grab and hold your attention? Does the writing have a clear main idea? Is the main idea supported with enough details? Are the ideas presented in a clear and reasonable order? In your evaluation, write at least one comment on what is good about the paragraph and at least one comment on what needs to be improved. (Focus on content and organization. Don't worry at this point about spelling, grammar, or punctuation errors.)

A strange sea creature that people rarely see because it lives in deep waters is the giant squid. Giant squids can grow up to sixty feet long. There are old sea stories about giant squids attacking boats. They wrap their tentacles around them. Rows of sucking disks line the arms. The giant squid's eyes are huge, up to fifteen inches wide. Boy, I wouldn't want to meet one, would you? Old sailors called giant squids sea monsters.

____

____

____

____

____

____

____

____

Name ______________________ Date ____________ Class ____________________

Peer Evaluation

Peer evaluation is a review of one writer's work by another writer. Here are some guidelines for the writer whose work is being evaluated.

- Make a list of questions for the peer evaluators. Which parts of your paper worry you?
- Keep an open mind. Don't take your evaluators' suggestions as personal criticism.

Here are some guidelines for the peer evaluator.

- Tell the writer what's good about the paper. Give the writer some encouragement.
- Focus on content and organization. The writer will catch spelling and grammar errors when proofreading.
- Be sensitive to the writer's feelings. State your suggestions as questions, such as "What does this mean?" and "Can you give an example?"

Exercise Suppose that you are evaluating the paragraph below for one of your classmates. Is the writing interesting? Is it well organized? Is it clear? Write at least five helpful questions or suggestions for the writer of this paragraph.

> Languages are interesting. Everyone has a native language. English is the native language of about 350 million people. Chinese is the native language of about a billion people. Spanish is the native language of about 300 million people. Even though English is not the native language of as many people as Chinese is. Still, English is the most widely spoken language in the world. The written Chinese is called kanji. Kanji is 4,000 years old. Japanese people use kanji too, but spoken Japanese is completely different than spoken Chinese. But each kanji represents one word or idea. To read a Chinese newspaper, you would have to have memorized at least 2,500 kanji.

1. ____

____

2. ____

____

3. ____

____

4. ____

____

5. ____

____

Name ____________________ Date ____________ Class ____________________

Revising

When you **revise,** you make changes to improve your paper. There are four main ways to revise.

- You can **add** new information to help your audience understand your main idea. Add words, phrases, sentences, or whole paragraphs.
- You can **cut** or take out repeated or unnecessary information and unrelated ideas.
- You can **replace** weak or awkward wording with more precise words or details.
- You can **reorder** or move information, sentences, and paragraphs for logical order.

Exercise Study the revisions made to the following paragraph. Then answer the questions below.

The scientists who first made radium in 1898, Pierre and Marie Curie, ~~did not~~ *refused to* take out a patent. They said that radium belonged to everyone. Ernest Hemingway, who gave his Nobel Prize medal to a religious ~~place~~ *shrine* in Cuba, said, "You don't ever have a thing until you give it away." Several ~~good~~ *important* inventors in history have felt the same way Hemingway did. *Today, radium is used to treat cancer and other diseases.* Wilhelm Roentgen, who discovered X-rays in 1895, refused to apply for a patent on his process or to take any money from it. He too felt that his discovery should belong to everyone. ~~I feel that way too.~~ John Walker, the Englishman who ~~made~~ *invented* matches, never patented his invention. He believed that matches should be public property.

1. Why did the writer move the sentences about Hemingway to the beginning of the paragraph?

____

____

____

2. Why did the writer replace the word *place* with the word *shrine* in the first sentence about Hemingway?

____

____

____

3. Why did the writer add the sentence "Today, radium is used to treat cancer and other diseases"?

____

____

____

4. Why did the writer replace the words *did not* with the words *refused to* in the sentence about the Curies?

____

____

____

5. Why did the writer cut the sentence "I feel that way too"?

____

____

____

Name ______________ Date __________ Class ______________

WORKSHEET 13 Proofreading and Publishing

When you **proofread,** you carefully reread your paper. You correct mistakes in grammar, usage, capitalization, spelling, and punctuation. One way to proofread is to use the following guidelines.

1. Is every sentence a complete sentence, not a fragment?
2. Does every sentence begin with a capital letter and end with the correct punctuation mark?
3. Do plural verbs have plural subjects? Do singular verbs have singular subjects?
4. Are verbs in the right form? Are verbs in the right tense?
5. Are adjective and adverb forms used correctly in making comparisons?
6. Are the forms of personal pronouns used correctly?
7. Does every pronoun agree with its antecedent (the word it refers to) in number and in gender?
8. Are all words spelled correctly? Are the plural forms of nouns correct?

After you proofread, you're ready to **publish,** or share your writing. Some ways to publish your work include reading what you've written to your classmates or to a group of friends, displaying your work on a school bulletin board or in the library, keeping a folder of your writing to share with family and friends, and sending your writing to a newspaper or magazine.

COMPOSITION

Exercise A: Proofreading Use the checklist above to proofread the following paragraph. Using a dictionary and your handbook to help you, cross out incorrect items and write corrections above them.

Communication is faster today than it was just a few hundred years ago. Queen Isabella did not get word of Columbus's discovery in 1942 until five months. After Columbus had landed. France did not get word that Lincoln had been asassinated until two weeks after his death. in 1969, Neil Armstrong's message from the moon took 1.3 seconds to arrive on earth. In the 1990's, we have fiber-optic wires that can conduct 800 million pieces of information in one second. Its no wonder that some people think we may be able to get information about events *before* they occur!

Exercise B On the lines provided, write three suggestions for ways that you might publish an essay on UFO sightings.

____

____

____

Name ______________________ Date ____________ Class ______________________

WORKSHEET 14

The Aim and Process of Writing

Aim—The "Why" of Writing

WHY PEOPLE WRITE	
To express themselves	To get to know themselves, to find meaning in their own lives
To share information	To give other people information that they need or want; to share some special knowledge
To persuade	To convince other people to do something or believe something
To create literature	To be creative, to say something in a unique way

Process—The "How" of Writing

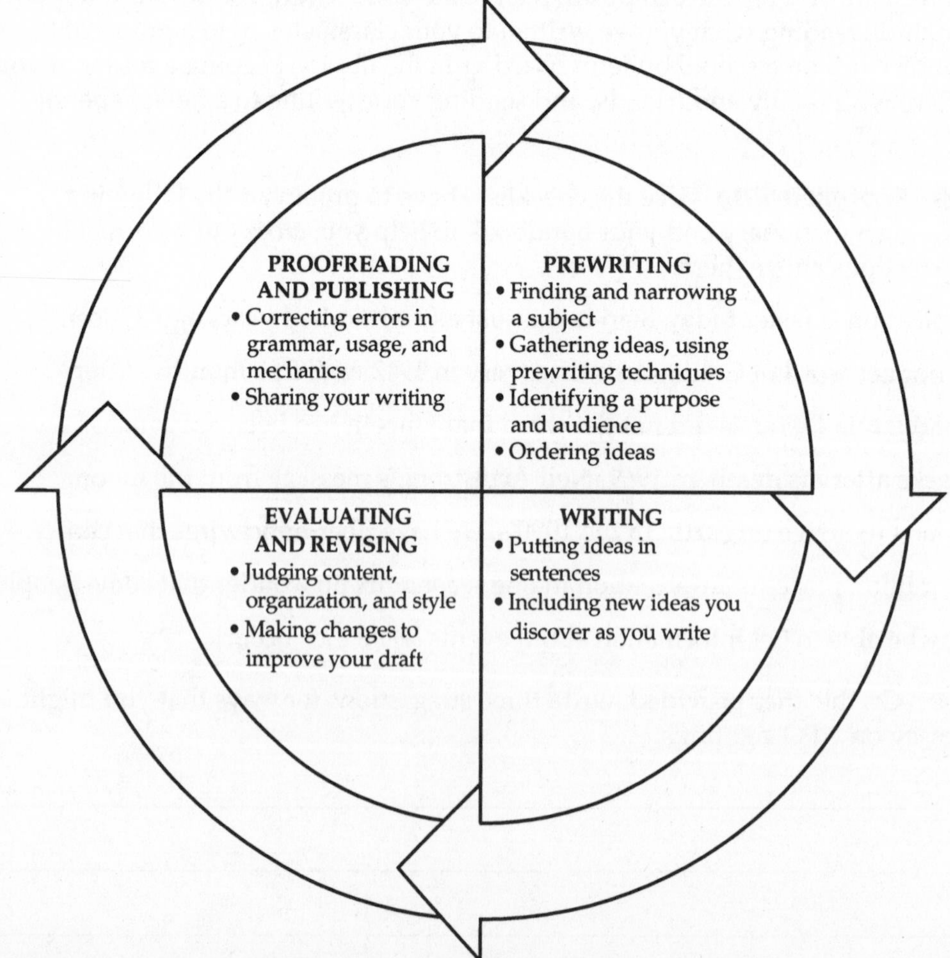
PROOFREADING AND PUBLISHING
• Correcting errors in grammar, usage, and mechanics
• Sharing your writing
PREWRITING
• Finding and narrowing a subject
• Gathering ideas, using prewriting techniques
• Identifying a purpose and audience
• Ordering ideas
EVALUATING AND REVISING
• Judging content, organization, and style
• Making changes to improve your draft
WRITING
• Putting ideas in sentences
• Including new ideas you discover as you write

Name ______________________ Date ____________ Class ______________________

Chapter 18: Paragraph and Composition Structure

WORKSHEET 1 The Paragraph's Main Idea

Every paragraph must contain a *main idea*. The **main idea** is the idea around which the entire paragraph is organized. It is what the paragraph is about.

Exercise On the line provided, write the main idea of each paragraph below.

EXAMPLE: 1. The wheel is one of the most important inventions of all time. It first appeared in Mesopotamia more than five thousand years ago. Today it appears everywhere. The wheel makes it possible to move large loads easily.

Main idea: *the importance of the wheel*

1. What instruments did early people use to write with? Some used stones, bones, and sticks. Others used clay tablets. Eventually people came up with various kinds of ink and paper. The ink we use today is a modern invention; so are lead pencils.

Main idea: ____

2. The first lamps were made when people realized that they could create light from burning oil. These early lamps were made out of hollow rocks filled with animal fat. The lamps lit up caves and made it possible to see at night.

Main idea: ____

3. A stethoscope is one of the most frequently used medical devices. It is used to listen to the lungs and heart. A person wearing a stethoscope can also detect the sounds of blood vessels. Even the heartbeat of an unborn baby can be heard through a stethoscope.

Main idea: ____

4. The silicon chip is now used in everything from refrigerators to binoculars. But where does silicon come from? Silicon is a chemical element usually found in a combined form known as silica. Silicon is dark gray in color and very hard. One common form of silica is quartz.

Main idea: ____

5. Artists have many ways of creating a drawing or painting. Some prefer to sketch on white paper with drawing pencils, charcoal, or ink. Others use colored pencils, pastels, or watercolors on white or colored paper. Acrylics and oil paints are used to create beautiful color landscapes, portraits, and still-life paintings on canvas.

Main idea: ____

Name ______________________ Date ___________ Class ______________________

WORKSHEET 2

The Topic Sentence

The **topic sentence** states the main idea of a paragraph. It can occur anywhere in a paragraph. Often it is either the first or second sentence. Sometimes a paragraph has no topic sentence, especially if it is a narrative paragraph that tells about a series of events. The reader has to add up the details to figure out what the paragraph is about.

Exercise Underline the topic sentence in each of the following paragraphs.

EXAMPLE: 1. Traditionally, festivals have been an important part of Iroquois life. In festivals the Iroquois give thanks for the blessings of nature. In the Maple Festival, the people give thanks for the trees and the syrup. Other Iroquois festivals include the Corn Planting Festival, the Strawberry Festival, and the Green Corn Festival, all of which celebrate planting and reaping. There is also a New Year Festival.

1. At the time when Europeans were first settling in North America, each Iroquois village had its own storytellers. The storytellers went from longhouse to longhouse. They also told stories at festival time. The Iroquois people listened carefully to the storytellers and remembered what they said. Storytellers were an important part of the Iroquois way of life.

2. In those days, Iroquois women dressed both for warmth and protection as well as for the sake of beauty. The soft deerskin skirts and dresses of the Iroquois were both practical and attractive. Iroquois women also adorned themselves with bright porcupine quills and beads made from shells and animal teeth. They also dyed their hair.

3. Iroquois men built the dwellings, made tools, and hunted for food. They cleared the land for planting, and they also fought enemies. The jobs of the Iroquois were divided between men and women. The women planted, gathered, and prepared food. They made the clothing and blankets and cared for the children.

4. What games did the Iroquois play? In one favorite sport, the Iroquois formed two teams on a large field. Each side had a goal post and used a spoon-like stick to carry or throw the ball over that goal. Does this game sound familiar? The Iroquois played what has become our modern-day game of lacrosse.

5. The "highways" of the early Iroquois were streams and rivers. To travel on them, the Iroquois used canoes. Canoes were the basic means of Iroquois transport. They were lightweight and made from bark. Canoes enabled the Iroquois to carry things over distances and to travel across bodies of water.

Name ______________________ Date ___________ Class ____________________

Using Sensory Details

Supporting sentences give specific details that explain or prove the main idea of the paragraph. One way to support a main idea is to use sensory details. Sensory details are words that appeal to one of the five senses—sight, hearing, smell, touch, and taste. Vivid sensory details help your reader clearly imagine what you're writing about.

Exercise A Read the following paragraph. Then complete the chart below, listing one detail from the paragraph that appeals to each of the five senses.

I'll never forget the day I spent at World of Water amusement park. Before we even entered the park, I could see the huge slides looming high above the walls surrounding the grounds. One slide stood about one hundred feet high and seemed to plunge straight down. People went down the slide cheering, whooping, laughing, choking, and sputtering on mouthfuls of water. There was also a wave pool, where people relaxed on tubes and floated gently on the aqua water until a sudden crash of waves churned the pool, toppling riders and causing screams of panic! I tried everything at least once, always baking in lines in the hot sun before splashing through the water again. On the way home, we stopped for a delicious fish dinner. That night, my skin smelled of chlorine and sunblock, and my body was sore from hours of exercise, but I was ready to go back again.

Sight	
Hearing	
Touch	
Taste	
Smell	

COMPOSITION

Exercise B Choose one of the following topics or one of your own. Write the topic. Then complete the chart with sensory details related to the topic. Include two details for each of the five senses.

POSSIBLE TOPICS: a tradition in my family — the best surprise ever — my favorite neighborhood (or town or city)

Topic: ____

	Detail 1	Detail 2
Sight		
Hearing		
Touch		
Taste		
Smell		

Name ____________________ Date ____________ Class ____________________

Using Facts and Examples

The main idea in a paragraph can be supported by *facts* or *examples*. A **fact** is a statement that can be proved true by directly observing or by checking a reliable reference source.

FACT: Abraham Lincoln was the sixteenth U.S. president.

OPINION: Abraham Lincoln was the best U.S. president. [An opinion, like the one expressed in this statement, can't be proved.]

Examples are specific instances or illustrations of a general idea.

Word processing, video games, and telecommunications are examples of how computer software is used.

Exercise A Read the following prewriting notes for a paragraph that tells about the invention of plastics. Cross out any facts that do not support the main idea.

In the 1860's, Alexander Parkes made the first partly synthetic plastic.

Parkesine, his plastic, could be molded into different shapes.

In many supermarkets today, customers are asked whether they want paper or plastic bags.

Bakelite was the first truly synthetic plastic.

Bakelite was invented in 1909.

Today, people are developing new ways to recycle plastics.

Synthetic plastics were first developed from substances in petroleum oil during the 1920's and 1930's.

Exercise B For each topic sentence below, write the kind of supporting detail (*facts* or *examples*) you think would be most effective in developing a paragraph. Then write two details of the kind you have chosen.

EXAMPLE: 1. Bats need protection from humans if they are to survive.
facts—Many species are on the federal endangered species list. There is an international organization dedicated to saving them.

1. Last summer, our neighborhood block party was full of surprises.

____

____

____

2. The Olympic games have a long and interesting history.

____

____

____

Name ______________________ Date ____________ Class ______________________

Chapter 18: Paragraph and Composition Structure

WORKSHEET 5 Unity in Paragraphs

A paragraph has **unity** when all the sentences support, or tell something about, one main idea. In the following paragraph, the sentence that has been crossed out does not support the main idea and destroys the unity of the paragraph.

Do you know what relative humidity is? Relative humidity is the amount of moisture in the air relative to the total amount of moisture the air can hold. Relative humidity is an important factor in health and comfort, especially during winter months when indoor air is heated. Dry indoor air can cause respiratory problems, skin irritations, and itching eyes. ~~Colds are another common problem in the winter.~~ The use of humidifiers and vaporizers can help increase relative humidity and therefore reduce these problems.

Exercise Each of the following paragraphs has one sentence that ruins the unity. Try your skill at finding the sentences that don't belong. [Hint: First, decide what the main idea is. Next, decide whether each supporting sentence is closely connected to the main idea.] Draw a line through each sentence that doesn't belong in its paragraph.

1. A well-known folk tale from Vietnam is called "The Buffalo Boy." It is about a boy who looks after water buffaloes in the rice fields and discovers the miraculous powers of the banyan tree. In one story he rises up to the sky while hanging on to the root of a banyan tree. The people of Vietnam say you can see the outline of the boy in the moon at night. The apparent face of the moon is really just craters.

2. Olives were an important part of life in ancient Greece. Wheat was scarce. Olive oil was used in cooking and also in lamps. Special laws were created to make sure that the land around Athens was used for olive trees rather than for any other purpose. Olive oil also was traded for other goods.

3. The street felt like an oven to Tamara as she walked toward the park. It was a hot day for baseball practice. She wondered if the Cardinals game would be on television that evening. Tamara told herself she couldn't let the heat slow her down, though. The coach would be deciding today who would start in the season's first game. And she wanted to be playing third base.

4. Canoes are made for many different kinds of water. White-water canoes are for use in fast, rock-filled streams. They're made to turn quickly to avoid obstacles. Other canoes are made for lakes and quiet rivers. They don't turn too quickly, so they won't be your first choice for use on a river with lots of rapids. On the other hand, they're easy to paddle in a straight line. You can also find canoes that are made to carry either one or two people. Before choosing a canoe, think about what kind of water you'll be using it in.

COMPOSITION

Name ______________________ Date ____________ Class ______________________

Coherence in Paragraphs A

A paragraph has **coherence** when a reader can easily tell how and why ideas are related. Transitional words and phrases are used to connect ideas in a paragraph. Here are some common transitions.

Transitions Showing Time/Narration			
after	finally	immediately	then
before	first, second, etc.	next	until
during	following	often	when
Transitions Showing Place/Description			
above	beside	in	there
along	down	into	to
around	from	next	under
before	here	over	where

Exercise On the lines provided, write the transitions from the above list that connect the ideas in each of the following paragraphs.

1. I was the first to cheer when I heard we were taking a class trip to New York City. Before I traveled to New York, I read some guide books to see what was there.

Transitions: ____

2. First, I did some reading. Then I wrote to the Chamber of Commerce for information on sites I wanted to see. I knew I had to see Ellis Island after I read the description of the new museum and grounds there. I also knew I wanted to get a view from high above the city.

Transitions: ____

3. After we got to the city, we immediately went to the Metropolitan Museum of Art. Next, we had lunch in a pizza shop. In the afternoon, we walked along Fifth Avenue until we were too exhausted to take another step.

Transitions: ____

4. When it was dark, we saw New York from the top of the World Trade Center. I gazed down at the city's countless lights. Finally, we returned to the hotel, where I slept contentedly.

Transitions: ____

5. The following day we went to Ellis Island. We walked around the grounds. There I stepped into the world of generations of immigrants who helped to make our country great.

Transitions: ____

Name ______________________ Date ___________ Class ________________

Chapter 18: Paragraph and Composition Structure

Coherence in Paragraphs B

Transitional words and phrases are used to connect ideas. Here are some common transitions.

Transitions for Comparing and Contrasting Ideas		
also	another	similarly
although	but	too
and	however	yet
Transitions Showing Cause and Effect/Narration		
as a result	for	so that
because	since	therefore
Transitions for Showing Importance/Evaluation		
first	mainly	then
last	more important	to begin with

Exercise Choose appropriate transitional words and phrases from the above list to connect the following ideas.

1. Bell-bottom pants were popular in the 1960's and 1970's, ____________________ they were completely out of style by the 1980's.
2. Shoulder pads are often worn in jackets. ____________________, people's shoulders sometimes look wider or broader than they actually are.
3. The style in hemlines is always changing, ____________________ so are the colors that are fashionable each fall.
4. It can be costly to pay a lot of attention to current styles ____________________ styles change so rapidly.
5. Certain classic styles are a good investment ____________________ they never seem to go out of style.
6. The oversized look in sweaters was popular in the 1980's. ____________________ style of this period was baggy trousers.
7. ____________________, Janis bought several pairs of stretch pants. Then she searched for shirts to match.
8. Some of this year's popular fabrics require dry cleaning; ____________________, Ralph decided not to buy them.
9. It is fun, ____________________ costly, to be in style.
10. Stephanie likes this year's new styles and would like to buy several items; ____________________, she knows they will go out of style soon.

COMPOSITION

Name ______________________ Date ____________ Class ____________________

Description: Using Spatial Order

When you want to tell in your writing what something is like or what it looks like, you use **description.** In a description, sensory details provide effective support. Often, you'll use **spatial order**—the order in which items are arranged in space. Here is an example of a description that uses spatial order.

Near the entrance to the theme park is a giant float of cartoon space characters. They point to the entrance, where a moving sidewalk takes guests to various places in the park. The first stop, near the entrance, is the World of Tomorrow Pavilion, where visitors can look at exhibits and see a film. The second stop, in the center of the park, is Future Rides, where all kinds of rides await those brave enough to go on them. The last stop, at the far end of the park, is the Future Food and Beverage Center, which is located in front of the Future World Gift Shop. On the perimeter of the park are a first-aid station and rest areas.

Exercise A Read the description of the theme park again. Then, on the lines provided, list the following details in the order of their distance from the entrance of the park. The last detail has been filled in.

DETAILS: first-aid station | entrance to moving sidewalk | giant float | Future Rides | Future Food and Beverage Center | Future World Gift Shop | World of Tomorrow Pavilion

____

____

____

____

____

____

first-aid station

Exercise B You and a friend decide to meet at the theme park. She has never been there. You tell her to meet you at the Future World Gift Shop. Write clear directions that will make it easy for your friend to find the spot. Or if you wish, draw a map.

____

____

____

____

Name ________________ Date __________ Class ______________

Narration: Using Chronological Order

In **narration,** you tell how a person or situation changes over a period of time. You may use narration to tell a story or incident, to explain a process, or to explain causes or effects. Often, you'll use **chronological order**—the order in which events occur.

Exercise Can you tell a story about being frightened? Can you tell the causes and effects of not cleaning up your room for a month? The following exercises will give you some practice in telling about events in the order in which they happen. Follow the directions for each item.

1. Choose one of the topics below as the subject of a story. Circle the letter of the topic you chose, and make up three or more events that might be in the story. Arrange all of the events in chronological order. Use your imagination.
   a. A mysterious light follows your family's car down a lonesome country road one night.
   b. A tall, shy, new student enters your school. He doesn't really fit in at first, but soon the situation changes.

   Events: ________________

   ____

   ____

   ____

2. Circle the letter beside one of the following activities. Then list three or more steps you'd need to take in order to perform this activity. Arrange the steps in chronological order.
   c. how to boot up (start) a computer
   d. how to clean up your room

   Steps: ________________

   ____

   ____

   ____

3. Write a brief cause-and-effect explanation of something that has happened to you. Tell the sequence of events in chronological order, showing how one event caused another, how the second event caused something else to happen, and so on. Give at least four events in all.

   ____

   ____

   ____

   ____

Name ______________________ Date ____________ Class ______________________

Classification: Using Logical Order

When you **classify,** you tell how a specific subject relates to other subjects that belong to the same group. You classify by defining or by comparing and contrasting. Usually, writers use **logical order**—grouping related ideas together—in paragraphs that classify.

Exercise A Think about two subjects that are alike enough to be compared and different enough to be contrasted. Write at least one statement that tells how these subjects are alike and one statement that tells how they are different.

You might compare and contrast one of the following pairs of subjects (or think of your own):

- being a child and being a teenager
- good science fiction movies and bad science fiction movies
- living in a large city and living in a small community

Topic: ____

Alike: ____

____

____

____

Different: ____

____

____

____

Exercise B On the lines provided, tell about a Clydesdale horse by using the classification strategy of defining. First, define what a Clydesdale is by telling its general class. Then list all the characteristics that distinguish it from other breeds. (If you need some information about the animal, use an encyclopedia or talk to an owner.)

____

____

____

____

____

____

____

____

____

Evaluation: Using Order of Importance

Evaluating is the process of judging something's value, deciding whether something is good or bad. You have to give reasons, or support, for your opinion. A good way to arrange your reasons is by **order of importance**. You can emphasize one reason by putting it first or last in the paragraph.

Exercise What's your evaluation? Why do you think so? On the lines provided, write your evaluation of each of the following subjects. Give three reasons for your opinion. List your reasons in order of importance with the most important reason first.

EXAMPLE: **Topic 1:** *our school's basketball team*

Evaluation: *It's a very good team.*

Reasons: (1) *Our center is five foot ten.*

(2) *Our guards are very quick.*

(3) *Players who are not even starting players are also good shooters.*

1. the street or road you live on
2. a book you've read lately (or a movie you've seen recently)
3. the newest fad in clothes

Topic 1: ______________________________

Evaluation: ______________________________

Reasons: (1) ______________________________

(2) ______________________________

(3) ______________________________

Topic 2: ______________________________

Evaluation: ______________________________

Reasons: (1) ______________________________

(2) ______________________________

(3) ______________________________

Topic 3: ______________________________

Evaluation: ______________________________

Reasons: (1) ______________________________

(2) ______________________________

(3) ______________________________

Name ______________________ Date ____________ Class ____________________

Planning a Composition

The **main idea** of your composition is the major point that you want to make about your topic. It's what you want your audience to focus on when they read your composition.

Exercise A Are you throwing away things that could be recycled instead? The writer who took the following notes became interested in recycling after hearing about the problems of too much trash. Read over the notes, and decide on a main idea for a composition on recycling. On the lines provided, write down the main idea.

You can set up a recycling center in your home or school.
Try not to buy items in jars or boxes that can't be recycled.
Find out how to get a community recycling program started.
Don't accept food that's in plastic containers at fast-food restaurants.
Separate your trash, and throw away only what can't be recycled.
Don't wrap your lunch in plastic.
Buy or make canvas or nylon grocery bags and lunch sacks that you can use again.
Don't buy things you don't really want or need.

Main idea: ____

____

Exercise B Think about each of the following topics. On the lines provided, write what you would choose as your main idea if you were writing a composition on that topic.

1. early pioneers in the American West

   Main idea: ____

   ____

2. unusual hobbies

   Main idea: ____

   ____

Name ______________________ Date ___________ Class ______________________

Early Plans

An **early plan,** also called an **informal outline,** is one way of sorting your ideas to make the job of writing easier. You put items in groups and then arrange your groups in order. Follow these steps to group ideas.

- Group items that have something in common with each other.
- Write a heading for each group to show how the items in it are related.
- Set aside any items that don't seem to fit. You can delete them or fit them in later.

Then you can order the ideas in each group. Here are some common ways to order ideas: (1) *chronological* (time) *order,* (2) *order of importance,* (3) *spatial* (space or location) *order.*

Exercise A Read the following items. Sort the items and separate them into three groups. On the lines provided, list the items in each group, and write a heading at the top of each list.

mowing the lawn	stamp collecting	trimming hedges
aerobics	weeding the garden	running
painting	model ship building	swimming

1. ______________	2. ______________	3. ______________
______________	______________	______________
______________	______________	______________
______________	______________	______________
______________	______________	______________

Exercise B Following are some details for a composition about Booker T. Washington. Number the details from 1–5 in chronological (time) order.

______ After the Civil War, Booker T. Washington, poor and homeless, decided that he wanted to go to school.

______ In his second year at the Hampton Institute, Washington's teacher was Natalie Lord, who encouraged him in his speaking ability.

______ He arrived at the Hampton Normal and Agricultural Institute dusty and ragged from his many homeless days.

______ Shortly after entering the Hampton Institute, Washington came under the influence of General Samuel Chapman Armstrong, who became Washington's role model.

______ The head teacher of the Hampton Institute was impressed by Washington's willingness to work hard and so allowed the boy to enter the school.

Name ______________________ Date ___________ Class ____________________

Chapter 18: Paragraph and Composition Structure

Formal Outlines

When you write a **formal outline,** you use letters and numbers. These letters and numbers label main headings and ideas that belong below those headings. A **topic outline** states ideas in single words or phrases. A **sentence outline** states ideas in complete sentences.

Exercise There are five blank spaces in the formal topic outline below. Use each of these five ideas to complete the outline.

Heart that pumps blood
Marrow inside bones
Spinal cord that is the "roadway" for nerves
Lungs that hold oxygen for the body
Involuntary muscle

Title: The Body
Main Idea: There are six major body systems.

I. Skin
  A. Outer layer
  B. Middle layer
  C. Inner layer
II. Bones
  A. Joints between bones
  B. ____________________
III. Blood
  A. ____________________
  B. Arteries that carry blood
  C. Veins that carry blood
IV. Breathing
  A. Nostrils and mouth that take in oxygen
  B. Trachea that carry oxygen to the lungs
  C. ____________________
V. Nerves
  A. Brain where all nerves begin and end
  B. ____________________
VI. Muscle
  A. Voluntary muscle
  B. ____________________

Name ______________________ Date ___________ Class ___________________

WORKSHEET 15

The Introduction

A good **introduction** captures the reader's interest and presents the main idea of the composition. Three ways of capturing a reader's attention are

- asking a question
- telling an anecdote (a short, interesting story)
- stating an intriguing or startling fact

Exercise Can you recognize the three ways of writing introductions? Working with two or three classmates, try to identify the technique used in each of these introductions. Write your answers on the lines provided.

1. There's a mystery in the sky. Centuries ago, ancient astronomers wrote about it. But when later astronomers looked for it, most of them thought the ancient astronomers were wrong. The mystery in the sky is whether there is a tenth planet, out beyond Neptune and Pluto. Many scientists believe Planet X is lurking out there waiting to be rediscovered!

____

2. *Do, re, mi, fa, sol, la, ti, do.* Did you ever wonder where in the world such words came from? An Italian monk named Guido d'Arezzo used the first syllable of each line of a Latin hymn to represent the music scale. Guido taught music in the monasteries, and the musical note system he developed made his work easier. Many people believe he is the inventor of written music.

____

3. Susanne woke up early on the morning of her thirteenth birthday. Someone had tied a string to the foot of her bed. On the string was a note that said, "Follow me." She put her hand on the string and started walking. The string led first to her brother's room, where he and their parents were waiting to go with her while she followed the string. It was the beginning of the most exciting birthday Susanne ever had.

____

4. The ancient Egyptians believed that intelligence was located in the heart. Since then medical science has advanced a great deal. We now know that intelligence is based in the brain, a three-pound mass of nerve cells located in the head.

____

5. Several years ago, as I stood waiting for a bus, a great blue heron came swooping down. It landed on the corner next to a newspaper stand, looked around at the traffic for a moment, and then flew off. The sight of that magnificent bird in such an unlikely place made me realize how important it is to bring nature into the city. The best way to do that is by creating more parks.

____

Name ______________________ Date ____________ Class ______________________

The Body

The **body** of a composition develops the main idea with paragraphs. Each paragraph supports or proves a main point by developing it with supporting details.

Exercise Each numbered item below needs either a main idea or a supporting idea. Add either a main idea or a supporting idea that makes sense. (You might use an encyclopedia to find some interesting ideas.)

1. **Main idea of composition:** ______________________

   Supporting idea 1: Bears hibernate throughout the winter.
   Supporting idea 2: Caterpillars hibernate throughout the winter.
2. **Main idea of composition:** Eating right is an important part of keeping healthy.
   Supporting idea 1: People should avoid eating foods high in fat, salt, or sugar.
   Supporting idea 2: ______________________

3. **Main idea of composition:** ______________________

   Supporting idea 1: The Kwakiutl Indians of the Yukon gave gifts to compete with other tribes.
   Supporting idea 2: In Japan, gift-giving is a way of being polite.
4. **Main idea of composition:** ______________________

   Supporting idea 1: Some dinosaurs were only the size of modern-day hens.
   Supporting idea 2: The brachiosaurus, the largest dinosaur, weighed about eighty-five tons.
5. **Main idea of composition:** Many young animals become independent faster than human babies do.
   Supporting idea 1: Horses are able to walk soon after they are born.
   Supporting idea 2: ______________________

Name ______________________ Date ___________ Class ______________________

Unity and Coherence in Compositions

A good composition has *unity* and *coherence*. A composition has **unity** when each body paragraph develops a topic related to the main idea. A composition has **coherence** when its ideas appear in a sensible order and are connected to one another. Paragraphs in a composition are often connected using **transitions** such as *first, therefore, in conclusion, however,* and *eventually*.

Exercise A Each numbered list below contains a main idea and three topics. Circle the topic that does not relate to the main idea.

1. Marsupials are a unique group of mammals.

   Kangaroos and opossums are marsupials.

   Marsupial mothers carry their babies in pouches.

   Rabbits have strong hind legs, also.

2. Viruses are difficult to cure.

   The incurable common cold is caused by a virus.

   Sharks do not develop cancer.

   Scientists don't understand viruses completely.

Exercise B Each numbered item below contains two short paragraphs. On each line, write a transition that might be used at the beginning of the second paragraph to connect it to the first.

1. Young children love to play with colored modeling dough. Luckily, such dough is easy and inexpensive to make. You can whip some up in your kitchen in no time at all.

   [transition], assemble all the materials that you need. These include a saucepan, some flour, a wooden spoon, some food coloring, a box of salt, and some cream of tartar.

   ____

2. For several years now, our state has received less than its usual amount of rainfall. At the same time, our population has been growing, and demand for water has increased. We now find ourselves facing a severe water shortage.

   [transition], as your governor, I am asking that you do what you can to conserve water. Put off washing the car. Don't leave the tap running. Limit the time that you spend in the shower. Small changes such as these can make a big difference.

   ____

Name ______________________ Date ___________ Class ______________________

The Conclusion

A **conclusion** helps readers know that your composition has come to an end. Here are some ways you can conclude a paper.

- Refer to your introduction.
- Restate the main idea.
- Close with a final idea.

Exercise In the following brief notes for two compositions, you will find the main idea and several supporting details. For each composition, write a sentence or a few sentences that you think would be a good conclusion.

1. **Main idea:** Horses are faithful, proud, beautiful animals.

   Supporting details: Horses can develop loyalty to humans.

   Horses seem to express some human emotions.

   Horses have a physical beauty and grace.

   Conclusion: ____

   ____

   ____

2. **Main idea:** Although clothing fashions change frequently, popular fashions tend to return.

   Supporting details: Women's skirt lengths have gone up and down by many feet over the last twenty years. However, the most popular length has been just below the knee. Women's pants styles have gone from capris to bell-bottoms and back to capris (now called leggings) in forty years.

   Men's pants went from baggy and pleated with cuffs (in the 1950's) to tapered and narrow with no cuffs (in the 1960's). In the early 1990's, they went back to baggy and pleated with cuffs.

   Conclusion: ____

   ____

   ____

Name ______________ Date ________ Class ______________

Choosing a Subject

Research reports give information about a subject, use print and nonprint sources, and provide lists of sources for the information. In planning a research report, you first must choose a subject. **Freewriting** is one way to come up with a subject.

Exercise A To begin thinking about subjects for a research report, use the lines below to freewrite answers to the following questions.

1. What do I wonder about? ______________________

2. What's important to me? ______________________

3. What have I read or seen lately that I'd like to know more about? ______________________

Exercise B Ideas for subjects can come from many areas. Under each subject area below, write two possible subjects for a research report.

hobbies and interests

1. ______________________
2. ______________________

occupations of family and neighbors

1. ______________________
2. ______________________

neighborhood and community

1. ______________________
2. ______________________

books, magazines, and newspapers

1. ______________________
2. ______________________

movies and television

1. ______________________
2. ______________________

COMPOSITION

Name ________________________ Date ____________ Class ______________________

Narrowing a Subject

After deciding on a general subject for a research report, you need to narrow your subject. That is, you need to focus on just one part of it. Each subject contains many smaller topics. Before deciding on a topic, ask yourself the following questions.

- Can I find enough facts about this topic? Where?
- Is my topic too broad for a short report? Or is the topic too narrow? (If the topic is too narrow, you may have trouble finding enough information.)
- Do I have time to get the information I need? (If you have to send away for information, how long will it take to get it?)
- Is the topic interesting enough to hold my attention? (You'll be more willing to put extra time and effort into a topic you like.)

One way to narrow a subject is to make a cluster chart. Write the subject in the middle of a piece of paper, and circle the subject. Then brainstorm to come up with ideas related to your subject. Write these down and circle them. Draw lines to connect the circles. Continue until you fill the page. Here's an example of a cluster chart on the subject of space. The chart contains four good topic ideas.

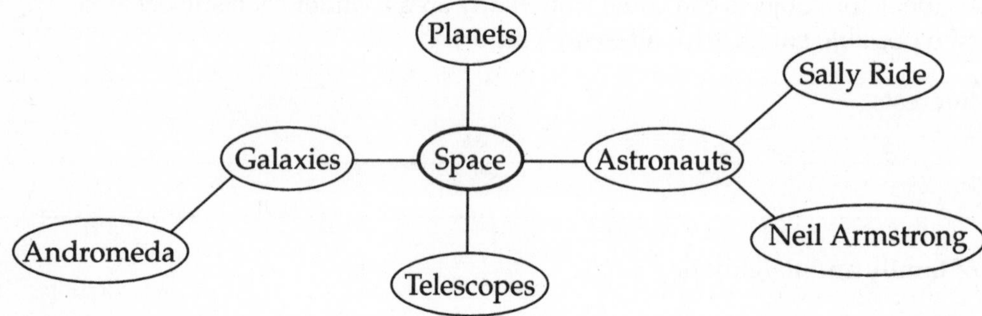

Exercise Use the space below to make a cluster chart. Choose your own subject, or use one of these two subjects: games or pets. Begin by writing the subject in the center circle. After you have finished your cluster chart, study it to find a narrow topic. Write your topic at the bottom of this page.

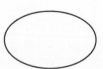

Topic: ____

Name ______________________ Date ___________ Class ______________

Thinking About Audience and Purpose

The basic **purpose** of your research report is to give information to your readers. The information consists mostly of facts and the opinions of experts. Your first **audience** probably will be your teacher and classmates, but reports might be for different audiences. Don't tell them what they already know. But don't confuse them, either. Explain ideas that are new to them, and define words they may not know.

Exercise A Think about the audience for a report on pandas or for a report on a topic of your own choice. Then answer these questions on the lines provided.

Topic: ____

1. What is it likely that my audience already knows about the topic?

____

____

____

2. What new or unusual information might interest and surprise my audience?

____

____

____

Exercise B You are writing a report on giant snakes to give both your teacher and classmates facts about the snakes. Below is some information you can use in your report. Which information would you put in your report? On the line under each piece of information, state whether or not you would use the information in your report. Explain why you would or would not use each piece of the information.

1. *Giant* means "big."

____

2. One giant snake, the anaconda, can be as long as thirty feet.

____

3. I hate snakes.

____

4. Boa constrictor babies are born live; python babies are hatched from eggs.

____

5. There are many kinds of snakes.

____

Name ______________________ Date __________ Class ____________________

Chapter 19: The Research Report

Making an Early Plan and Asking Questions

Your **early plan,** or informal outline, for your report will list the main ideas that you want to cover. To find the information for your early plan, ask yourself questions. You can start with the ***5W-How?*** questions: *Who? What? When? Where? Why? How?* The questions will help guide your research and keep you focused on your topic. Here, for example, is a list of questions on the subject of killer whales.

Who has studied killer whales in the wild?
What do killer whales eat?
When do killer whales have to come up for air?
Where are killer whales found?
Why are killer whales called "killers"?
How do killer whales communicate with one another?

Exercise You're planning a research report on a topic of your own or on the following topic: schools in Japan. On the lines provided, write six questions about the topic.

Topic: ____

Question 1: Who ____
____
____?

Question 2: What ____
____
____?

Question 3: When ____
____
____?

Question 4: Where ____
____
____?

Question 5: Why ____
____
____?

Question 6: How ____
____
____?

Name ______________ Date ______________ Class ______________

Finding and Evaluating Sources

Your library and your community contain many valuable sources of information for research papers. The following chart lists some of the sources that are available.

Library Resources	Community Resources
Encyclopedias	Museums
Books	Supermarkets
Magazines	Nature centers
Newspapers	Hospitals or clinics
Booklets and pamphlets	Colleges
Videotapes and audiotapes	Government offices
Slides	Interviews with experts

When you're researching a topic, you need to *evaluate* the sources of information. To **evaluate** means to determine something's strengths and weaknesses. Not all of your sources will be equally useful. Here are some questions that will help you evaluate, or judge, the usefulness of a source.

- **Is the source nonfiction?** You're looking for facts.
- **Can you trust your sources?** Are the sources respected and reliable?
- **Is the information current?** You need the latest available information.
- **Is the information objective?** Be sure all sides of a topic are presented.

Exercise On the line provided, write a topic for a research report. If you don't have a topic, look for sources on a hobby that interests you. Then follow the directions below.

Topic: ______________________________

1. **Print Sources.** Go to the library and look up three different printed sources of information about your topic. List these sources.

____

____

____

2. **Nonprint Sources.** Think of at least two nonprint sources that you could use for an article about your topic. List these sources.

____

____

____

COMPOSITION

Name ______________________ Date ___________ Class ____________________

Listing Sources and Taking Notes

Keep track of your sources by making **source cards** on index cards or sheets of notebook paper divided in half. Write the name of each source on a separate card, and give each card a source number. Write the source number in the upper right-hand corner of the source card.

When taking notes, let your early plan and questions about your topic guide you. Scan through the sources for information that relates to your headings and your questions. The tips below can help you take efficient notes.

- Use a separate 4" × 6" **note card** or half a sheet of paper for each source and for each note.
- Use abbreviations and short phrases.
- Use your own words. If you copy someone's exact words, put quotation marks around the words.
- Label each card by writing at the top a key word or phrase that tells what the card is about.
- Put the source number in the top right-hand corner of each note card.
- In the bottom right-hand corner of each card, write the number of the page where you found the information.
- Take notes from each of your sources.

Exercise A Below are the Modern Language Association (MLA) guidelines for listing sources from a book.

Books: List author, title, city of publication, publisher, and copyright year.

Hamilton, Edith. *Mythology*. Boston: Little, Brown, 1942.

On the lines below, write information correctly for a source card for a book that you have written entitled *Surviving Middle School*, published in 1993 by Ican Press, New York.

____

____

____

Exercise B On an index card or half a sheet of paper, use your own words, short phrases, and abbreviations to take notes from the following paragraph.

Another writer who describes the life of urban African American youths is Gwendolyn Brooks. In the chapter "Home," for example, from her novel *Maud Martha*, Brooks beautifully describes the painful emotions of a family faced with the possibility of losing their home because mortgage payments cannot be met. Brooks's novel is not strictly autobiographical, but the Home Owners' Loan Corporation that intrudes in "Home" *was* a reality for the young author. In spite of adversity, Brooks went on to win a Pulitzer Prize.

Name ______________ Date ________ Class ______________

Organizing and Outlining Information

After gathering most of your information, you need to organize it. Separate your note cards into stacks with the same or similar labels. Think of a heading to identify each stack. Decide on the order of your main headings—perhaps order of importance or chronological (time) order. Then sort the cards in each stack to make subheadings for your outline. Next, create an outline from your main headings and subheadings. A **formal outline** uses letters and numbers to show the relationships of ideas. Here is the beginning of such an outline, which serves as a table of contents for the reader.

Outline: I. Major heading
- A. Subheading
  - 1. Detail
  - 2. Detail
- B. Subheading

Exercise You have gathered information for a report on "Natural Disasters in the United States." Now you are ready to write your formal outline. Following is your list of headings and subheadings. Figure out an appropriate order, and place them in the outline form below.

Tornadoes outside the "Alley"	Inland floods	Floods
Mississippi River	Tornado Alley	Tornadoes
Coastal floods	Missouri River	Why tornadoes occur
Where tornadoes occur		

Natural Disasters in the United States

I. ______________________
- A. ______________________
- B. ______________________
  - 1. ______________________
  - 2. ______________________

II. ______________________
- A. ______________________
- B. ______________________
  - 1. ______________________
  - 2. ______________________

COMPOSITION

Name ______________________ Date ____________ Class ______________________

Chapter 19: The Research Report

Writing a First Draft

Below are some notes you have taken for a research report on killer bees. One of the notes is a paraphrase of information from a source. The other is a direct quotation.

Bees in the United States 1

Where they'll go depends on mild winters. Could live year-round in parts of the U.S.: as far north as San Francisco and S. Maryland, all Ala., Miss., La., S. Tx., Ariz., Va., N.C., & S.C.

pp. 34-35

Bees in the United States 2

"Killer bees will venture to the northern United States in summertime; however, they will perish during the cold winters."

p. 72

Exercise On a separate sheet of paper, use both notes above to write a paragraph for your report. Paraphrase, or state in your own words, the direct quotation. [Note: In your final draft of an actual report, you would give credit to the sources you used to create your report. For this paragraph, write the source number and page number in parentheses after you have used information from the source. Insert the citation in parentheses just before the end mark of the sentence in which you have used that source's information. The source number appears in the upper right-hand corner of the note card. The page number appears lower right.]

Name ______________________ Date ___________ Class ______________________

Evaluating and Revising

Evaluating a report means determining its strengths and weaknesses. **Revising** a report means making changes to improve it. If the answer to any of the following questions is no, your report may need revisions. You could add sources or facts, or you could replace or reorder information.

- Does the report use several different sources?
- Does the report consist of facts and the opinions of experts?
- Is the report in the writer's own words? If someone else's words are used, are they in quotation marks?
- Is the information well organized?
- Is the introduction interesting, and does it tell what the report is about?
- Does the conclusion bring the report to a close?
- Is the list of sources in correct form on a separate sheet at the end?

Exercise Here are the changes the writer made in one paragraph while revising a research report titled "The Invasion of the Killer Bees." Look at the changes carefully. Then, on the lines below, answer the questions that follow.

(No one can survive a hundred or more stings.) Killer bees are extremely nervous, and they are also fighters. Native bees chase people ^for a yard or so^ when they are bothered. Africanized bees, however, will chase for more than half a mile. Their poison is no different from the poison of ordinary bees, but they come after people in a big swarm. ~~I wouldn't want them chasing after me!~~ Dr. Kenneth Schuberth of the Johns Hopkins medical institutions says, "When you get that much venom in your system at once, it's like receiving a giant snake bite."

1. Why did the writer move the first sentence to a new place in the paragraph? Where does it make more sense? ______________________

____

2. Why did the writer add the words *for a yard or so* to the third sentence? [Hint: Does the reader need this information?] ______________________

____

3. Why did the writer cut the sentence *I wouldn't want them chasing after me!*? ______________________

____

4. Why did the writer add quotation marks to the last sentence? ______________________

____

COMPOSITION

Name ______________________ Date ____________ Class ____________________

Chapter 19: The Research Report

Proofreading and Publishing

Proofreading is reading carefully for mistakes in spelling, capitalization, usage, and punctuation, and then correcting them. **Publishing** is sharing your report with others.

Exercise A: Proofreading The following paragraph is from a report on spirituals, songs sung by slaves. One famous spiritual is "Swing Low, Sweet Chariot." Proofread the following paragraph. Cross out any errors, and write the word, letter, or punctuation mark correctly in the space above the line.

Spirituals were sang by slaves on southern plantations. Frederick douglass a former slave, said that slaves were generally expected to sing as well as to work. Most of the songs were very sorowful. Many of them spirituals are still sung today. They were often about a better life to come.

Some of the spirituals had codes in them. For example, Go Down, Moses is a spiritual based on the bible story about the Israelites, who were slaves in egypt. Moses was sent to ask the pharoah to set the Israelites free To the African American slaves singing this Spiritual, the words were also a plea to their masters to "Let my people go."

Exercise B You've written a research report on spirituals. Think of five specific ways to publish your report. List your ideas on the lines provided.

1. ______________________________
2. ______________________________
3. ______________________________
4. ______________________________
5. ______________________________

Name ______________________ Date ____________ Class ______________________

Resources

The Dewey Decimal System

Every book in your library is labeled with a number and letter code to help you to find the book. That label is the book's **call number.**

The **Dewey decimal system** is a method for organizing nonfiction books in libraries. It has ten general numerical subject classifications. They are listed below.

000–099	General Works (encyclopedias, periodicals, etc.)
100–199	Philosophy (includes psychology, conduct, etc.)
200–299	Religion (includes mythology)
300–399	Social Sciences (economics, government, law, etc.)
400–499	Languages (dictionaries, grammars, etc.)
500–599	Science (mathematics, chemistry, physics, etc.)
600–699	Technology (agriculture, engineering, aviation, etc.)
700–799	The Arts (sculpture, painting, music, photography, sports, etc.)
800–899	Literature (poetry, plays, orations, etc.)
900–999	History (includes travel and biography)

Fiction books are shelved in alphabetical order by authors' last names. If the author has written more than one book, the books are shelved in alphabetical order by the first word of their titles (not counting *A, An,* or *The*).

Exercise A On the lines provided, write the general subject area of books with the following call numbers.

1. 750 ______________________
2. 430 ______________________
3. 620 ______________________
4. 219 ______________________
5. 333 ______________________
6. 140 ______________________
7. 990 ______________________
8. 842 ______________________
9. 555 ______________________
10. 049 ______________________

Exercise B Look at each of the descriptions of books below. On the line provided, write *N* for nonfiction. Write *F* for fiction.

______ 1. a novel by Mark Twain

______ 2. a biography of Toussaint L'Ouverture

______ 3. a book about the history of Cuba

______ 4. a mystery written by a Latin American author

______ 5. a book of short stories by African authors

Name ______________________ Date ____________ Class ______________________

The Card Catalog

To find the call number of any book you're looking for, use the *card catalog*. The **card catalog** is a cabinet of drawers containing alphabetically arranged cards. Fiction call numbers can be found in either the *author cards* or the *title cards*. Nonfiction call numbers can be found in author cards, title cards, or *subject cards*. Sometimes a card contains a "see also" note. This cross-reference directs you to another section of the card catalog that has more information on the same subject. An **on-line catalog** is a computerized version of the card catalog. Here is a picture of an author card.

972.014 D **Davies, Nigel, 1920–**
The Aztecs, a history.—Macmillan, 1973
—(Aztecs—History)

You will often use the subject card catalog when you are doing reports for school. Suppose you're looking for a book about dinosaurs. You look in the subject card catalog under *D* for *dinosaurs*. All the library's books on dinosaurs will have a card in that file. Each card gives the author, the title, and a brief description of the book.

Exercise Each item below gives you one piece of information about a book. Write which card catalog you would look in to find the book's call number. Write *A* for author cards. Write *T* for title cards. Write *S* for subject cards. (Note: Authors are listed last name first. Titles of books are italicized.)

______ 1. *The Call of the Wild*

______ 2. reptiles

______ 3. London, Jack

______ 4. South American Indians

______ 5. *Old Yeller*

______ 6. Bradbury, Ray

______ 7. Liberia

______ 8. Sandoz, Mari

______ 9. *Frederick Douglass*

______10. Hughes, Langston

Name ______________________ Date __________ Class ______________________

The Parts of a Book

Most nonfiction books contain the nine parts listed below. The information that each part provides is given.

JACKET:	description of book and author
TITLE PAGE:	full title, author, publisher, and place of publication
COPYRIGHT PAGE:	date and place of first publication and any revisions
TABLE OF CONTENTS:	titles of chapters or sections with their page numbers
LIST OF ILLUSTRATIONS:	pictures, charts, maps, diagrams, and their page numbers
APPENDIX:	additional information about subjects in book
GLOSSARY:	definitions of difficult words
BIBLIOGRAPHY:	names of books used as references by the author
INDEX:	topics in the book with page numbers where they can be found

Exercise Where would you look in an earth-science textbook to answer each of the following questions? (Don't worry about actually answering the question. Just write what part of the book you would use to find the answer for each.)

1. When was the book first published? ______________________
2. What is a *tectonic plate*? ______________________
3. Where can I find information about volcanoes? ______________________
4. Has the book been revised? ______________________
5. Which chapter discusses mountains? ______________________
6. What sources did the author use to write the book? ______________________
7. Where in the book can I find information about gems? ______________________
8. On what page does the chapter on earth's formation begin? ______________________
9. Where was the book published? ______________________
10. I read the discussion about stalactites in Chapter 12. Where might I find more information about stalactites? ______________________

Name ______________________ Date ____________ Class ____________________

Using Reference Materials

The following list describes special reference sources and the kinds of materials and information they contain.

VERTICAL FILE: up-to-date subject file containing pamphlets and newspaper clippings with government, business, and educational information

MICROFORMS: pages from newspapers and magazines that are reduced for viewing on a screen

ENCYCLOPEDIAS: multiple volumes of articles on general subjects

BIOGRAPHICAL REFERENCES: information about outstanding people

SPECIAL BIOGRAPHICAL REFERENCES: information about outstanding people in particular fields or groups (e.g., *Biographical Dictionary of American Sports*)

ATLASES: maps and geographical information

ALMANACS: up-to-date information about current events, statistics, and dates

BOOKS OF QUOTATIONS: famous quotations indexed by subject

BOOKS OF SYNONYMS: lists of words that are synonyms

REFERENCE BOOKS ABOUT LITERATURE: information about various works of literature

READERS' GUIDE TO PERIODICAL LITERATURE: index of articles of more than one hundred magazines

Exercise Each question below asks for a piece of information that you can find in a special reference. From the list above, write the special reference that would give you the answer.

1. What did President Woodrow Wilson do in 1917? ____________________
2. Where can some recent magazine articles on Poland be found? ____________________
3. What is another word that has the same meaning as *cold*? ____________________
4. Where are the Azores islands? ____________________
5. What is the *aurora borealis*? ____________________
6. What is the population of Terre Haute, Indiana? ____________________
7. What is on the front page of the *Chicago Tribune* for March 17, 1990? ____________________
8. Is there a government pamphlet about inoculation? ____________________
9. How many novels did John Steinbeck write? ____________________
10. Where was Jesse Owens, track and field star, born? ____________________

Name ______________________ Date ___________ Class ______________________

Using the Newspaper

A daily newspaper has a variety of reading materials in its various sections. The following chart shows contents that you may find in a typical newspaper.

WHAT'S IN A NEWSPAPER?		
WRITER'S PURPOSE/ TYPE OF WRITING	READER'S PURPOSE	READING TECHNIQUE
to inform news stories sports	to gain knowledge or information	Ask yourself the *5W-How?* questions.
to persuade editorials cartoons reviews ads	to gain knowledge, to make decisions, or to be entertained	Identify points you agree or disagree with. Find facts or reasons the writer uses.
to be creative or expressive comics newspaper columns	to be entertained	Identify ways the writer interests you or gives you a new viewpoint or ideas.

Exercise Using a copy of the daily newspaper from home or your library, answer the following questions. Use the lines provided.

1. Is there a special identification or title for each section of this newspaper? List below the sections of the newspaper.

   ____

   ____

2. Find an article that gives you information about a specific event in world news, sports, or entertainment. Find answers to the *5W-How?* questions *(Who? What? When? Where? Why? How?)* and list them briefly below.

   ____

   ____

3. Find an editorial or a letter to the editor. Identify what the writer wants you to think or do. What facts or opinions does the writer use to try to persuade you?

   ____

   ____

4. Find a cartoon that you think is intended to persuade you. Explain your selection.

   ____

   ____

Name ______________________ Date ___________ Class ____________________

Using the Dictionary A

Dictionaries differ in the amount and kinds of information that they contain. An **unabridged dictionary** of English is very large and may contain around 460,000 words. A **college** or **abridged dictionary** is shorter and contains perhaps 160,000 words. There are also smaller **school dictionaries** for students and **paperback dictionaries.**

The words listed in a dictionary are called **entries.** Entries are listed in alphabetical order. To help you follow this order, each page of entries has a pair of **guide words** at the top. The first guide word is the first entry on the page; the second guide word is the last entry on the page.

An abridged college dictionary contains many more words than a school dictionary does. Consider, for example, the words found between *Wales* and *walkie-talkie* in two dictionaries:

Webster's New World Dictionary: Student's Edition	*Webster's New World Dictionary:* Third College Edition
Wales	Wales
walk	Walesa, Lech
walkaway	Waley, Arthur
walker	Walhalla
walkie-talkie	walk
	walkabout
	walkaway
	walker
	walkie-talkie

The student dictionary has five entries where the college dictionary has nine.

Exercise Use an unabridged dictionary in your school or public library to answer the following questions. The words that you will need to look up in the dictionary appear in boldface type in the questions below.

1. Of what nationality is **Lech Walesa**? ______________________________

2. **Arthur Waley** was a translator of literature from what countries in Asia?

3. What does the term **walkabout** mean in Australia? in Great Britain? ____________

4. If after a battle, a general were to say, "That was a **walkaway,**" what would he or she mean?

5. What other spelling of **Walhalla** is commonly used? ____________________

Name ______________________ Date ____________ Class ____________

Using the Dictionary B

Information found in dictionaries includes

- **Entry word.** The entry word shows how the word is spelled and how it is divided into syllables. The entry word may also show capitalization and alternate spellings.
- **Pronunciation.** The pronunciation, which follows the entry word, is shown by the use of *accent marks, phonetic symbols,* or *diacritical marks.* **Accent marks** show which syllables of a word are said more forcefully. **Phonetic symbols** represent specific sounds. **Diacritical marks** are special symbols placed above the letters to show how they sound. A **pronunciation key** explains the sounds represented by these symbols.
- **Part-of-speech labels.** These labels indicate how the entry word should be used in a sentence. Some words may be used as more than one part of speech.
- **Other forms.** These spellings may show plural forms of nouns, tenses of verbs, or the comparative forms of adjectives and adverbs.

Exercise A Use a dictionary to answer the questions below.

1. Is there a *t* sound in the word *depot?* ______________________
2. Divide the word *duplicate* into syllables. ______________________
3. Which syllable is accented when *conduct* is a noun? ______________________
4. Which syllable is accented when *conduct* is a verb? ______________________
5. How is the *digm* pronounced in *paradigm?* ______________________

Exercise B Use a dictionary to find the part of speech of each of the following words.

1. brisk ______________
2. already ______________
3. alphabetize ______________
4. fiend ______________
5. into ______________
6. although ______________
7. themselves ______________
8. scruffy ______________
9. soon ______________
10. oh ______________

Exercise C Use a dictionary to answer the following questions.

1. What is the plural form of the word *son-in-law?* ______________________
2. What is the correct past tense form of the verb *swim?* ______________________
3. Is the word *lice* singular or plural? ______________________
4. What is (or are) the plural form(s) of *amoeba?* ______________________
5. List other forms of *normal.* ______________________

Name ______________________ Date ____________ Class ______________

Using the Dictionary C

An **etymology** is the history of a word. In a dictionary entry, the etymology usually appears just before the definitions. If you look up the word *corral* in a dictionary that gives etymologies, you might see an etymology that looks like this:

[Sp < *corro,* a circle, ring < L *currus,* cart < *currere,* to run]

This means that *corral* comes from a Spanish word, *corro,* meaning "a circle or ring." The Spanish word came from a Latin word, *currus,* meaning "cart," which in turn comes from the Latin word *currere,* meaning "to run." In most dictionaries, abbreviations such as *Sp* for *Spanish* and symbols such as < for "comes from" are explained in a guide to abbreviations and symbols. You can usually find this guide either at the beginning or at the end of the dictionary.

Exercise A Find the guide to abbreviations and symbols in your dictionary. On the lines provided, write the abbreviations that your dictionary uses for the following words.

1. German ______________
2. Old French ______________
3. Spanish ______________
4. Arabic ______________
5. Yiddish ______________
6. Chinese ______________
7. Old English ______________
8. Danish ______________
9. English ______________
10. Iranian ______________

Exercise B Use a dictionary to answer the following questions about etymologies. Look up the italicized words.

1. From whose name does the word *boycott* come? ______________________________

   ____

2. The name of the country *Australia* comes from a Latin word, *australis.* What does *australis* mean? ____

   ____

3. What four words were combined to create the word *radar*? ______________________________

   ____

4. The word *corps* means "a body or group of people." What language did the word come from, and what did it mean in that language? ______________________________

   ____

5. What do the letters *AWOL* stand for? ______________________________

   ____

Name _______________ Date _________ Class _______________

Using the Dictionary D

Contents of a dictionary entry include

- **Examples.** Phrases or sentences may demonstrate how the defined word is used.
- **Definitions.** If there is more than one meaning, definitions are numbered or lettered.
- **Special usage labels.** These labels identify words that have special meaning or are used in special ways in certain fields.
- **Related word forms.** These various forms of the entry word are usually created by adding suffixes or prefixes.
- **Synonyms and antonyms.** Sometimes **synonyms,** words that are similar in meaning, and **antonyms,** words that are opposite in meaning, appear at the end of a word entry.

Exercise A Use a dictionary to answer the following questions. Look up the italicized words. Then look for usage labels that point out special definitions.

1. What does the word *composition* mean to a printer? _______________

2. What does the word *draw* mean in card playing? _______________

3. What does the word *draw* mean in golf? _______________

4. What does the word *first* mean in music? _______________

Exercise B Use a dictionary to answer the following questions. Use the lines provided.

1. What is a related word form of the word *heroic*? _______________

2. What is an example of the use of the word *mint*? _______________

3. What are two definitions of the word *resource*? _______________

4. Give one antonym for the word *dexterous*. _______________

Name ______________________ Date ___________ Class ____________________

Personal Letters

A **personal letter,** sometimes called a **friendly letter,** is often a good way to communicate with a friend or a relative. Like a conversation, a friendly letter contains a specific, personal message from you to the person you're communicating with. The purpose of a personal letter is to express emotions and ideas.

Exercise A On the lines below, write a personal letter to a friend on a topic of interest to both of you. For example, you may write about a new hobby, a book, a movie, a sporting event, or something else that is of interest to you both.

Dear ____________________,

Your friend,

Exercise B On the lines provided, write a personal letter to a relative. You may want to tell about something that has happened in your immediate family, something that has happened in your community, or how and what you are doing in school.

Dear ____________________,

Love,

Social Letters

A **social letter** is a courteous announcement or response concerning a particular event. Social letters may include *thank-you letters, invitations,* or *letters of regret.*

A **thank-you letter** is sent to tell someone that you appreciate his or her taking time, trouble, or expense to do something for you. Always respond promptly, and try to say something specific about the kindness that the person has done for you.

An **informal invitation** is a request for someone to attend an occasion. Include specific information about the occasion, the time and the place, and any other special details your guest might need to know (such as that everyone should dress casually).

A **letter of regret** is written to inform someone that you will not be able to accept an invitation. If the letters *R.S.V.P.* (an abbreviation for "please reply" in French) appear on the invitation, it's especially important to send a written reply.

Exercise A The following are characteristics of social letters. Write *T* for thank-you letter. Write *I* for invitation. Write *R* for letter of regret.

_______ 1. Send if you cannot attend.

_______ 2. Tell why the gift is special.

_______ 3. Include the place of the event.

_______ 4. Say something in addition to thanking the person.

_______ 5. Tell what to wear to the event.

Exercise B You have been invited to a friend's house party but cannot attend because your grandparents will be in town for an overnight visit on the date of the party. On the lines provided, write a short letter of regret.

____

____

____

____

____

____

____

____

____

____

Name ______________________ Date ____________ Class ____________________

The Parts of a Business Letter

There are six parts of a business letter. The **heading** includes your address and the date of the letter. The **inside address** contains the name and address of the person to whom you are writing. The **salutation** is the greeting. It is almost always *Dear* and then the person's name. The **body** is the main part of the letter. The **closing** is the polite ending. *Yours truly, Sincerely,* and *Sincerely yours* often are used as closings. The **signature** is handwritten directly below the closing. Beneath the signature, type or print your name.

The two forms of a business letter are *block form* and *modified block form.* When you use **block form,** every part of the letter begins at the left margin, and paragraphs are not indented. When you use **modified block form,** the heading, the closing, and your signature each start to the right of the center of the page. The first line of each paragraph is indented.

When you write a business letter, use a polite, respectful, and professional tone and standard English. State the reason for your letter clearly and promptly. Also, be sure to include all necessary information.

A business letter should be typed single-spaced (with an extra line between paragraphs) or neatly handwritten (using black or blue ink) on plain, unlined 8 1/2" × 11" paper. Center the letter on the page with equal margins on the sides and at the top and the bottom. Use only one side of the paper. Avoid crossing out mistakes, or making smudges, erasures, and ink blots. Check for typing errors and misspellings.

Exercise Each item below is all or part of one of the six parts of a business letter. Write *H* if it is the heading. Write *I* if it is the inside address. Write *S* if it is the salutation. Write *B* if it is the body. Write *C* if it is the closing. Write *SIG* if it is the signature.

______ 1. Dear Ms. Mahoney:

______ 2. As I told you on the phone, I am a magician and tuba player.

______ 3. Ms. Alice Mahoney
14 Peabody Lane
Sea Bright, New Jersey 07760

______ 4. October 16, 1994

______ 5. Yours truly,

Name ______________________ Date ___________ Class ___________

Types of Business Letters

You write a **request letter** to ask for information about a product or a service or to request sample materials. In an **order letter,** you ask for something specific, such as a free brochure advertised in a magazine or an item of merchandise that is listed in a catalog when you don't have a printed form. In a **complaint** or **adjustment letter,** you report an error or state a specific complaint. When writing such letters, register your complaint as soon as possible, be sure to mention specifics, and keep the tone of your letter calm and courteous. In an **appreciation** or **commendation letter,** you express your appreciation, gratitude, or praise for a person, group, or organization. State exactly why you are pleased.

Exercise On the lines provided, write a business letter for one of the situations below. Use your own return address, but make up any other information you need to write the letter.

1. Your parents said you could spend two weeks this summer at the youth camp of your choice. Write to the Circle 1 Summer Camp, located at 3333 Route 1 in Festus, Missouri 63028.
2. Write a letter of appreciation or commendation to an individual or organization you would like to thank or congratulate for outstanding efforts or performance.
3. Write a letter of complaint about a piece of broken merchandise from a mail-order business.

Name ______________________ Date ____________ Class ______________________

Addressing Envelopes and Completing Printed Forms

Follow these guidelines to address an envelope: (1) Place your complete return address in the top left-hand corner of the envelope. (2) Center the name and address of the person or organization to whom you are writing on the envelope. For a business letter, the name and address to which the letter is being sent should exactly match the inside address of the letter. (3) Use standard two-letter postal abbreviations for state names, and use ZIP Codes.

Follow these guidelines to complete printed forms: (1) Look over the entire form before you begin. (2) Take note of any special instructions, such as "Please print clearly" or "Use a pencil." (3) Read each item carefully. (4) Supply all the information requested. You can use a dash or the symbol *N/A,* which means "not applicable," to indicate that some information does not apply to you. (5) Proofread your completed form. Make sure you have given all requested information. Check for errors, and correct them neatly.

Exercise A Suppose you need to address a letter to someone you know. Write the necessary information on the lines below.

____
____
____

____
____
____
____

Exercise B Write C for correct or *I* for incorrect on the blank next to each of the following statements about printed forms.

______ 1. If a question on a printed form does not apply to you, you should ignore it and leave the answer line blank.

______ 2. When a question applies to you, you need to supply all the information requested.

______ 3. You should ignore special instructions unless someone asks you to read them.

______ 4. You should look over the whole form before you start writing.

______ 5. When you make an error, you should correct it neatly.

Name ______________________ Date ___________ Class ____________________

Resources

Manuscript Style A

A **manuscript** is any typed or handwritten composition. Use the following guidelines as you make a final copy of your paper.

Handwritten Papers: Use regular 8 1/2" × 11" lined paper and blue or black ink. Write legibly. Do not skip lines unless your teacher tells you to do so.

Typewritten Papers: Use regular 8 1/2" × 11" typing paper. Avoid very thin (onionskin) paper and erasable paper. Use a fresh black ribbon. Double-space between lines.

Word-processed Papers: Use letter-sized sheets or continuous-feed paper that separates cleanly along the edges. Make sure that the printer you use can produce clear, dark, letter-quality type. Check with your teacher to be sure that the typeface you plan to use is acceptable. Double-space between lines.

Whether your paper is handwritten, typed, or word-processed, use the following format.

- Use only one side of a sheet of paper.
- Leave one-inch margins at the top, sides, and bottom of each page.
- Indent the first line of each paragraph five spaces from the left margin.
- Number all pages (except the first page) in the upper right-hand corner, one-half inch from the top.
- Follow your teacher's instructions for placement of your name, the date, your class, and the title of your paper.
- Make corrections neatly. To insert a word or a short phrase, use a caret mark (‸) and add the word(s) immediately above it.

Exercise On the blanks provided, write C for correct or *I* for incorrect for the following statements.

EXAMPLE: ___*I*___ 1. Use only erasable paper for typewritten manuscripts.

______ 1. Only the first page of your manuscript should be numbered.

______ 2. Indent the first line of each paragraph five spaces from the left margin.

______ 3. Use very thin, onionskin paper for your manuscripts.

______ 4. Papers should be partly typed and partly handwritten.

______ 5. A caret mark is used to remove words from a sentence.

______ 6. Typewritten papers should be double-spaced.

______ 7. Use any color ink for handwritten papers.

______ 8. Your paper should include your name, date, class, and title.

______ 9. Word processors should never be used for manuscripts.

______10. Use both sides of the paper.

Name ______________________ Date ___________ Class ____________________

Resources

Manuscript Style B

Few **abbreviations,** shortened forms of words or phrases, are used in the text of a formal paper. But many others are used to save space in tables, notes, and bibliographies.

Certain abbreviations such as *Mr., Mrs., Sr., Jr., Dr.,* and *Sen.* are acceptable when used with a person's name. If they do not accompany a name, spell out the words.

Dr. Lawrence will see you.	The **doctor** will see you.
Gov. Ann Richards	Please speak, **Governor.**

Abbreviate given names only if the person is most commonly known that way. Leave a space between two such initials, but not between three or more.

Susan **B.** Anthony **E. B.** White **J.E.B.** Stuart

The abbreviations A.M., P.M., A.D., and B.C. are acceptable when they are used with numbers.

9:15 **A.M.** 10:45 **P.M.** 700 **B.C.** **A.D.** 12

After spelling out the first use, abbreviate the names of agencies and organizations commonly known by their initials.

FIRST USE: **Federal Bureau of Investigation** SECOND USE: **FBI**

In text, spell out the names of states whether they stand alone or follow another geographical term. Use traditional abbreviations for state names in tables, notes, and bibliographies. Use two-letter postal abbreviations only in addresses that include the ZIP Code.

TEXT: **Nebraska** TABLES, ETC.: **Nebr.** WITH ZIP CODE: **NE**

Exercise: Proofreading Rewrite the following sentences to correct manuscript style.

1. My teacher, M. L. K. Johnson, is an admirer of author Pearl S. Buck (1892–1973).

   ____

2. Pearl S. Buck was born in W. Va., but spent most of her life in China.

   ____

3. Mister Johnson says that as a child, Buck spoke Chinese before she learned English.

   ____

4. At two o'clock P.M. on the Public Broadcasting Service, we are going to see Public Broadcasting Service's dramatization of *The Big Wave,* a story that Miz Buck wrote about Japan.

   ____

   ____

5. A prof. spoke about Buck's writing and told us she won the Nobel Prize for literature in 1938.

   ____

Name ______________________ Date ___________ Class ______________________

Manuscript Style C

A number that states "how many" should be spelled out if it can be expressed in one or two words. Otherwise, use numerals.

five rocks **one hundred** runners **5,770** customers **twenty-four** minutes

Spell out numbers that express order, such as *first* and *fourth*. If they represent the day of the month, use numerals only.

the **fifth** person on September **16** **twenty-first** year

In your writing, use **nonsexist language**—language that applies to people in general, both male and female.

In the past, many skills and occupations excluded either men or women. Now that most jobs are held by both men and women, language is adjusting to reflect this change. When you are referring to humanity as a whole, use nonsexist expressions rather than gender-specific ones.

SEXIST: **chairman, stewardess** NONSEXIST: **chairperson, flight attendant**

Sometimes the antecedent of a pronoun may be either masculine or feminine. In such a case, use both masculine and feminine pronouns to refer to it.

Any **camper** who wants to help dig should bring **his** or **her** own shovel.

You can often avoid the awkward *his or her* construction by substituting an article (*a, an,* or *the*) for the construction or by rephrasing the sentence.

Each **camper** who wants to help dig should bring **a** shovel.

Campers who want to help dig should bring **their** shovels.

Exercise: Proofreading On the line provided, correct the manuscript style in each of the following sentences.

1. On July eighth, the nomination was not decided until the 57th ballot.

____

2. The 1st chairman of the committee was Laura McGown.

____

3. There are 17 wild turkeys resting in that field.

____

4. Everyone coming to the picnic should bring his or her own plate, cup, and tableware.

____

5. It took us thirteen days to find 25 pictures for the collage.

____

Name ____________ Date ________ Class ____________

Resources

WORKSHEET 18 Review

Exercise A Each of the items below is a piece of information about a library book. On the line provided, write what card catalog you would use to find the book—*author, title,* or *subject*. (Note: Authors are listed last name first. Titles of books are italicized.)

1. Haiti ____________
2. Kwanzaa, an African American holiday ____________
3. *Grandpa and the Statue* ____________
4. Giovanni, Nikki ____________
5. Kurdish refugees ____________

Exercise B You need to find the following pieces of information in a book about the Cherokee Nation. On the line provided, write which part of the book you would use to answer each question.

1. On what page does Chapter 4 start? ____________
2. On what page is the Trail of Tears described? ____________
3. I read about Chief John Ross in Chapter 10. Is there additional information about him in the book? ____________
4. When was the book first published? ____________
5. What does the word *treaty* mean? ____________

Exercise C Write the reference you might use to find the following information.

1. What happened last week in your community's city council meeting? ____________
2. What are some details about the life of Haile Selassie? ____________
3. What is the typical life span of an Indian elephant? ____________
4. Where is Bangkok? ____________
5. What is the population of the Sudan, in Africa? ____________

Exercise D Use a dictionary to answer the following questions. Use the lines provided.

1. When is the word *roman* capitalized and when is it not? ____________

   ____
2. Divide *habitat* into syllables. ____________
3. Give the parts of speech for the word *fall*. ____________
4. What usage labels are given for the word *relief*? ____________

   ____

5. What is the etymology of the word *khaki*? ______________
6. What is one synonym of the word *fear*? ______________
7. What is an antonym for the word *opposite*? ______________
8. What is an example of the use of the word *manner*? ______________
9. On which syllable is the accent in the word *radiometer*? ______________
10. What does the word *biscuit* mean to someone in England? ______________

Exercise E Consider each of the following situations. Write *T* if you would write a thank-you letter. Write *I* if you would write an invitation. Write *R* if you would write a letter of regret.

______ 1. You cannot attend your uncle's wedding.

______ 2. You are putting together a surprise party for your best friend.

______ 3. Your grandmother sent you a fruit basket when you were in the hospital.

______ 4. You want to have a party at your house next Sunday afternoon.

______ 5. Your friend's parents took you to a restaurant last weekend.

Exercise F The following list gives the six parts of a business letter. Number the list from 1 to 6 in the correct order, from top to bottom.

______ 1. Closing ______ 4. Inside address

______ 2. Signature ______ 5. Heading

______ 3. Body ______ 6. Salutation

Exercise G Read the following body of a complaint letter. Then, on the lines provided, list four things that are wrong with the letter.

Last year, I received a horrible product from your company. You people must be very silly. I have never had such a useless thing as this thing that you sent me. I would like you to do something about it as soon as possible. Or else.

1. ______________________________

2. ______________________________

3. ______________________________

4. ______________________________

RESOURCES

Exercise H On the blanks provided, write C for *correct* or *I* for *incorrect* about the following statements about envelopes and printed forms.

______ 1. On a printed form you should fill in all blanks, whether or not the question applies to you.

______ 2. You should read any special instructions on a printed form.

______ 3. On an envelope, the name of the person to whom you are mailing the letter appears in the upper left-hand corner.

______ 4. You should always proofread a form after filling it out.

______ 5. Always spell out the names of states on an envelope.

Exercise I On the blanks provided, write C for *correct* or *I* for *incorrect* about the following statements about manuscript form.

______ 1. Number all pages of your manuscript except the first page.

______ 2. Indent ten spaces from the left margin.

______ 3. Skip every other line on a handwritten manuscript.

______ 4. Use a caret mark to indicate an addition to the paper.

______ 5. Use only one side of each sheet of paper.

Exercise J: Proofreading On the lines provided, correct the manuscript style of each of the following sentences.

1. Egyptian writing dates to around 3300 before Christ.

   ____

2. My aunt, M.E. Lightree, went to work for the Federal Bureau of Investigation in 1965, and now my cousin also works for the Federal Bureau of Investigation.

   ____

   ____

3. Last week two thousand five hundred seventy-nine people attended our 1st track meet.

   ____

4. When we flew to Dallas, Tex., both the male and female stewardesses were very nice to us.

   ____

5. When each helper arrives, ask him to start sorting the books.

   ____

Name ______________________ Date ____________ Class ____________________

Appendix: Diagraming Sentences

Diagraming Subjects and Verbs

A **sentence diagram** is a picture of how the parts of a sentence fit together. To diagram a sentence, first find the simple subject and the simple predicate, or verb, and write them on a horizontal line. Then separate the subject and verb with a vertical line. Keep the capital letters, but leave out the punctuation marks, except in cases such as *Mr.* and *July 11, 1992.*

Horses gallop.

Horses | gallop

To diagram a question, first make the question into a statement. Then diagram the sentence.

Are you going to the store?

you | Are going

To diagram an imperative sentence, place the understood subject *you* in parentheses on the horizontal line.

Clean your room.

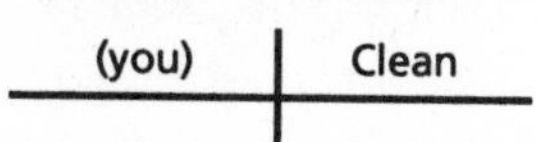

Exercise On a separate sheet of paper, diagram only the simple subject and the verb in each of the following sentences. Remember that simple subjects and verbs may consist of more than one word.

EXAMPLE: 1. Gwendolyn Brooks has been the poet laureate of Illinois.

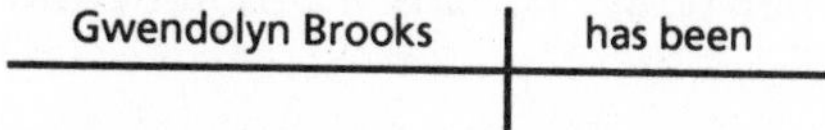

1. Angela just returned from Puerto Rico.
2. She was studying Spanish in San Juan.
3. Listen to her stories about her host family.
4. She really enjoyed her trip.
5. Have you ever been to Puerto Rico?

Name ______________________ Date __________ Class ______________________

Diagraming Compound Subjects and Compound Verbs

To diagram a compound subject, put the subjects on parallel lines. Then join them by a dotted line on which you write the connecting word (the conjunction).

Sharks and **eels** can be dangerous.

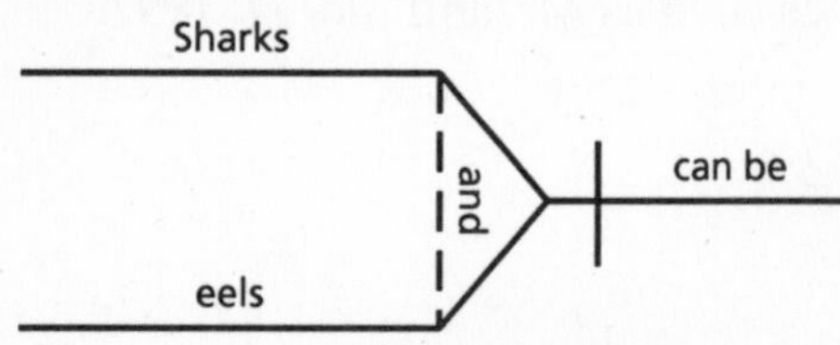

A compound verb is diagramed in the same way.

The cowhand **swung** into the saddle and **rode** away.

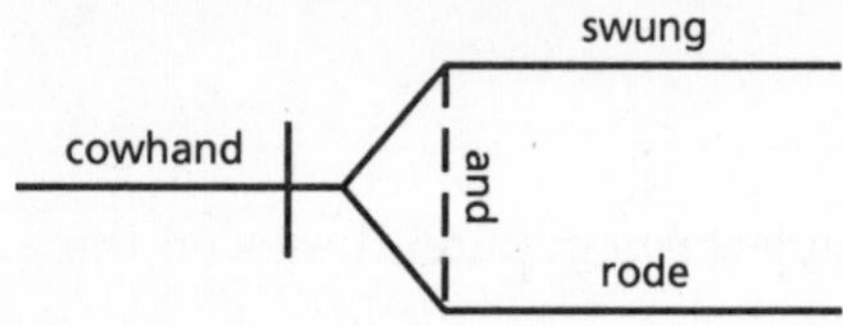

Alice Walker **has written** many books and **received** several prizes for them.

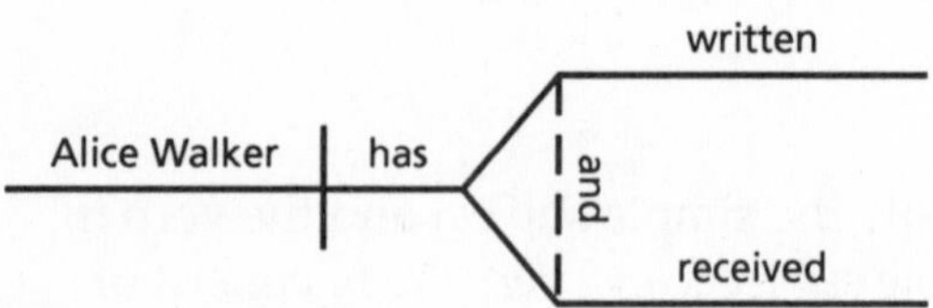

A sentence with both a compound subject and a compound verb combines the two patterns.

Rosa Parks and **Martin Luther King, Jr., saw** a problem and **did** something about it.

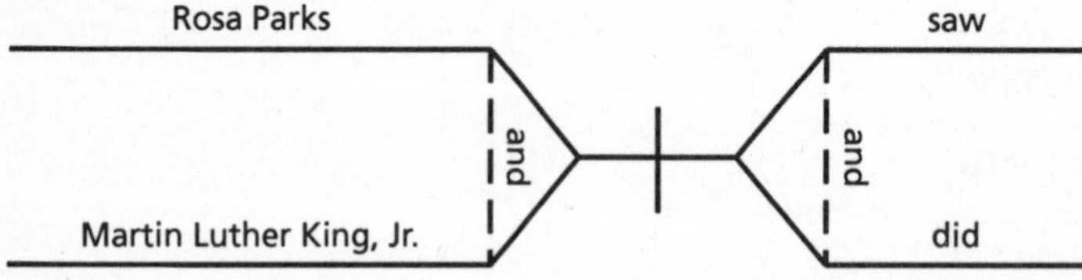

Exercise On a separate sheet of paper, diagram the simple subjects and the verbs in the following sentences.

1. Everyone knows and likes Mr. Karras.
2. Hurricanes and tornadoes are frequent during the summer.
3. Julio and Rosa were frying tortillas and grating cheese for the tacos.
4. Jade Snow Wong and Amy Tan have written books about growing up in San Francisco's Chinatown.
5. Shells and driftwood littered the beach.

Name ______________________ Date ____________ Class ______________________

Diagraming Adjectives and Adverbs

Adjectives are written on slanted lines connected to the words they modify. Notice that possessive pronouns are diagramed in the same way adjectives are.

dark room

room
dark

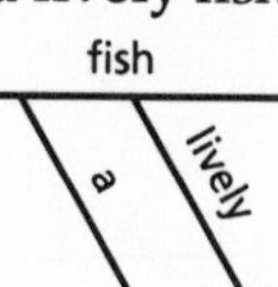

Adverbs are also written on slanted lines connected to the words they modify.

walks **briskly**

walks
briskly

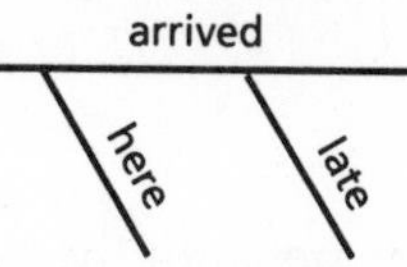

When an adverb modifies an adjective or another adverb, it is placed on a line connected to the word it modifies.

a **very** happy child

child
a
happy
very

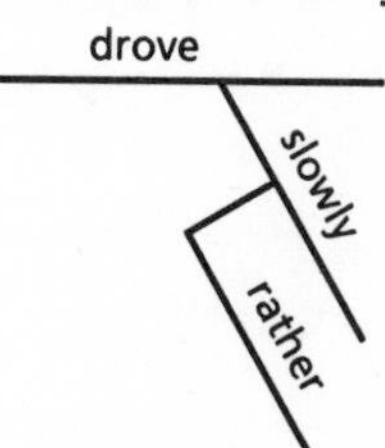

When a conjunction joins two modifiers, it is diagramed like this:

The **English** and **American** musicians played **slowly** and **beautifully**.

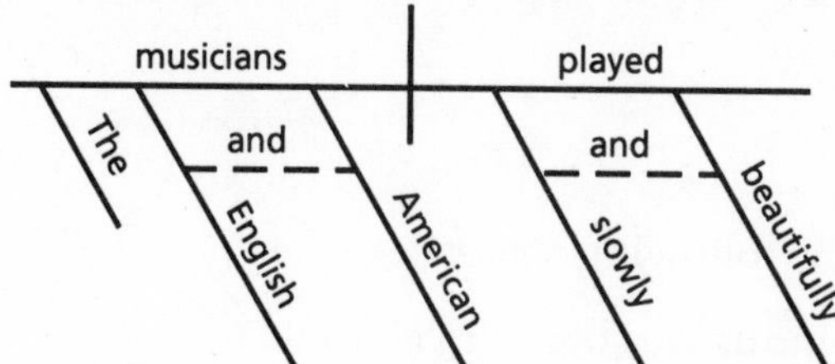

Exercise On a separate sheet of paper, diagram the following sentences.

1. The determined young Frederick Douglass worked extremely hard.
2. The talented actress spoke loudly and clearly.
3. Mei-Ling and her younger sister will arrive tomorrow.
4. That glue does not work very well.

Name ______________________ Date ___________ Class ______________________

Diagraming Direct Objects and Indirect Objects

A direct object is diagramed on the horizontal line with the subject and the verb. A vertical line separates the direct object from the verb. Notice that this vertical line does not cross the horizontal line. The second example below shows how to diagram a compound direct object.

We like **pizza**.

We | like | pizza

Lizards eat **flies** and **earthworms**.

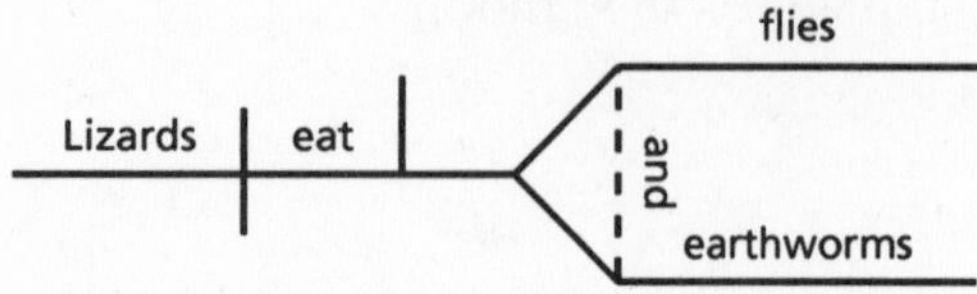

An indirect object is diagramed on a horizontal line beneath the verb. The verb and the indirect object are joined by a slanting line. The second example below shows how to diagram a compound indirect object.

Marisol brought **me** a piñata.

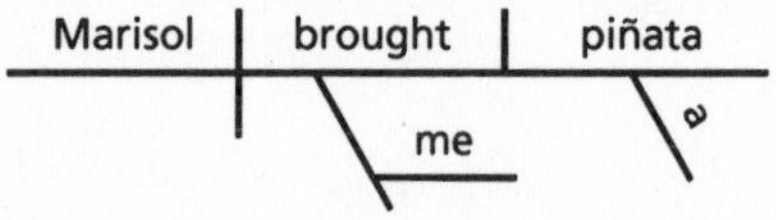

Marisol | brought | piñata

me

a

Tanya gave the **singer** and the **dancer** cues.

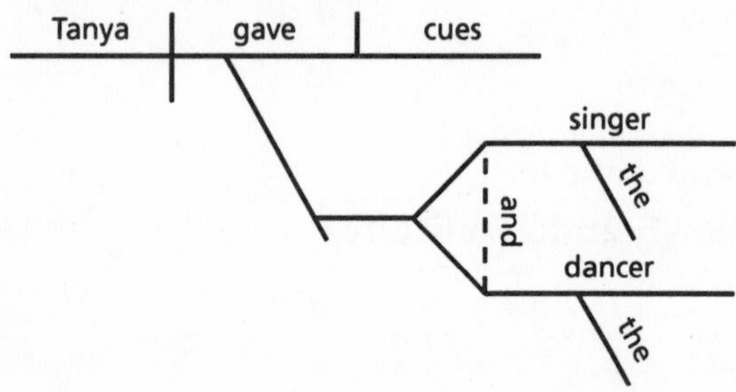

Exercise On a separate sheet of paper, diagram the following sentences.

1. He sent the American Red Cross and Goodwill Industries his extra clothes.
2. My aunt knitted Violet and me sweaters.
3. Kim drew us a quick sketch.
4. Gerardo and Wendie are organizing the play and the refreshments.
5. Did you clean the bathroom and the kitchen today?

Name ____________________ Date ____________ Class ____________________

Diagraming Subject Complements

A subject complement (predicate nominative or predicate adjective) is diagramed on the horizontal line with the subject and the verb. A line slanting toward the subject separates the subject complement from the verb. Some examples below show how to diagram compound subject complements.

PREDICATE NOMINATIVE: Barbra Streisand is a famous **singer**.

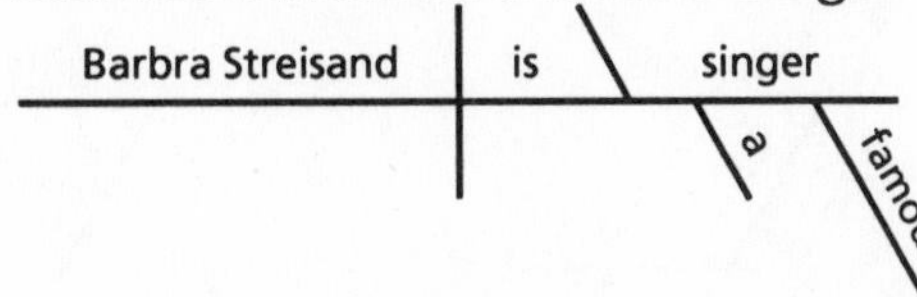

COMPOUND PREDICATE NOMINATIVE: Clara is a **student** and a volunteer **nurse**.

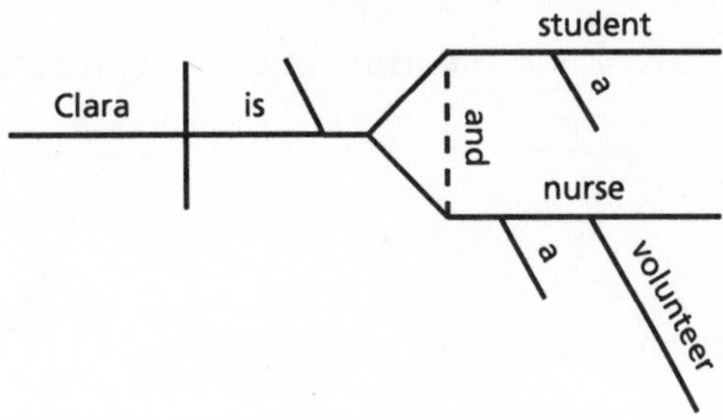

PREDICATE ADJECTIVE: She was extremely **friendly**.

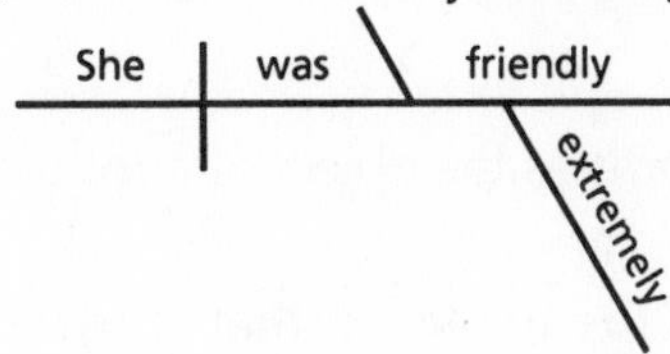

COMPOUND PREDICATE ADJECTIVE: We were **tired** but very **happy**.

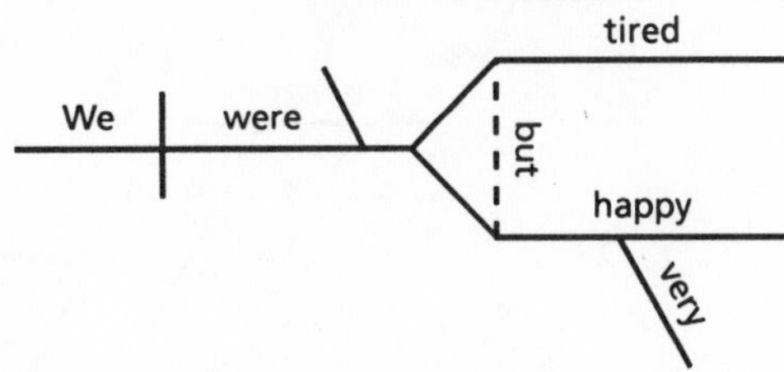

Exercise On a separate sheet of paper, diagram the following sentences.

1. Turtles are reptiles.
2. Their tough bills look sharp and strong.
3. Turtles may grow very old.
4. Is this the largest freshwater turtle?
5. Painted turtles really do look painted!

Name ______________________ Date ____________ Class ______________________

Diagraming Prepositional Phrases

A prepositional phrase is diagramed below the word it modifies. Write the preposition on a slanting line below the modified word. Then write the object of the preposition on a horizontal line connected to the slanting line. Some examples below show prepositional phrases with compound objects.

ADJECTIVE PHRASES: traditions **of the Sioux** gifts **from Nadine and Chip**

traditions
of
Sioux
the

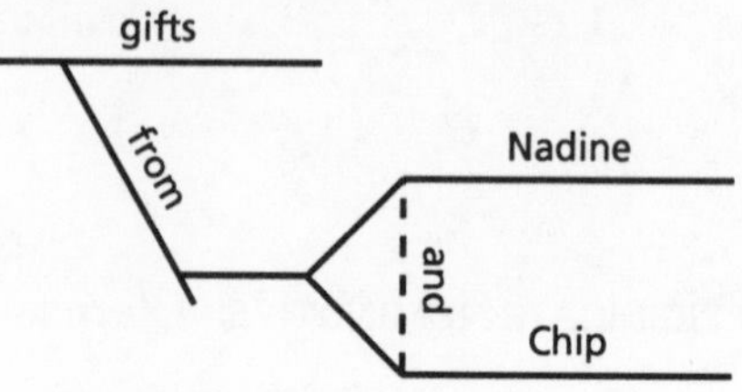

ADVERB PHRASES: awoke **in the morning** searching **for the gerbil and the hamster**

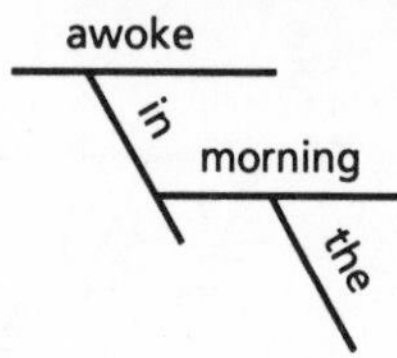

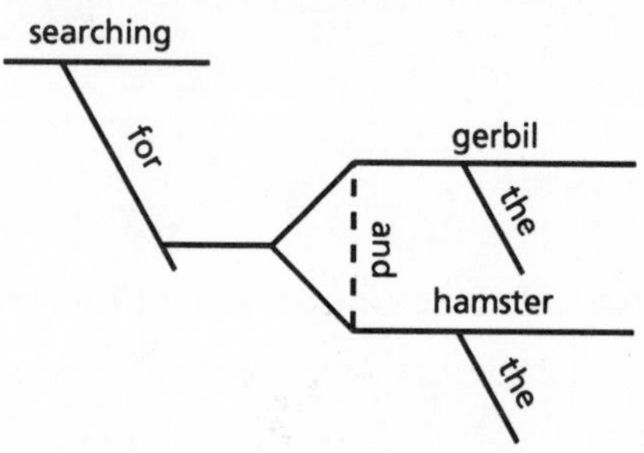

When a prepositional phrase modifies the object of another preposition, the diagram looks like this:

Richard Wright wrote one **of the books on that subject.**

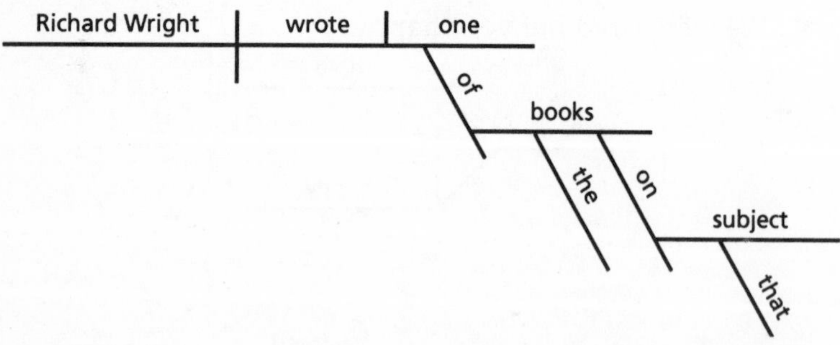

Exercise On a separate sheet of paper, diagram the following sentences.

1. The director of that movie about the Civil War was chosen for an Academy Award.
2. A play about Cleopatra will be performed tonight.
3. Leroy usually practices with his band.
4. Stevie Wonder has written songs about love and freedom.
5. I admire the paintings of Marc Chagall.

Name ______________________ Date ___________ Class ______________________

Diagraming Subordinate Clauses

Diagram an adjective clause by using a broken line to connect the relative pronoun and the word that it relates to. [Note: The words *who, whom, whose, which,* and *that* are relative pronouns.]

The students **whose projects are selected** will attend the regional contest.

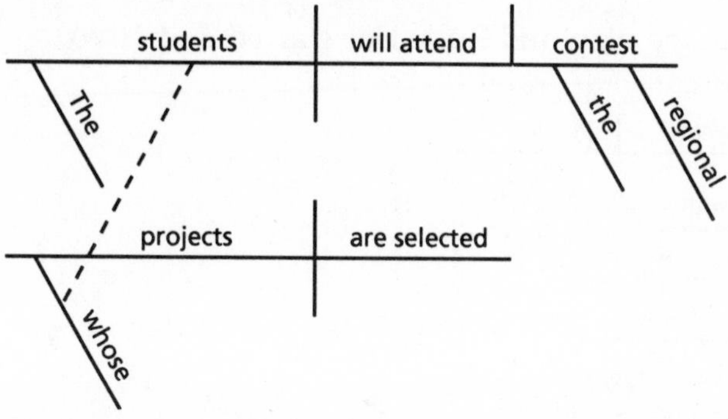

Diagram an adverb clause by connecting it with a broken line to the word it modifies. Write the subordinating conjunction on the broken line. [Note: The words *after, because, if, since, unless, when,* and *while* are common subordinating conjunctions.]

If I study for two more hours, I will finish my homework.

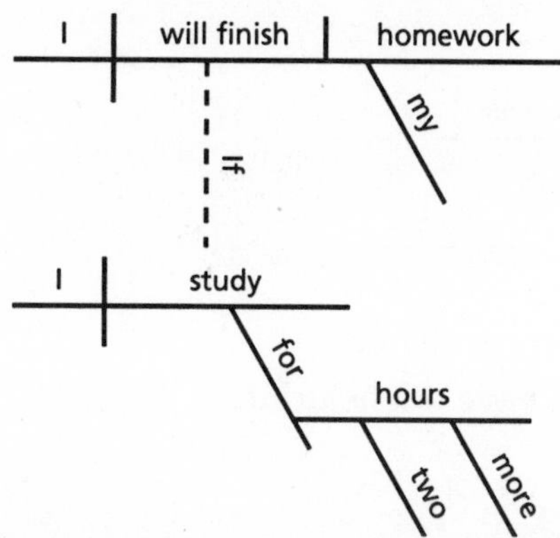

Exercise On a separate sheet of paper, diagram the following sentences.

1. Proverbs are sayings that usually give advice.
2. Because the day was very hot, the cool water felt good.
3. If it does not rain tomorrow, we will visit Crater Lake.
4. Janice and Linda found some empty seats as the movie started.
5. When I got home, I rested on the sofa.

Diagraming Sentences Classified by Structure

SIMPLE SENTENCE: Ray showed us his new bike. [one independent clause]

COMPOUND SENTENCE: Ossie Davis wrote the play, and Ruby Dee starred in it. [two independent clauses]

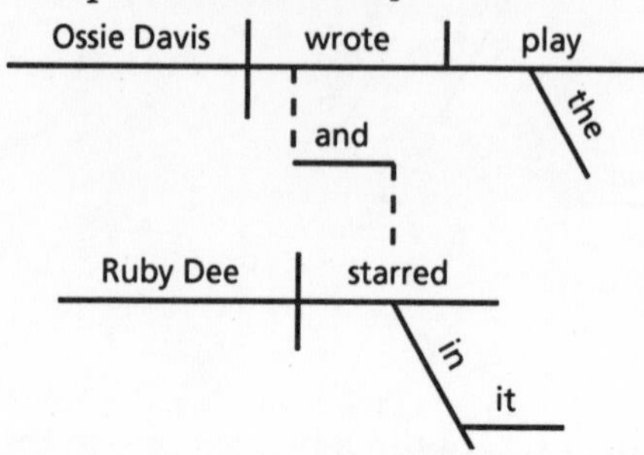

COMPLEX SENTENCE: Altovise has a carving **that was made in Nigeria**. [one independent clause and one subordinate clause]

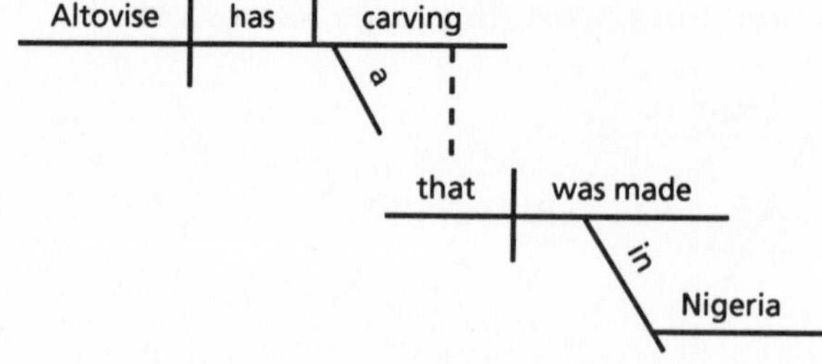

Exercise On a separate sheet of paper, diagram the following sentences.

EXAMPLE: 1. Lucas likes that new CD, but I have not heard it.

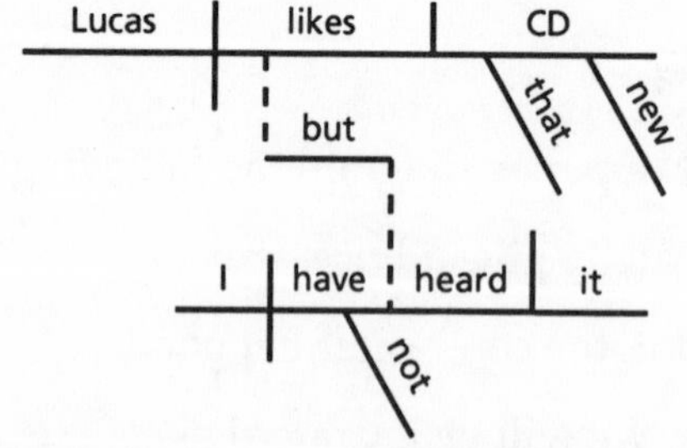

1. Sally Ride was the first American woman who flew in space.
2. Luis Alvarez was an atomic scientist, but his son became a geologist.
3. All of the children screamed as the roller coaster began its descent.
4. Sandy Koufax is my baseball hero, but my sister prefers Henry Aaron.